A Purple State of Mind

Craig Detweiler

HARVEST HOUSE PUBLISHERS

EUGENE, OREGON

This work published in association with the Conversant Media Group, P.O. Box 3006, Redmond, WA, 98007.

ConversantLife.com is a trademark of Conversant Media Group. Harvest House Publishers, Inc., is a licensee of the trademark ConversantLife.com.

Cover by Abris, Veneta, Oregon

Back cover author photo © Don Milici

A PURPLE STATE OF MIND
Copyright © 2008 by Craig Detweiler
Published by Harvest House Publishers
Eugene, Oregon 97402
www.harvesthousepublishers.com

Library of Congress Cataloging-in-Publication Data
Detweiler, Craig, 1964-
A purple state of mind / Craig Detweiler.
     p. cm.
Includes bibliographical references.
ISBN-13: 978-0-7369-2460-3
ISBN-10: 0-7369-2460-4
1. Christianity and culture. I. Title.
BR115.C8D48 2008
261.0973—dc22

                                                        2008012038

Printed in the United States of America

     08 09 10 11 12 13 14 15 16 17 / VP-SK / 12 11 10 9 8 7 6 5 4 3 2 1

Download a Deeper Experience

Craig Detweiler is part of a faith-based online community called ConversantLife.com. At this website, people engage their faith in entertainment, creative arts, science and technology, global concerns, and other culturally relevant topics. While you're reading this book, or after you have finished reading, go to www.conversantlife .com/craigdetweiler and use these icons to read and download additional material from Craig that is related to the book.

Resources: Download study guide materials for personal devotions or a small-group Bible study.

Videos: Click on this icon for interviews with Craig and video clips on various topics.

Blogs: Read through Craig's blog and articles and comment on them.

Podcasts: Stream ConversantLife.com podcasts and audio clips from Craig.

conversant life .com

engage your faith

To Zoë and Theo
and the next generation

May you find abundant life in God.

An Appreciation

Every book is a community project. Sure, an author spends hours at the keyboard in a lonely room. But writing begins with listening. It is sparked by conversations overheard, by trends noted, by things we hear on TV. A stranger may ask us a haunting question. Our children may blurt out a funny phrase. A spouse may listen to our rants. *A Purple State of Mind* is a community project. It is an ongoing conversation. This book and the movie that inspired it were forged in the marketplace of ideas. They are works of public theology. Consequently, I am grateful for my friends and advocates throughout this endeavor.

The movie *Purple State of Mind* would not have begun without John Marks' interest in having a long, thoughtful conversation. John has been a faithful foil at each stage of this journey. His rapier wit and voracious mind made it a delightful ride. We took a leap of faith together, and I'm amazed by how well the movie turned out. Our gracious producers, John Priddy, Ed Priddy, and Mark Priddy supported us throughout the arduous process. Uber-editor Greg Bayne provided the perspective we desperately needed to finish the project. The talented staff of Priddy Brothers Productions kept us on task, especially the tireless efforts of Anna McMurphy.

This book started with the enthusiasm of Stan Jantz and Bruce Bickel. Their vision for a more conversant faith community aligned with my hopes for *Purple State of Mind*. Peter Schumerth has been the Conversant man with a marketing plan. Harvest House demonstrated their faith in ConversantLife.com through the leadership of Bob Hawkins. My editor, Terry Glaspey, guided the process with a remarkably gentle and compassionate hand. The sharp eyes of my copy editor, Gene Skinner, kept this book on track through several iterations.

The love of my family animates my daily life. My sweet Caroline serves as my primary partner in this story called life. We have walked through dark passages that tested our faith. Yet our commitment to each other has never wavered. She is a true helpmate, the better half that balances my worst inclinations. Caroline is a superb editor, a brilliant thinker, and a compassionate follower of Jesus. She serves her community in ways that challenge me and restore my faith. She came from a blue country of Chicago to the red ways of Charlotte, North Carolina. We've forged *A Purple State of Mind* in the sandy soil of California. I am forever changed by the grace of God she pours into my body and soul every single day.

I write for my children, hoping to carve out room for them to roam. Their boundless curiosity requires a wide berth. Unfortunately, the attacks of September 11 threatened their abilities to explore, to enter into cultural plunges with anticipation rather than fear. Perhaps *A Purple State of Mind* toward countries around the world will carve out the safe place for all our children to relate to others around the globe. This book is dedicated to Zoë and Theo. Thank you for turning abundant life in God into a lived reality. May your hearts be drawn to the color purple, the royal hue of Christ the King.

Contents

Beyond Red and Blue

Introduction

Why are the most "tolerant" people so intolerant of Christians? Why do gay people insist on parading their lifestyles? Why does Hollywood put so much sex and violence in their movies? Do they have any morals at all? Why are the public schools so afraid of religion? How can liberals so blindly toe the Democratic Party line? Growing up in North Carolina and then serving as a professor in Christian colleges, I have been surrounded by people who feel assaulted by the media. Many of them are solid citizens, looking to preserve their Christian homes. They moved to the suburbs to be near their church and their kids' schools. They cherish and protect their freedom. They want to be left alone to do their jobs, love their families, and raise their children. They honestly do not understand why they are the targets of ridicule and the focus of legislation. If this sounds like you, this book is written for you.

Why do Christians hate gay people? Why are they so judgmental? Do they enjoy protesting? Why do Christians create such cheesy art? Are they ignorant? Why are they so scared of science? Why do they place such blind faith in the Republican Party? Living in Southern California, working in the entertainment business, I am surrounded by people who feel condemned by the Christian community. Many of them are artistic types raised in strict Southern homes. They fled to California to pursue their dreams. They cherish and protect their freedom. They want to be left alone to do their jobs, love their families, and raise their children. They honestly do not understand why they are the targets of ridicule and the focus of legislation. If this sounds like you, this book is also written for you.

A purple state of mind begins from a position of humility rather than pronouncement. It starts by listening, really listening, before we speak. (It emphasizes our two ears rather than our one mouth!) It seeks to understand how we have all contributed to the rancorous divisions in American life. It suggests what we can do to heal the breach. It avoids a binary approach to life and embraces a more tripartite, even Trinitarian, view of reality. My goal is to bring people into a broader, more God-honoring conversation. We must get beyond the unhelpful polarization of red and blue states and move into the more majestic color purple, meeting under the purple reign of Christ.

Christians need a different kind of apologetic. We have been so offensive for so long that we must begin with apologies rather than arguments. I have tried to demonstrate this in my interaction with John Marks in the feature documentary *Purple State of Mind*. This book provides a behind-the-scenes peek at our relationship. What was I thinking during our long, rambling conversations? Why did I often answer his questions with more questions? Are my convictions so superficial that I offered only halfhearted answers? On the contrary, my passion for Christ and the beauty of God's kingdom makes me more hesitant to adopt only black-and-white responses to a colorful world. I am energized by the possibilities for Christianity within the postmodern context. Rather than the divisive either/or policies of the past, this new era will be characterized by a both/and approach to faith and culture. A purple state of mind blends the best of ancient Christian practices to forge our future.

To some, a purple state of mind may sound lukewarm. Isn't purple rooted in compromise, a blending of red and blue shades of belief? Shouldn't we be single-minded in our focus? Shouldn't a firm faith result in bold proclamation? The apostle Peter encourages us to always be ready to give an answer for the hope that resides within us (1 Peter 3:15). Are we prepared? We've been trained to give an answer through extensive study and scholarship. A substantial body of excellent research has equipped people to argue for the Christian faith.

I am eager to communicate the grace of God, the wonder of Christ's love, the comforting presence of the Spirit. Yet all too often, we overlook the later portion of Peter's challenge. We are told to make our defense with gentleness and respect. Yet how much gentleness and respect do we see in the public square? Most Christians I see on television look angry and frustrated. They often have little respect for their interviewers and even less for those who oppose them. We look more like rabid attack dogs rather than godly sheep. The King James translation urges us to answer with meekness and fear. Who wants to follow a pastor who is meek? Isn't faith the opposite of fear? A purple state of mind measures words carefully. It defuses arguments rather than escalating controversies. Such Christlike leadership has been in remarkably short supply.

We have also overlooked the impetus for our gentle and respectful responses. Our biblical mandate is to give an answer to everyone *who asks*. It starts with people's curiosity—when we walk with such authentic hope that our friends and neighbors are intrigued. They may wonder, how do we remain so calm under pressure? How do we juggle the rigorous demands of contemporary life? How do we retain hope despite all the bad news around us? Unfortunately, we often shout scripted answers to questions people aren't asking. Frankly, we have done such a poor job of embodying the love of God that I find almost no one eager to hear more about Jesus. Instead, people want to know why Christians are so judgmental. They don't understand how we can cast our allegiance on one political party. They can't figure out why we are so obsessed about only two issues—abortion and homosexuality. Our actions have caused confusion. The questions are not sparked by the hope within us but by the anger that emanates from us.

Our fears and frustrations have served as an effective fulcrum.[1] We've been mobilized to write letters and complain to our congressmen. We've been urged to boycott Walt Disney World. We've been ushered to the theater in support of Mel Gibson's *The Passion of the Christ*. Historian Garry Wills points out how political strategist Karl Rove

> shaped the hard core of the Republican Party around resentments religious people felt over abortion, homosexuality, Darwinism, women's liberation, pornography and school prayer…Rove made the executive branch of the United States more openly and avowedly religious than it had ever been, though he had no discernible religious belief himself. His own indifference allowed him to be ecumenical in his appeal to Protestants, Catholics and Jews.[2]

Some viewed the resulting rancor as progress. In his resignation speech, disgraced House Republican leader Tom DeLay ridiculed those who "lament the bitter divisive partisan rancor." He considered such polarizing partisanship "not a symptom of democracy's weakness but of its health and its strength."[3] Yet some of those who contributed to the resentments have begun to recant.

Conservative columnist Cal Thomas and liberal commentator Bob Beckel reflected upon their experience of the front lines of the culture wars. They begged their readers to find common ground:

> We're two guys who spent a lot of years in the polarizing business, but on opposing sides…We helped write the game plan, and we have participated in everything from getting money out of true believers to appearing on television to help spread the contentious message. In many cases, we wrote the message. We know the gig, and it's just about up.[4]

They recognize that the politics of division has reached a dead end. In *Crazy for God,* Frank Schaeffer reflects on growing up in L'Abri under the shadow of his father, Francis Schaeffer. Much of the Schaeffers' work served as the philosophical underpinnings of Christian cultural engagement. In retrospect, the younger Schaeffer told John W. Whitehead,

> The other thing I began to understand is that in dismissing the whole culture as decadent, in dismissing the public school movement as godless, in talking about anybody who opposed them as evil, the Religious Right was only a mirror image of the New Left. Thus, the Religious Right and the New Left are really two sides of the same coin. What gets left out is a basic discussion about the United States and the reality of living here, the freedoms we enjoy and the benefits of a pluralistic culture where people are not crushing each other over beliefs. This gets lost.[5]

We're suggesting that both sides are drawing the last, desperate gasps of their failed projects.

Already, a host of books have described the breach. In *God's Politics,* Jim Wallis suggested, "God is not a Republican or a Democrat." Arriving in the wake of the 2004 presidential election, Wallis' timely reminder turned into a surprising bestseller. Important historical background has been added by Garry Wills in *Head and Heart: American Christianities* (2007). He documents how the disestablishment of religion in America allowed faith to thrive via choice. In *A Secular Age* (2006), Charles Taylor (winner of the Templeton Prize) argued for the place of religion within the public sphere.[6]

How religious should our public discourse and government policies be? How pluralistic can the American experiment become? Answers from the left side of the aisle come from pastor Robin Meyers (*Why the Christian Right Is Wrong*), rabbi Michael Lerner (*The Left Hand of God: Taking Back Our Country from the Religious Right*), historian Randall Balmer (*Thy Kingdom Come: How the Religious Right Distorts the Faith and Threatens America*), and *Time* editor Amy Sullivan (*The Party Faithful: How and Why Democrats Are Closing the Gap*). Representatives on the far right include Ann Coulter (*If Democrats Had*

Any Brains, They'd Be Republicans), Bernard Goldberg (*Crazies to the Left of Me, Wimps to the Right*), and Newt Gingrinch (*Rediscovering God in America*).

Those attempting to navigate the messy middle include Gregory A. Boyd (*The Myth of a Christian Nation: How the Quest for Political Power Is Destroying the Church*), Becky Garrison (*Red and Blue God, Black and Blue Church*), and Joel Hunter (*A New Kind of Conservative*). Amy E. Black has offered help in *Beyond Left and Right: Helping Christians Make Sense of American Politics*. Marcia Ford contributed *We the People*. Even the 2008 presidential candidates came to agree with Brian McLaren's title, *Everything Must Change*. It is tough to add to so many extensive and insightful political tomes.

Most of the punditry about faith and politics comes from those who still believe in political solutions. What is distinctive about a purple state of mind? It doesn't locate the problems in politics. Yes, skilled leaders are important for brokering world peace. More courageous politicians may extend more equal opportunities to all. We need elected officials who seek justice and attack systemic evil. But the next generation knows that political realignments will not save us. We hunger for a more authentic approach to public life. We long to see genuine humility. We value creative conversations and practical solutions. The shifts we need are more theological than ideological. Our times call for a more embodied faith.

A purple state of mind starts with people rather than policies. This book is loaded with personal anecdotes. It doesn't call for the reformation of political parties. I don't expect to alter institutions. Our progress starts locally, in our supermarkets, in our schools, in our workplaces. We can start by dialoguing with people who disagree with us. As we listen to our neighbors, we may learn how to love them. Such cross-cultural encounters may broaden our interests and deepen our understanding. We may find ourselves paying attention to parts of the world we never noticed. Privatized faith may grow into global concerns. We can model what politicians used to know: People from opposite sides of the aisle or temple or mosque can work together for the common good. We can put aside self-interest long enough to seek liberty and justice for all.

The Chasm We've Created

How do we defuse the culture wars? The Christian community must own our part in the skirmish. We have plenty of reasons to be angry. We feel attacked, abused, and wronged. We have developed long lists of offenses. From Supreme Court rulings to Super Bowl nipple slips, we have aired our frustrations. Our complaints have been heard. To what end? Next time we want to add fuel to the fire, what would happen if we followed Jesus' enigmatic example instead? Goaded to fight, he picked up a cross. Backed into a corner, he chose to lay down his life. He unnerved his enemies by literally disarming himself.

Arguments can be constructive. Arguments can be instructive. But ours have been destructive: petty, personalized, and unyielding. Consider the biblical warning of Titus 3:9, "But avoid foolish controversies and genealogies and arguments and quarrels about the law, because these are unprofitable and useless." Second Timothy 2:23 is similar: "Don't have anything to do with foolish and stupid arguments, because you know that they produce quarrels." What fruit has our culture war produced?

In his prescient book, *They Like Jesus but Not the Church* (2007), Dan Kimball describes the gulf we've created. Our evangelistic efforts often begin with the bridge illustration, a simple way to depict the gospel in graphic terms. This pillar of the four spiritual laws places humanity and God on opposing cliffs. We are separated by sin. Only the cross of Christ can span the divide. Jesus reconciled humanity and God in his sacrificial death. Through faith in Christ, we can cross over to God.

Unfortunately, too many Christians have spent the last 30 years building another gap. It is almost impossible to talk about Jesus without hearing complaints about Christians. The objections that opened this book dominate our discussions. "Why are Christians so anti-intellectual? Are they always so negative? Who appointed them the morality police?" We cannot deliver the good news about Jesus because we've created a chasm of confusion. Dan Kimball writes, "We have created this chasm with our rhetoric and attitudes, which have led people today to harbor negative perceptions of Christians and Christianity that prevent them from trusting us and being interested in the gospel…this new chasm keeps them from ever getting to the sin chasm."[7] People do not object to Jesus. They just reject his people.

So how do we remove the barrier we've erected through our polarizing and politicized faith? A purple state of mind builds bridges across the culture. It finds common ground rather than bones of contention. We should always be prepared to give a reason for the faith that lies within us. But we should offer that reason only when we've earned the right to speak, when we've demonstrated our faith with such authenticity that others are desperate to discover what compels us. Unfortunately, we've been quick to speak and slow to listen. We've engaged in greater and less effective rhetoric at each stage of the misguided culture war. Consequently, my apologetics begin with apologies.

I apologize for my self-righteousness, my hypocrisy, and my holier-than-thou attitude. I am sorry for the atrocities committed in the name of God. I am grieved by the racism, sexism, and homophobia propped up by specious and selective interpretations of scripture. How have we turned Jesus, the great defender of the poor, the hungry, and the hurting, into a hater? The military language we have adopted toward society (waging a culture war, engaging the culture, prayer as spiritual warfare) has placed us in opposition to those we seek to welcome into God's kingdom. Our language stems from an Old Testament world in which a minority people sought to resist foreign idols. Yet to equate ancient Israel with modern America is a vast misreading of history.[8] A Christian majority in a wealthy nation defended by massive firepower can hardly claim to be an embattled underdog. I am grateful for our national wealth and comfort. But to drive from spacious homes in large cars to plush churches in order to hear sermons about how persecuted we are is just silly. Poorer countries around the globe conflate our consumerism with our Christianity. Unfortunately, we have muddied those waters almost beyond recognition. A century of quiet, humble service may go a long way toward repairing the damage. Will the world ever know we are Christians by our love, by our concern for our neighbors, near and far?

Unfortunately, my worst fears have been confirmed by research done by the Barna Group about young Americans' perception of the word *Christian*. Jesus' followers are associated with hypocrisy, judgment, and attacks on homosexuals. We are seen as overly invested in political solutions to the world's problems. Barna pollster David Kinnaman concludes, "In studying thousands of outsiders' impressions, it is clear that Christians are primarily perceived for what they stand against. *We have become famous for what we oppose rather than who we are for*."[9] Positioning ourselves as "us versus them" has alienated people, separating all of us from the love of Christ that should compel us.

The era of "blue versus red" politics must end. *A Purple State of Mind* is an attempt to reframe the conversation, to approach people from a humble posture. How did we dig such a substantial hole for ourselves? This book will explore the roots of our anti-art, anti-culture, anti-intellectual tendencies. We will retrace our steps to figure out how we arrived here. What theological shifts do we have to make to escape our un-Christian behavior? In our image-saturated society, we may have to recover a visual faith. In a world wondering if Christianity makes any substantial difference, we must practice an integrated faith that connects our creeds with deeds. Through patient listening and perceptive seeing, we can put on the mind of Christ that responds in love to hurting people.

As Jesus traveled through public spaces and saw all the people's faces, he wept. Was it because of their sin? Their ungodliness? Their television programming? As he taught in synagogues and announced the kingdom of God, he attracted crowds. The Gospel of Matthew records that "when he saw the crowds, he had compassion on them, because they were harassed and helpless, like sheep without a shepherd" (Matthew 9:36). He didn't see a fallen people. He saw a hurting people. No judgment. No condemnation. Just overflowing compassion. Rather than respond with rage or despair, he begged God for more help. There is so much harvesting to be done, but so few people are willing to join the effort. Should we critique the culture from the sidelines? Condemn people who are already hurting? Or are we filled with Christlike compassion, recognizing how harassed and helpless people feel?

To understand the depths of our desperation, check the television schedule. Phobias abound on *Fear Factor*. *Desperate Housewives* depicts people looking for love in all the wrong places. *Grey's Anatomy* demonstrates how fragile our feelings remain. We're like the cast of *Survivor,* stuck on an island with people we can't trust. Can we create a community better than the one on *Kid Nation?* These shows wrestle with the alliances we forge. Am I better off seeking my own welfare? Should I connect with others?

One of the most popular shows, *Lost,* began with people from every tribe and nation crawling from a plane wreck. Like America after 9/11, they emerge dizzy and disoriented. They try to rebuild their lives out of the wreckage. All of them have a secret, a backstory they're hiding, something that needs to be made right. They're trapped in a purgatory, atoning for their sins. Despite their own problems, they tend to demonize others. Will the survivors band together in a time of crisis? Will we?

We desperately need people who will lead the way. *Heroes* also brings together people from different nations, cultures, and beliefs. We see tremendous sacrifices made to save humanity from self-annihilation. At a time when we desperately need heroes, Jesus calls us to serve others out of compassion. Do we see people as harassed and helpless, as lost? Are we willing to be part of the solution, to rise up as heroes to a hurting world? A purple state of mind examines the contemporary context. Stuck on our island, it looks for signs of life wherever they may be found. It sends up flares that highlight the enduring truths of scripture.

Two Friends, Three Decades

This project started with a phone call. My college roommate, John

Marks, was coming to California. He was doing research for a book about his journey out of Dallas, out of Christianity, out of the faith he left behind. He wanted to interview me, to reflect upon our transcendent and transitional sophomore year at Davidson College in North Carolina. John's book began while he was researching a story for *60 Minutes* on Jerry Jenkins and Tim LaHaye's best-selling Left Behind books. John served as a producer for Morley Safer, often preinterviewing subjects for their show. A Christian couple from Oklahoma asked John, "Will you be left behind?"[10] They turned the tables, actively witnessing to the reporter assigned to interview them. Rather than dismiss their inquiry, John decided to take their question seriously. Will he be left behind? John began by revisiting the place of his most vibrant Christian faith. He remembered a time when he prayed with conviction. He flashed back to his college roommate, me. John called, eager to figure out what happened to the faith he left behind.

In 1982, two young men, committed to Christ and obsessed with pop culture, shared a decidedly modest room in Belk Dormitory. Neither one of us was particularly neat. We inherited a rickety loft, allowing John's bed to serve as a couch. He covered it with a cheap Mexican blanket and other curios from south of the border. I took the top bunk because I wanted to sleep in peace without interruption. Davidson College's honor code allowed us to live with an open-door policy. People could enter at all hours of the day or night. John and I were night owls, so we grew accustomed to people dropping by on their way back from the library, from the college union, from a frat party. John and I were almost always awake, just starting to think about studying. We didn't mind the interruptions. Our late-night bull sessions covered the waterfront of ideas. Debates ranged from politics and art to women and usually, religion.

John and I could always find a movie or song to pontificate upon. The Clash, R.E.M., and Elvis Costello inspired us. We invited our hall mates to enter into the ring, to share our passion for punk, new wave, or American rock. John also championed soundtracks to old westerns—whether the vistas of John Ford, Howard Hawks, or Sergio

Leone. He was attracted to the Old West, to a mythical America of John Wayne riding on the range. As a native Texan, John wore cowboy boots and the occasional hat. Growing up in North Carolina, I wore Converse's Chuck Taylor high-tops, perfect for playing hoops or stomping across a punk club.

Our religious questions were never speculative. They were earnest, intense, and important. Having only recently decided to follow Christ, I brought an evangelical fervor to every encounter. I argued from assurance, challenging people to make more significant sacrifices. Our hall was filled with followers of Jesus from across the Protestant spectrum. We had lifelong Presbyterians, Baptists, and Episcopalians. I didn't care what people were raised on. What mattered was their personal relationship to Christ. How dedicated was their daily devotion to God? My outreach knew no bounds. From my fraternity to the family, I was a man on a mission, called to communicate Christ at all times. I attempted to steer conversations toward the Bible, toward God, toward matters of life and death.

John and I both served as small group Bible study leaders for Davidson Christian Fellowship. As the year went on, John's emphasis shifted from the letters of St. Paul to Bruce Springsteen's *Nebraska*. But neither one of us realized his move away from Bible study would eventually be followed by his renunciation of faith altogether.

Only years later did I discover just how judgmental my pronouncements appeared. Good news to me became bad news to others, an either/or choice that pushed people away from God's grace. I spent years drawing lines in the sand, challenging people to take a stand. "Which side are you on? Are you inside or outside of God's kingdom? Will you be left behind?"

I finally realized that the only lines Jesus drew in the sand humbled those who stood in judgment of others. When the Pharisees brought a woman caught in adultery before Jesus, he stood in solidarity with her (John 8). He put himself on the side of the sinner. And he challenged those who felt above or beyond reproach to consider the sin residing in their own hearts. Jesus drew a picture that reflected our own shortcomings, lest we consider ourselves more highly than we ought. Theologian Ray Anderson places Jesus' loyalties in perspective:

> If there are two sides to humanity, Jesus will be found on the wrong side. He was not a religious person, though he lived amid a religious society that prized appearance and cultivated piety as a discipline of outward form. Where lines were drawn between the sacred and the profane that tended to dehumanize and marginalize common people, he acted with uncommon decency toward those whose dignity was shredded by the disgrace that comes from misfortune, mistreatment and moral failure.[11]

When Jesus chose sides, he always ended up beside the poor, the oppressed, and the excluded. Despite my best efforts to claim Jesus was on my team, I found out I was all too often lining up on the wrong, self-righteous side. How could I get in line with Jesus, standing in solidarity with his causes, his people, his timing? This book is a form of apology, not like the classical apologetics that defend the faith, but an attempt to reframe the conversation.

Four Conversations

John Marks and I grew up in the red states of Texas and North Carolina. We got married and moved to the blue states of New York and California. After John's phone call, we embarked on a series of conversations, retracing our conservative Southern roots. We also visited each other's media-savvy workplaces in the most liberal of states. This book is organized around those four rambling conversations captured in the film *Purple State of Mind*.

Each conversation brought up particular issues. Quotations from the film launch each chapter. Snippets of dialogue are broken out in a unique font, laid out more like a screenplay. It is a form of eavesdropping on the kind of awkward and frank discussions we may have with our closest friends or family. The first conversation was held in Los Angeles at Biola University. It deals with our background—our beliefs, choices, and testimonies. Part two occurred outside Charlotte, North Carolina, at our alma mater, Davidson College. We went back to campus for our college reunion. It covers galvanizing experiences of faith and doubt, the events that tested us. For the third conversation, we met in John's hometown, Dallas, Texas. After eating barbeque, we dealt with our differences. The authority of scripture influenced our discussion of heaven, hell, and homosexuality. The final chapters take place in New York City, on the anniversary of 9/11. It is more of a rapprochement, seeking to hear and understand each other. What do Christians fear? When did John abandon his faith? What moments of grace and beauty can we all build upon? We hope our conversation can serve as an example. If we can discuss our differences in a civil manner, maybe others can too.

It is not necessary to see the film to follow the book. But our contentious conversations also exuded warmth, humor, and camaraderie. John brought his background as a reporter to our four meetings. He asked most of the questions, often putting me on the defensive. Hoping to correct the grandstanding that characterizes too much of contemporary Christianity, I often resisted his efforts to pin me down, to shoehorn my beliefs into preestablished stereotypes. Viewers of the film have left our exchanges frustrated by my reticence. "Why didn't Craig simply answer his questions?" This book will provide those answers.

Jesus could be evasive, especially when confronted by his detractors. He often bobbed and weaved, answering questions with his questions, telling stories that left his accusers frustrated and even more confused. Jesus constructed his parables like smart bombs that only detonated hours or days after the initial exchange. *A Purple State of Mind* (the book) is offered as a clarification, a more complete picture of the world I attempted to describe in *Purple State of Mind* (the movie). Here my most measured words won't end up on the cutting room floor.

The book is an extension of the vibrant discussions that have arisen following the film. The movie has played to audiences across the religious and political spectrum. We've screened at the New York

Theater Workshop in Greenwich Village, at Ebenezer's coffeehouse in Washington DC, and at the Alamo Drafthouse in Austin. We've been hosted by Episcopalians in Charlotte, Presbyterians in Atlanta, and Nazarenes in San Francisco. We've conversed with students at Davidson College, Baylor University, and the University of Iowa. We've played at film festivals in Boise, Idaho, Winston-Salem, North Carolina, and Los Angeles, California. This project is an instant conversation starter regardless of the setting.

Purple State of Mind (the movie) has inspired some unlikely partnerships. At the University of Maryland, InterVarsity Christian Fellowship and the Students for the Separation of Church and State co-hosted a screening. At New York University, The Navigators and the Atheists, Agnostics and Freethinkers Club joined forces. The questions that follow the screenings are as unique as each venue. A Baha'i in College Park wondered about the particularity of my beliefs. A Muslim in Texas understood my discomfort with the things said and done in the name of my religion. Baptists in Waco were ready to dunk my nonbelieving partner in a pond. An otherwise peaceful Buddhist wanted to punch me in the City of Brotherly Love. These conversations have been heated, personal, and passionate. We wouldn't have it any other way.

Yet amid all the diverse beliefs, we have been touched by the profound and nearly universal hunger for a new conversation. People are simply fed up with old scripts and predictable battle lines. They are no longer buying the divisiveness that the media keeps selling. We recognize that the rancor has grown too personal, too passionate, too destructive. At the end of each screening, questions invariably arise about how we get along. Not in a simple or saccharine sort of way. We don't think our differences should be buried. But we dare to suggest that honest disagreements need not separate us. We find common ground in our hopes, our dreams, our disappointments. The humanity that unites us is greater than the beliefs that divide us.

We are used to choosing sides and rooting for our team. We divide the world into categories: us and them, winners and losers, saved and condemned. We tend to see the cosmic struggle as good versus evil or God versus Satan. But does that describe the world accurately? We say, "There are two sides to every argument," but could there exist a third way?[12] Maybe God stands above our disputes. We worship a Trinitarian God. Perhaps the most powerful portrait of the Trinity comes from medieval Russian icon painter Andrei Rublev. He poured such love and care into creating his icon of the Holy Trinity (1410). It is a portrait of a dinner bathed in resplendant gold leaf. The Godhead looks more like three angels gathered around a table. Are the Father, Son, and Holy Spirit engaged in a three-way conversation? Could reality be tripartite rather than binary?

To a divisive, either/or world, I offer a both/and alternative. The title of each chapter in this book has *and* in the center. So rather than figuring how we differ from our friends and neighbors, I've chosen to find as much common ground as possible. Christ was not satisfied to live apart from his people. He entered into our predicament, putting on our problems, getting down to an approachable street level. Jesus lived out his faith in the marketplace of ideas, among people who actively disagreed with him. A purple state of mind pursues compromise out of conviction, conviction that God does not wish that anyone would perish.

This book will be organized around ten haunting questions that linger over the movie *Purple State of Mind*. They are rooted in personal experience but connected to recurring objections to the faith. This book will wrestle with the problem of evil, the danger of judging others, the folly of a disembodied faith. It will offer practical positions that can the fill the massive hole we have dug for ourselves. I hope to offer theological shifts, rooted in lived religion and resonant scriptures that will help us navigate a tenuous world.

I've saved the more controversial issues of homosexuality, global warming, and abortion for the latter portion of the book. These wedge issues have been helpful tools for both sides in galvanizing their supporters and raising money. The inflammatory rhetoric emanating from each camp has turned off those of us caught in the crossfire. We are eager to broaden the conversation, to recover forgotten aspects of Christian faith. But a purple state of mind is also patient, offering people time and space to have their say.

People with a purple state of mind do not place their faith in a political view or a party. Instead, they seek to put on the attitude of Christ (Philippians 2:5). The apostle Paul describes Christ as taking on the form of a servant, humbling himself, becoming obedient even in death. These are anything but power moves. So how do we serve our communities? How do we humble ourselves before our neighbors? What does following the way of Christ look like in our daily lives? God's kingdom is not of this world, but we are forced to live out our faith in tangible ways. Jesus' followers were both liberal and conservative. They ranged from government officials like Matthew to an independent-minded fisherman like Peter. Some, like Judas, leaned toward zealotry and rebellion. Others attempted to uphold the status quo. Jesus made room for a range of positions and strategies within his followers.

The film began in the wake of the 2004 election, and this book arrives on the eve of the 2008 election. The surprising victories in the Iowa caucuses of Barack Obama and Mike Huckabee portended surprising change. Voters in the heartland rejected the preestablished party candidates. They chose Christian contrarians instead. Both Obama and Huckabee sounded more like preachers than politicians in their victory speeches. After his historic triumph, Obama suggested, "We're not blue states and red states, we are United States." People are desperate for a change, not just of president but also of perspective.

If you think the world's understanding of the word *Christian* has never been clearer, this book is not for you. If you feel no conflict about how America has positioned itself on the global stage, this book is not for you. If you think the blurring of faith and politics has been helpful, this book is not for you. But if you long for an alternative, a third way that embraces our humanity while honoring Christ's divinity, keep reading.

What Is a Purple State of Mind?

1. A purple state of mind has grown tired of old arguments. It longs to get beyond the red state–blue state divide. It embraces the freedom of the 1960s and the responsibilities of the 1950s.

2. A purple state of mind has experienced the grace of God and extends it to others. It pursues goodness, purity, and holiness out of joy rather than burden. It is transformed and transforming, reformed and ever reforming.

3. A purple state of mind affirms the ancient orthodox creeds but connects them to practical deeds. It puts an equal emphasis on beliefs and practices, living out an embodied faith.

4. A purple state of mind communicates through words and images. It affirms art and artists. It seeks renewed metaphors of faith, hope, and love.

5. A purple state of mind experiences periods of doubt and depression, dark nights of the soul. It endures serious, unexpected trials. But rather than escape from pain, a purple state of mind confronts death and dying with confidence. It recognizes that Jesus conquered our worst fears, leading us even to embrace laughter.

6. A purple state of mind receives love and extends love. It recognizes the difference between love and sex. It is prepared to be disappointed by others, but it never despairs. Faith, hope, and love endure.

7. A purple state of mind embraces the Bible as God's living word, still speaking into our lives today. It understands the importance of dual listening, holding what we see in tension with what God says. A purple state of mind unearths hidden or neglected verses, following the Spirit's lead in ongoing revelation.

8. A purple state of mind does not stand in judgment over friends, family, or neighbors around the world. It takes heed of Jesus'

warning. Who's in danger of hell? Me. It pursues our heavenly calling, working toward the city of God. It cultivates the garden.

9. A purple state of mind loves children, all children, and works to ensure they have the healthiest, heartiest life possible. It adopts a holistic approach to ministry. It bridges generation gaps. A purple state of mind defends widows and orphans, seeking justice for all.

10. A purple state of mind takes the suffering of others seriously. It listens. Really listens. It doesn't put Band-Aids on bullet wounds. Rather, it attends to the size and scope of others' pain through pastoral caring and long-term relationships. It rests in the power of silence.

11. A purple state of mind searches for beauty and wonder. It finds a role within God's dramatic actions. It joins with others in performing God's words on the stage of life.

12. A purple state of mind follows and worships Jesus. It doesn't place faith in politics, in power, or in people. It adopts the long view. It is hopeful that despite the ugliness of today's situation, the reign of Christ will prevail.

These 12 principles will serve as the through line for *A Purple State of Mind*. We may not agree on every point. In wrestling with what it means to serve Christ in a new millennium, we draw upon the best of ancient faith practices to forge our future. As John and I sought common ground, we also agreed to disagree in a manner that kept our friendship intact. A mature faith will not feel threatened by differences of opinion or doctrine. Dealing with issues within Christian community should sharpen our minds, quicken our hearts, and strengthen our faith. Let's proceed!

California

Many consider Los Angeles a godless Sodom and Gomorrah. The misadventures of Britney Spears and Paris Hilton demonstrate how low the rich and famous can go. Yet from the early days of Hollywood, movie stars like Fatty Arbuckle could literally get away with murder. Glamorous images of sunshine and surf attracted people to L.A. The population in Southern California exploded in the 1950s. Teenagers cruised down the Sunset Strip. But then, images from the Watts riots of 1965 sent shockwaves across America. Which vision of Los Angeles would prevail? The fires following the Rodney King verdict demonstrated ongoing tensions besetting the City of Angels.

Despite its sinful reputation, Los Angeles' origins are profoundly spiritual. Catholic missionaries founded it as *La Ciudad de Nuestra Senora, la Reina de los Angeles*—"The City of Our Lady, the Queen of the Angels." The city hosted two of the most significant religious movements in twentieth-century Christianity. In 1906, a one-eyed, black preacher named William J. Seymour began a series of meetings marked by emotional outbursts, dramatic healings, and speaking in tongues. The Azusa Street Revival was a multiracial movement that spawned such dynamic denominations as the Assemblies of God, the International Church of the Foursquare Gospel, and the Church of God in Christ. Modern Pentecostalism started in a dilapidated warehouse along Azusa Street.

In 1908, Lyman Stewart, the co-owner of the Union Oil Company, teamed up with minister T.C. Horton to found the Bible Institute of Los Angeles. Concerned about the rise of science and scholarship potentially undermining the tenets of the Christian faith, Stewart also commissioned a 12-volume series called *The Fundamentals.* These pamphlets served as the basis for the fast-growing fundamentalist movement.

Perhaps proximity to Hollywood allowed the Bible Institute of Los Angeles (rechristened as the acronym, Biola) to merge conservative Christian faith with mainstream media. It published magazines like *The King's Business* and a broadcast from radio station KTBI. It now trains the next generation of filmmakers through a Cinema and Media Arts major. When Biola invited me to direct their film program, I was intrigued. I decided to educate our 200 student filmmakers through practical, professional experience.

We took 20 students to the 2005 Sundance Film Festival to show them the competitive world of independent film. As we watched the passionate, low-budget movies, I wondered why people of faith did not display similar courage. Why don't we make more bold, brave, and affordable independent films? I returned from Sundance ready to make a difference.

John Marks called to say he'd just sold a book to HarperCollins about faith and politics in America. My old college roommate was using his journey out of evangelical faith as the backdrop for the book. John wanted to come to Los Angeles to interview me. He asked, "Would you mind if I recorded our conversation?" The more I thought about that potential conversation, loaded with history and pregnant with awkward pauses, the more I decided there might be a movie within it. Surrounded by an empty studio, a wealth of equipment, and a host of eager film students, I had all the elements in place for a low-budget independent film. I told students on Monday that we were starting *Purple State of Mind* on Wednesday. And so the conversation began...

Freedom and Responsibility

1

How did the culture war begin? Was there a clear winner? Or did it devolve into a long, costly stalemate?[1] What can we learn from the battle? Perhaps we are not as polarized as we presume.[2] Political parties and pundits strive to distinguish themselves from the competition in the starkest possible terms. We use rhetoric to rail against one another while our core positions may involve only a slight divergence. We may be hardly separated rather than deeply divided. Can we move from an adolescent mind-set, shouting across the religious and political divide, into something more thoughtful, productive, and mature?

As a witness to the sixties and seventies, I've seen how destructive we can be—even toward ourselves. I've also lived through the comparative comfort of the Reagan era in the eighties. He turned back the clock to a prosperous vision of America before the social upheavals of the sixties. Can we uphold the vigorous freedom of the sixties alongside the rigorous responsibility of the fifties?

A purple state of mind pushes past the either/or squabbles of an earlier era. It adopts a both/and approach to following God and interacting with the world. It builds bridges rather than burning them. It seeks common ground rather than points of division. A purple state of mind attains maturity by knowing when and where to apply biblical truths to our blind spots.

John: I think this should be a candid discussion.

Craig: I want it to be first and foremost an honest conversation. Straightforward. Tell the truth. Nothing held back.

Were you alive when President John F. Kennedy was shot? While the world wailed, I was warm in my mother's womb. She was in the doctor's office, awaiting a checkup on my status. I was born two months after Kennedy was assassinated. I arrived after the initial shockwave, the outpouring of grief, and the confusion as to why such tragedy happens. But we all continue to wrestle with the conflicts that erupted in the wake of Kennedy's death.

I entered a world on fire. Throughout my childhood, there were riots in the streets, protests on campuses, scenes from Vietnam in the news. My parents attempted to shield me from much of the conflict, turning me on to Mr. Rogers rather than Walter Cronkite. Yet the palpable conflicts over civil rights, free speech, and the war draft spilled into newspapers, televisions, and casual conversations. The struggle for civil rights was more than a century in the making. Leaders like Rosa Parks and Martin Luther King were as patient as possible, given their long walk to freedom. Yet the positive steps created by the Civil Rights Act still moved too slowly for those trapped in the inner city. Riots in Watts and Detroit set cities ablaze. The mistakes of the Vietnam War constitute their own painful book. As images of the war filtered into our living rooms, resentment toward our leaders grew. Chaos reigned among protestors inside and outside the 1968 Democratic National Convention.

I knew my dad hated the protestors, but I didn't know why. Something about their appearance bugged him. It may have been their long hair, their scanty clothes, and their flagrant disregard of authority. The hippies seemed equally frustrated by people like my father. They were complaining about the man, the system, anyone over 30. Why were the protestors so angry? What was all the shouting about? A generation gap emerged over the war in Vietnam. The students were ostensibly resisting the draft. They did not want to serve in an endless, misguided war in Southeast Asia.

Behind the political policies were distinct lifestyle choices. The hippies were celebrating free love, plentiful drugs, and raucous rock music. My father was wondering what happened to hard work, paying taxes, and civic responsibility. Teenagers embraced freedom while adults trumpeted responsibility. These dueling notions of the American identity exploded into a full-blown culture war that has been raging ever since. Reporter Ronald Brownstein calls this second civil war "the great sorting out."[3]

A purple state of mind appreciates the competing ideals that launched the culture war. It recognizes the patriotism that resides behind both visions. It remembers how much capital was created by responsible citizenship in the fifties. It also celebrates the ingenuity unleashed in the freedom-loving sixties. We learned valuable lessons from both eras. A purple state of mind borrows from both, combining freedom and responsibility.

The Fifties Versus the Sixties

I have lived my entire life in the shadow of the 1960s. I've heard the stirring speeches of Martin Luther King and Malcolm X. I've mourned the assassination of Bobby Kennedy in Dion's song, "Abraham, Martin, and John." I've been taken to the Vietnam War in *Apocalypse Now.* How many television specials have I seen that retrace the upheavals of 1968? *Rolling Stone* magazine commemorates Woodstock or the Summer of Love every single year! Was it the best of times or the worst of times? Forty years on, we're still locked in an adolescent debate. We see it in the childish name-calling of Bill O'Reilly and Ann Coulter on the right or MoveOn.org and Daily Kos on the left.

Every American presidential election since the sixties has essentially been a referendum on that painful era. There were no clear winners in Vietnam. Like Rambo, we're still fighting. It is a dark era in American history most of us would rather not review (even though we must learn those lessons so we stop repeating them). The fissure generated in Vietnam lies behind our conflicted feelings over the war in Iraq. We can't talk rationally as a nation about important issues because of deep-seated, unresolved family dynamics. If you prefer the comparative calm of the fifties, then you know how to vote. If you uphold the progressive hopes of the sixties, then it is clear which candidate represents you. The only problem with this pattern is that many of us missed the fifties *and* the sixties. We're ready to move on, to live in this moment, to meet today's challenges rather than to relive yesterday's news.

Living with this conflict is comparable to listening to our parents argue. We've heard all the lines, all the rhetoric, and all the old grudges. We can recite them from memory, and we've been exhausted by the gridlock. We haven't bothered to speak up because we know our parents were too busy arguing to listen. The shouting match showed no signs of abating, so we let the circus pass us by. Instead of joining the conversation, we elected to start our own companies, clubs, and churches. The creative brain drain from civic activities has been well documented.[4] Those who were turned off by the partisan rancor eventually turned off the pundits on TV. We are on the Internet instead, arguing about the minutia that remains distinctly ours—music, movies, television, shopping. We don't want to be superficial. But with no creative political options, we opt out. If we hope to engage the next generation in public life, then this culture war, rooted in bitter recriminations, must stop. For the sake of our children and grandchildren, we must call a cease-fire.[5]

Those of us who've inherited this war have seen enough casualties. John Marks and I were born at the end of the baby boom and the beginning of Generation X. We understand the majority position and empathize with the minorities who've been sidelined by the sheer size of the opposition. Consider this book an effort to bridge the generation gap. I'm here to help those over fifty understand what is coming. I stand between the baby boomers and their children, brokering a truce. As a professor, I've invested heavily in Generation Y, hoping that they will enact enough changes to make room for my children—Generation Z!

Seeking Wisdom

Seek wisdom, not knowledge.
Knowledge is of the past; wisdom is of the future.

NATIVE AMERICAN PROVERB

I recount our recent history in an effort to fill in gaps in our understanding. We must comprehend where we've been if we hope to figure out where we're going. I've seen the abuses of power represented by Watergate. The special prosecutor's hearings interrupted hours of my favorite TV cartoons. (Did you realize that Hillary Clinton was part of the legal team investigating Nixon's White House? Republicans have struggled with her for a looooong time!) I watched Nixon's sad wave goodbye on the White House lawn. I also understand the faith embodied by the first "born again" president, Jimmy Carter. His Southern Baptist beliefs led him to broker peace in the Middle East. Yet I also endured the 444 days of the Iranian hostage crisis that accompanied his peaceful negotiations. After such international embarrassment, Americans desperately wanted to return to the fifties era of strength and power. Ronald Reagan played the part of forceful leader resisting the Soviet Union. The fall of the Berlin Wall and the collapse of Communism was a victory for freedom around the world.

Unresolved tensions about Vietnam, drugs, and the sixties fueled the vitriol hurled at the Clintons *and* the Bushes. Bill Clinton strapped on the mantle of President Kennedy, declaring himself "A Man from Hope." His appearance playing saxophone on *The Arsenio Hall Show* sent a clear signal that he embraced civil rights. As "entertainer in chief," Clinton demonstrated a mastery of the electronic medium. His obfuscations about inhaling marijuana and dalliances with White House intern Monica Lewinsky also sparked latent fears of sex, drugs, and rock & roll. (Did you realize that Monica's famous blue dress was found in her mother's apartment—in the Watergate complex?) To his detractors, Clinton represented too much freedom and not enough presidential responsibility. The impeachment proceedings against him were a recapitulation and payback for the embarrassment borne by the Nixon administration.

George W. Bush represented a return to the fifties. He may have engaged in alcohol abuse or cocaine use, but Bush confessed his sins and seemed genuinely contrite. He experienced the dangers of too much personal freedom and welcomed the responsibility he found in his newfound faith. While Clinton parsed verbs, Bush offered plain-spoken surety. He distanced himself from his patrician upbringing, adopting a Texas rancher lifestyle as a populist alternative. To those tired of Clinton's libertinism and excess, Bush offered a down-home throwback: cowboy boots and pickup trucks.

Yet all the tough talk in the world seemed insufficient in dealing with a nearly unseen enemy. How could a band of terrorists bring down the World Trade Center? They used our strengths against us, hijacking our own planes. They crashed into our most impressive symbols of financial prowess and military might. September 11, 2001, humbled and angered us. We marched into the Middle East with unprecedented firepower. Afghanistan fell almost without resistance. We submitted Iraq to "shock and awe." Unfortunately, Osama bin Laden and Al Qaeda proved they could not only run but also hide. We attacked nations, but our enemies were individuals. American technology ended up undermined by insurgents with homemade bombs. We terrorized others with torture at Guantanamo Bay and Abu Ghraib. We operated like a powerful empire but proved incapable of ferreting out an ideology. We desperately need leaders who can protect freedoms while serving as responsible world citizens. Such nuance has been lost in our prolonged and pointless culture war.

The next generation admires the civic responsibility of the fifties *and* the progressive art and music of the sixties. They have embraced a both/and view but have been alienated by either/or debates. A purple state of mind embraces freedom *and* responsibility. It takes the best of history but leaves the worst excesses (on both sides) behind. It blows away the purple haze hanging over our past. This chapter highlights key moments that got us into this mess. It will offer tangible proposals for moving on with maturity.

Nixon Versus Kennedy

For almost 50 years, we have been sorting out the choices represented by the first televised presidential debate, Republican Richard M. Nixon versus Democrat John F. Kennedy. On September 26, 1960, Vice President Nixon and Senator Kennedy squared off under the moderation of ABC's Howard K. Smith. Over 80 million viewers tuned into the debate, which pitted Nixon's experience (eight years as Eisenhower's vice-president) against Kennedy's comparative youth (one term as a U.S. senator). Both candidates offered hawkish opposition to the Communist threat represented by the Soviet Union. They debated issues of national debt, farm subsidies, welfare, and health care that continue to be unresolved. They drew distinctions about the role of government to stimulate economic growth. But Nixon and Kennedy diverged most significantly in style rather than substance.

Kennedy arrived at the debates looking tan, rested, and energetic. Nixon looked haggard, having recently fought off the flu. He refused to don makeup, figuring his forceful words would rule the day. Those who listened to the debate on the radio found Nixon the victor. Yet those watching the debate on tiny black-and-white televisions saw something else. They saw Nixon sweat while Kennedy smiled. Although Nixon was only five years older than Kennedy, his demeanor seemed comparatively ancient in outlook and energy. Nixon's noticeable five-o'clock shadow didn't help either.

Nixon learned the connections between style and substance too late in the campaign. Makeup covered his beard in three subsequent television debates. But Kennedy gained just enough confidence and votes to capture the closest general election of the twentieth century. Just one-tenth of 1 percent of votes separated Kennedy from Nixon. Americans have remained almost equally divided ever since.

The legacy of John F. Kennedy remains remarkably hopeful and progressive. Consider the optimism behind his war on poverty. Having watched the Russians beat Americans into orbit, Kennedy redefined the terms of the space race. How much chutzpah did it take to engage in a race to the moon? His version of American government looks almost absurdly hopeful in hindsight.

When Richard Nixon campaigned for president in 1968 (and for reelection in 1972), he promised an alternative to the vexing Vietnam War. Nixon expanded the Cold War efforts to include Cambodia and Laos. He presented a stronger America that refused to be intimidated. At the same time, Nixon engaged in a remarkable array of diplomatic missions to China and the Soviet Union. He met his adversaries face-to-face, winning surprising concessions and forging unexpected alliances.

Behind their policies, presidents Kennedy and Nixon represented divergent attitudes toward profound social change within America. The Kennedy years brought glamour to the White House. Entertainers like Marilyn Monroe sang sultry birthday greetings to President Kennedy. An air of celebration could also be read as a reign of permissiveness. A Democratic administration presided over the explosion of sex, drugs, and rock and roll. Progressive politics coincided with experimentation and unrest. The Nixon presidency offered a return to law and order. Freedom took a backseat to responsibility. In 1971, President Nixon identified drug abuse as public enemy number one in the United States. He created the Special Action Office for Drug Abuse Prevention (it became the Drug Enforcement Administration in 1973). We've been fighting America's longest war, the war on drugs, ever since.

Purple Haze

Jimi Hendrix' song "Purple Haze" epitomizes the fuzzy grasp of reality that accompanied drug experimentation in the sixties. The title allegedly arose from a powerful batch of LSD served to Hendrix by Owsley Stanley. Some have also attributed it to a strain of purple marijuana. Hendrix said the inspiration arrived in a dream. Whatever the derivation, "Purple Haze" is rooted in altered states of consciousness. Released in 1967, "Purple Haze" served as the psychedelic anthem for San Francisco's summer of love. The key to the song's eerie sound is harmonic dissonance. Jimi's guitar is tuned in B-flat, while Noel Redding's bass plays E octaves. Such discordant sounds matched the era perfectly. A clash of cultures resulted in something jarring and new. Jimi didn't just play rock music, he offered the Jimi Hendrix Experience.

Consider the transcendent promises contained in his phrase, "'Scuse me while I kiss the sky." Some heard it as a sexual provocation, a pledge to kiss a guy. But the sound made it clear that his sights were set in the great beyond. At his seminal appearance at the Monterey Pop Festival, Jimi transported the crowd to a higher state of consciousness. He demonstrated the otherworldly power of raw feedback, playing his guitar behind, above, and beyond himself. Hendrix stepped into the role of sexual shaman, licking, caressing, and stroking guttural sounds from his Stratocaster. In setting his guitar on fire during "Wild Thing," Hendrix offered his gifts to the rock gods. It is an incantation, sacrificing his most precious possessions to the altar of altered states.

Unfortunately, Jimi's life ended up in a similar state of self-immolation, falling to pieces just as suddenly and tragically. The Experience Music Project in Seattle serves as a permanent archive for all things Hendrix. EMP founder Paul Allen spent part of his Microsoft millions acquiring Hendrix memorabilia, bringing it back to Jimi's hometown of Seattle. It is a memorial to a musical messiah. The hall dedicated to Jimi is fittingly called "Sky Church."

To others, "Purple Haze" demonstrated a world utterly adrift. The idyllic visions of Woodstock were undercut by the horrific murder at Altamont. With Hell's Angels serving as security, 1969's other free concert (at Altamont Speedway in Northern California) ended in death rather than musical bliss. Every time *Rolling Stone* magazine presents another rosy retrospective of the sixties, I wonder why it refuses to acknowledge the dark side of psychedelia. How can it hold up Hendrix, Joplin, and Jim Morrison as departed saints, when they are also exhibits A, B, and C in the perils of drug abuse? They were amazing and stupid at the same time. Great talents squandered by excess. So when parents who lived through the worst of the sixties attempt to spare their children the same amount of destructive experimentation, I applaud. "Just say no" arose from painful, lived experience. It may have been simplistic, but it was preferable to self-destruction.

Recent films like *Drugstore Cowboy, Trainspotting,* and *Requiem for a Dream* capture both the allure and the demolition of drugs. They provide an audio-visual approximation of a drug trip. Their images are intoxicating and attractive—the ultimate music videos. Yet their message is clear: Despite the attraction, do not be deceived—drugs will kill you. They serve as cautionary tales for a stylish era. Today's students have largely learned from the painful past. Rates of teenage pregnancies, drug use, and violence have hit 40-year lows. The parents from a turbulent era raised remarkably respectful, well-behaved kids. Demographers Neil Howe and William Strauss noted the surprising generational shift:

> Boomers started out as the objects of loosening child standards in an era of conformist adults. Millennials are starting out as the objects of tightening child standards in an era of non-conformists adults. By the time the last Millennials come of age, they could become…the cleanest-cut young adults in living memory.[6]

To a large degree, Generation Y has embraced the family values of the 1950s. But its rebellion remains wrapped in the profane packages of the 1960s.

Consider the violent, R-rated film *Fight Club* (1999). It is a scathing critique of consumer culture and middle-class values. We follow Jack, the bored protagonist, on a brutal slide into an underworld of macho self-abuse. Jack longs for genuine feeling, even if he must shed blood to achieve it. So while Jack may be a mild-mannered bureaucrat by day, he rallies his friends for bare-knuckled bar fights at night. *Fight Club* unleashes the fragile postmodern male id with frightening results. What begins as an invigorating alternative devolves into Project Mayhem, a prescient precursor to the terrorist attacks of 9/11. Schizophrenia leads to destructive nihilism.

This is contrasted by the diagnosis offered by the toughest puncher in the club, Tyler Durden. He summarizes the isolation of a generation raised in affluence rather than upheaval:

> Advertising has us chasing cars and clothes, working jobs we hate so we can buy s— we don't need. We're the middle children of history, man. No purpose or place. We have no Great War. No Great Depression. Our Great War's a spiritual war...our Great Depression is our lives. We've all been raised on television to believe that one day we'd all be millionaires and movie gods and rock stars. But we won't. And we're slowly learning that fact. And we're very, very p— off.

When I showed *Fight Club* to a class of undergraduate students, they nodded in recognition. They connected with Tyler's frustration. During a class discussion afterward, a student announced, "We're rebels." When I asked what they were rebelling against, he said, "Our parents." This all sounded more than vaguely familiar, so I pushed further. "What does that look like?" The students answered, "We don't want to be like our parents. Drinking. Doing drugs. Getting lots of divorces...we're rebels!" The most rebellious behavior imaginable? Abstinence!

While baby boomers harrumph about presidential candidates' ancient drug use, their children are begging for them to grow up. Parents complain to MTV about Britney Spears' kiss with Madonna. Switchboards light up from viewers shocked by Janet Jackson's nipple slip during the Super Bowl halftime show. Yet the next generation lets out a collective yawn. They've already seen it, done it, or dismissed it. They identify with the band Weezer, which recorded a song titled "Tired of Sex." They are ready to move on, past the provocation to more substantive issues. Rivers Cuomo of Weezer asks, "Oh, why can't I be making love come true?"

A New Conversation

Craig: My introduction to what it meant to follow Jesus was to be a laughingstock. It meant bad hair, bad makeup, and bad TV. Is this what I signed up for? This whole tension of red state and blue state, this is the tension that I live with—how do I own my own people who so make me cringe on a regular basis? This nomenclature of left and right, red and blue is not helpful right now.

John: It's not meant to be helpful. It's meant to do exactly what it does. I'm not happy with what people on the traditional left, or Democrats, say is their worldview. I honestly don't know if they have one. I'm as weary as anybody in this country of the politically correct dialogue, which basically says, "I'm a victim and you're not. No, *I'm* a victim and *you're* not." It's useless. It's done. It's dead. Postmodernism is dead. All those answers on the secular side are basically dead.

John Marks and I stand between generations. We are old enough to understand the boomers' intra-generational issues, yet we're still young enough to identify with the discontent of those who followed. We embarked on a purple state of mind because we're desperate for a new paradigm, hungering for a different set of talking points. We each risked alienating our constituencies. Coming from evangelical Christianity, I am part of the fifties tribe, which is struggling to protect home and hearth. As a journalist, John Marks identifies with the political left and their tattered ideals. We both find ourselves embarrassed by those we represent. I ask how God's people could have turned Jesus into a hater. John questions why allegedly free-thinking people are so close-minded when it comes to religion. A purple state of mind tries the patience of both sides. It runs the risk of disloyalty for the sake of a larger goal.

We must put the past behind us. We can no longer afford to be divided over issues of sexuality and drug use when global crises demand our attention. To lead the world, we must get past our adolescent fixation on who did what to whom. The rumor mills that trumped up charges against the Clintons in Whitewater or George W.

Bush with evasion of the Vietnam War have done nothing but distract us. How much negative energy has been expended on investigations that went nowhere? We've been busy digging up dirt when we should have been building roads and schools. We tore down a government in Iraq rather than solidifying our own ability to lead by example. Shame on us for obsessing over the past instead of investing in the future. No wonder voters in 2008 longed for change.

The Gospel According to Austin Powers

Our desperate need for freedom and responsibility rests in the seemingly contradictory letters of the apostle Paul. He applied his godly advice in a unique way for the audience he was addressing. To Corinthian Christians navigating a libertine culture, he preached caution. Corinth was noted for temples dedicated to Apollo and Aphrodite. Worship at these temples often included sex with temple prostitutes. They were thought to serve as conduits for the divine. An intimate sexual encounter on temple grounds was comparable to an experience with the gods. So imagine how confused early Corinthian Christians may have been about what constituted proper worship of Christ. Their understanding of Christian freedom knew no bounds. Paul urged the Corinthian church to exercise spiritual discipline, to get their house in order. He insisted they "flee from sexual immorality" (1 Corinthians 6:18). To those who claimed, "Everything is permissible," Paul responded with a chastening, "Everything is not beneficial" (1 Corinthians 10:23).

In Corinth, even eating meat could involve idolatrous activity. The local cults of Apollo and Aphrodite controlled so much of the public consciousness and economy that new believers were encouraged to examine the sources of their food supply. Food sacrificed to idols may not be contaminated physically, but Paul challenged the Corinthian to demonstrate sensitivity toward those who may have confused or conflated eating with idolatry. Paul urges the Corinthian believers to take responsibility for their Christian brothers and sisters. To a chaotic church, he preaches order, propriety, and maturity.

Yet to the uptight church in Galatia, Paul preaches freedom. The new believers clung too closely to their Jewish roots. Perhaps out of fear of persecution, the local church leaders insisted that new Christians adopt the rigorous (old) rules of Hebraic law. Gentile converts were expected to get circumcised according to Jewish ritual. Paul considers such attempts to bind people to ancient purity laws as a threat to the gospel of grace. He insists, "It is for freedom that Christ has set us free. Stand firm, then, and do not let yourselves be burdened again by a yoke of slavery" (Galatians 5:1). He begged the Galatian Christians to loosen up, to relax their standards in the name of Christ.

Was Paul contradicting himself? By no means! In each letter, he concludes with an appeal to love. To the legally minded Galatians, Paul summarizes the law in a single command, "Love your neighbor as yourself" (Galatians 5:14). To the battling Corinthians who confused sex with love, Paul spells out the attitudes and actions that constitute love. "Love is patient, love is kind. It does not envy, it does not boast, it is not proud" (1 Corinthians 13:4). He preaches freedom to Galatia and responsibility to Corinth because they each need to apply the message in a unique way.

Unfortunately, we often fail to identify our particular blind spots. Legalistic churches will often reiterate the call to purity given to the Corinthians. Lax churches will return to Paul's letter to the Galatians to justify more license. Those who need freedom cling to responsibility. Christians who need to learn responsibility insist upon the freedom Paul grants to Galatia. Those who have ears to hear, let them hear.

Austin Powers: International Man of Mystery urges us toward maturity. In the comedic conclusion, Austin gets the drop on a surprised Dr. Evil. But Evil remains unflappable and punches Austin's buttons: "We're not so different, you and I. However, isn't it ironic that the very things that you stand for—free love, swinging parties—are all now, in the nineties, considered to be evil?" Austin retorts, "No, man, what we swingers were rebelling against is uptight squares like you whose bag was money and world domination. We were innocent, man. If we'd known the consequences of our sexual liberation we would have done things differently, but the spirit would have remained the same. It's freedom, baby, yeah!" Austin Powers connects wisdom, experience, and the spirit all in one interrelated package. Dr. Evil offers a challenge: "Face it—freedom failed." With the sounds of the sixties anthem "What the World Needs Now Is Love" playing in the background, Austin concludes, "No man, freedom didn't fail. Right now we've got freedom *and* responsibility. It's a very groovy time." Even sassy movie stars can capture profound truths.

It is not freedom versus responsibility. It is not the law and order of the Republican Party *or* the liberal policies of the Democratic Party. We need a strong military to defend our freedoms. We need unregulated markets to encourage innovation. We need social agencies to check our greed and support "the least of these." We must find freedom *and* responsibility *between* the parties. We must learn to listen to Paul's competing calls. Christian maturity incorporates the whole of scripture and applies it to an integrated life. We must be aware of our history. We must recognize how we've become so divided. We must grow up as a nation, moving on to freedom and responsibility rather than dragging each other into ancient history. The radical claims of Paul continue to challenge us. Libertines may need to give up some freedoms for the health of others. Conservatives may need to unwind enough for the Spirit to enter in.

Adolescence is an experiment in self-governance. It is about identifying your own strengths and weaknesses, learning to moderate. Sometimes we fall on our faces from too much excess. At other times, we shrink back from opportunities we should have seized. Highly responsible people may sprint to early success and wake up 20 years later, wondering what all the compliance wrought. They will long for freedom. Those raised in a borderless environment will have to find a roadmap that shows where the blind curves and dangerous precipices are located. Maturity arises when those maps have been internalized, when familiarity with biblical wisdom coincides with personal experience. We appreciate the gift of freedom, but we also recognize when enough is enough. Only with our house in order can we begin to focus outwardly. We do not merely play thought police, checking and correcting others. Rather, we take on the deeper challenge of walking beside others, inviting them to join us on the journey. It's a very groovy time.

Grace
and
Goodness

2

From Watergate to Monica-gate, the office of the president has been undercut by ethical lapses. The scandals that discredited televangelists in the eighties were followed by a billion dollars in judgment against the Catholic church for covering up sexual abuse by priests. Enron trumped up earnings statements and burst Wall Street's bubble. Journalists assigned to investigate such malfeasance turned out to be creating their own fiction. Clearly, we are a culture in ethical crisis. The biblical book of Judges describes a time when "Israel had no king; everyone did as he saw fit" (Judges 17:6). We are living in an era of equally shifting standards. There are plenty of reasons to despair.

While confidence in our institutions plummets, the next generation demonstrates a profound interest in doing the right thing. Neil Howe and William Strauss characterize the Millennial generation as hardworking, team oriented, and achieving. They suggest that they'll be known for "a grassroots reconstruction of community, teamwork, and civic spirit. They're doing it in the realms of community service, race, gender relations, politics and faith."[1] They long to rescue war orphans in Uganda, to take on sexual trafficking in Thailand, and to engage in fair trade.[2] Note the shift in the million-selling songs of rock band Linkin Park. Initially, they were desperate to find "Somewhere I Belong." Their anger was directed at others who disappointed them. They were "Numb." On their album *Minutes to Midnight,* they still need to "Bleed It Out," but they also explore "What I've Done." They express a willingness to face themselves, to cross out what they've become en route to letting go of what they've done. The music video connects the dots between global problems and personal responsibility. In the face of environmental and economic crises, they offer a musical prayer to let mercy come and wash away what we've all done. Solving issues of poverty, injustice, and health care will require sacrifices from all of us.

Today's students are the best behaved in my lifetime. Despite high-profile cases like Columbine, teen crime is way down. Many are willing to forgo experimentation with sex and drugs for the sake of a larger goal.[3] The rise in Christian college enrollment may be tied to their hunger to live with purity and purpose. They demonstrate a strong sense of personal responsibility, taking on jobs to help pay for books and tuition. The next generation is tireless in its efforts, but these kids are nearly worn out. They have been sheltered by their parents yet still feel pressured to achieve. They are exhausting themselves in pursuit of goodness, beauty, and truth.

I'm glad they want to do the right thing, but they must grasp grace first. Despite their best intentions, striving to attain goodness will not work. They'll be burnt out abolitionists, environmentalists, and teachers. How can we build a sustainable personal economy? What is needed to maintain servanthood? We can only reverse the tide of irresponsibility while still walking in the grace of God. This chapter will contrast my spiritual journey with John Marks' experience of Jesus. I entered via grace. John started his Christian commitment in goodness. Could these divergent means be connected to our long-term results?

Craig: My whole spiritual search, I connect to the films of Martin Scorsese. I see *Raging Bull* as a senior in high school,

and I say, that's me! I am that raging bull, I am that caged
animal. I am that self-destructive.

Saint Augustine confessed to stealing an apple. I'll confess to boost-
ing a pack of baseball cards. As a ten-year-old, my life of petty crime
was exhilarating and horrifying at the same time. In junior high, I
skipped school with some of my more delinquent friends. We walked
to the local mall. On a dare, we each stole a pair of sunglasses, hiding
them in the front of our pants. Mine were bright red with blue trim—
very seventies. I never wore them again.

I'm no saint. But evidently, such chicanery is a precondition for
canonization. Like St. Augustine, I have a sin problem. We all do. I
am two-faced. I project an image of wholeness while protecting my
seamier side. As a teenager, I became an expert at satisfying adults and
currying my peers' favor. This meant punctuality at school and party-
ing on the weekend. Good grades chased by good times. Nothing is
impressive or exceptional about such activities; they just represent your
garden-variety duplicity.[4] Nevertheless, I still tend to protect my dirty
laundry. If pressed, I may admit to premarital sex, but I'd rather not go
into details. Drinking and drugs I set aside as my business, not yours.
Yet, a certain amount of confession is necessary if we have any hope of
recovery. I have an addiction to sin. We all do.[5] It is easy to recognize
it in others. We can point out the fallacies in people and institutions.
We look at a fractured world and agree, "It's not the way it's supposed
to be."[6] But how do we tell our story without reveling in our own dirt?
Can we document our sinfulness without celebrating it?

A purple state of mind recognizes our limitations. It has reached
the end of a rope and reached up for a lifesaving hand. A purple state
of mind has experienced the grace of God and extends it to others.
It is transformed and transforming, reformed and ever reforming.
It strives to see clearly, to put on the mind of Christ. The pursuit of
purity flows out of radical grace. A purple state of mind connects the
dots between personal piety and the public good.

Martin Scorsese's hard-hitting movie *Raging Bull* (1980) gave me a sneak preview of the dangerous road ahead of me. Robert De Niro's Oscar-winning performance as self-destructive boxer Jake LaMotta held up a cracked, R-rated mirror to my fractured psyche. Jake LaMotta won the world middleweight boxing championship in 1949. Yet he couldn't sustain relationships. He alienated his brother, his wife, everyone who cared about him. In *Raging Bull,* LaMotta loses his championship belt and ends up alone in a jail cell. He bangs his head against the wall, begging, "Why? Why? Why?" He cries, "I am not an animal!" Such self-destruction looks positively primeval. By the end of the film, a washed-up, overweight Jake LaMotta works as an entertainer in a low-life lounge. Backstage, he recites Marlon Brando's famous speech from *On the Waterfront.* Brando's poignant admission, "I could have been a contender instead of a bum, which is what I am" mirrors LaMotta's own descent. It is a devastating, depressing conclusion to the ultimate cautionary tale.

As the screen fades to black, Scorsese dedicates *Raging Bull* to his mentor from New York University film school, Haig Manoogian. He follows that with quotations from the Gospel of John where Jesus heals a blind man. In John 9, Jesus mixes his spit with the local dirt to create a healing mudpack. The locals want to know how Jesus accomplished such a miracle. When they ask the blind man to explain the process, he responds with utter simplicity. His words haunted and intrigued me: "One thing I do know. I was blind but now I see" (John 9:25).

Surely, Jake LaMotta was blind to his self-destruction; he became his own worst enemy. Such blindness seemed familiar. I knew how blocked and frustrated I felt with my own situation. But seeing was another story. Clarity would be wonderful. My mind raced with the possibilities: to gain self-control, to understand the forces that animate this life, to walk with focus. This brutal film awakened my deep longing to see.

Raging Bull allowed me to see myself in sharp relief. It echoes the biblical letter of James: "Anyone who listens to the word but does not do what it says is like a man who looks at his face in a mirror and, after looking at himself, goes away and immediately forgets what he looks like" (James 1:24). Living one life is hard enough. Juggling two lives is exhausting. By the time I graduated from high school, I'd had enough. I was ready to start over. I began attending Young Life, a high-energy and relational youth ministry. At Young Life, I first heard the words *personal relationship* and *Jesus Christ* in the same sentence. To my self-destructive habits, Young Life offered a simple but costly option. I could exchange my tired and tattered duplicity for a single-minded focus. I considered this potent offer.

Following Jesus looked awfully attractive as a freshman in college. Cut off from family and friends, I was ready to start anew. None of my old life necessarily bound me. I was invited to a weekend camp at Young Life's Windy Gap. The speaker talked about the cost of discipleship, something I had already considered. Jesus' challenge in Luke 9:24 made sense: "If anyone would come after me, he must deny himself and take up his cross daily and follow me." Was I willing to be "all in"? In October 1981 at Windy Gap, I committed all I knew about myself to all I'd heard about Jesus. It resulted in an immediate internal leap. My guilt was lifted, my spirit quickened. As the final line of my favorite film, *Casablanca,* says, "It was the beginning of a beautiful friendship."

Grace

John: That quickening you're talking about—that's a beautiful word. How?

Craig: My early days with Jesus were the biggest high I'd ever experienced. That's for real. I woke up in the morning and I'm just like, "I'M ALIVE! Look at the sky, it's so blue! Look at those plants, they're so green! I love Jesus; he loves me. My senses started tingling.

I came back from camp with a goofy grin on my face. Grace and forgiveness overwhelmed me. I was stunned by such freedom. I got involved in Davidson Christian Fellowship, joining a small group Bible study. I ate up every word we studied. I started practicing personal

Bible reading as well. I couldn't believe how radical and refreshing Jesus could be. All fall, I bounded across campus with a song in my heart. No amount of homework could dampen my joy. Having been granted a new lease on life, I couldn't imagine being burdened by common, everyday complaints. I sailed through classes on a spiritual high. Rather than unbearable, the lightness of my being was positively lilting. My newfound faith flowed out of every pore. I couldn't contain my literal "en-theos-iasm."

How could I explain something so ridiculous? Grace makes no mathematical sense. All the debts in my account were wiped off the books. With amazing grace, to bring up the past is a waste of time. Despite my best efforts to drag myself back through the mud of my own making, God had moved on. Old skeletons? Cleared out. Old business? Forgotten. Old news? Redeemed. There is no condemnation (or even recollection!) in Jesus Christ. We can take a lifetime to grasp the wideness of God's mercy. To forget it is far too easy. To reject it is absolutely tragic.

What an amazing fear-fighting agent! I brimmed with confidence, aware that "with God all things are possible" (Matthew 19:26). I memorized the promise that "no temptation has seized you except what is common to man. And God is faithful...he will also provide a way out" (1 Corinthians 10:13). I approached final exams knowing "I can do everything through him who gives me strength" (Philippians 4:13). I felt like more than a conqueror through him who loved us (Romans 8:37).

Yet my crusade was also loaded with compassion. To those who struggle with self-image, God said, "You're beautiful." To those obsessed with others' opinions, God said, "You're preapproved with me." To those who had been abused, God said, "I remember, I weep, I comfort, and I restore." Grace changes the rules of the game. It places us on a different playing field altogether. There are still lines, but there is so much room to roam. Why obsess over the edges when there is so much playing to be done? And yet we struggle to appropriate this new reality. It is far too easy to turn religion into a rule rather than a release.

Goodness

John: My experience of Jesus happened in the context of somebody who was already sort of very straight-laced. I kind of went to Sunday school. I didn't even listen to rock and roll until I was sixteen. And you know what my first album was that opened my eyes? It was Queen's *News of the World*, which isn't even rock and roll. It's pathetic.

Goodness knows, goodness is in short supply. Evil is easy to portray onscreen, but goodness is rarely dramatized. Nice characters come off as more saccharine than sweet. Innocence is often viewed as naïveté. Over time, the purity of Pollyanna has become associated with foolishness, a failure to grasp reality. Are Christians living in the real world? Or as we've been accused, are we so heavenly minded that we're no earthly good? In the brilliant fantasy His Dark Materials trilogy, Philip Pullman inverts John Milton's *Paradise Lost*. Pullman suggests that Adam and Eve's fall was a good thing. Humanity should seek knowledge. In seeking self-determination, we arrive at true wisdom. For Pullman, the fall from grace was fortunate rather than catastrophic. While American audiences roundly rejected the cinematic version of the trilogy's first book, *The Golden Compass,* we have widely embraced the notion that innocence is undesirable.

Consequently, I am so impressed by the goodness of so many Christian students. They honestly want to do the right thing. They are willing to forgo cheap thrills for a higher calling. In an age of instant gratification, the rise of abstinence became headline news. *Newsweek* ran a cover story on "The New Virginity."[7] *GQ* sent a reporter to Biola.[8] They profiled one of my film students, shocked that a hunk like Jacob could postpone sexual activity until marriage. ABC's *Nightline* turned the story into a segment on this strange species known as Christian college students.[9] The Biola students answered correspondent Jake Tepper's questions with aplomb. A reporter from *The New York Times Magazine* even moved into a Biola dormitory.[10] She found the same commitment to personal piety. But amid the model behavior, she also uncovered some interesting exceptions. Students revealed their struggles with homosexuality, their frequenting of gay bars, and the lure of alternative lifestyles. Goodness is tough to maintain even within a Christian college bubble. Only from an experience of grace can we walk in enduring goodness.

I indulged most of my appetites in high school. Growing up, the legal drinking age was only 18. Even in junior high school, almost everyone had an older brother or sister who could and would buy the beer. My innocence did not make it through a spring break beach trip. Charlotte area high schools descended upon Myrtle Beach for an unholy week of debauchery. We felt it was our duty to ingest as much alcohol and hook up with as many partners as possible. We accomplished our goals within 48 hours. I lost my virginity on a bleary Easter morning. I recall feeling vaguely guilty about the connection on the calendar. But we still had five more disgusting days to go. By the end of the week we were literally sick of ourselves. To consider God's grace in that context was truly shocking. How can Jesus embrace such a degraded person?

In high school, I was a sinner in need of a Savior. John Marks was a nice person trying to be nicer with Jesus. It is tough to be rescued from a position of strength or comfort. We may appreciate the beauty of Christian doctrine, the sacrifice embodied in the cross, but if we're basically good people practicing a decent life, what difference does Jesus make? Rather than a help, the rigors of Christian behavior can become a burden. Being good can become a buffer from truly experiencing life. Perhaps our divergent journeys arise from those early choices we made. I was burnt out on sin by age 17. John had barely started. Which path is preferable?

As a Christian college professor, I had students that were generally bright, compliant, and sweet. I recall a casual reference I made in class to Glenfiddich. It was met by blank stares. They had no idea that Glenfiddich was a Scotch, let alone how it tasted. I was touched by their limited life experience. In an era of overindulgence, how rare and refreshing! Yet they also had a hard time grasping how much freedom they'd been granted. In class, they asked questions about what was forbidden rather than what was permissible. They wanted me to draw clear boundaries on what they could see, what they could say, what they could portray. They struggled with parental disapproval, afraid of being judged by the kinds of films they wanted to make. Their gifts and callings were at war with their upbringing. Too many don'ts had crimped their creativity and blocked out the wealth of dos. I admire the high standards embraced by my Christian students, but my heart also aches for those who have been raised to simply color inside the lines. Too many focus only on toeing the outer edges rather than enjoying the broad spaces between them.

If I could have given my Christian college students one graduation gift, it would have been Philip Yancey's seminal book *What's So Amazing About Grace?* Yancey grasps how precious and rare grace remains "our last best word." Yet he writes about his own struggles to turn a theological concept into a lived reality. Sadly, Yancey's Christian college education did not help. "I realized that in four years I learned almost nothing about grace."[11] How could a movement founded on forgiveness have heaped guilt rather than grace upon its students? Christian counselor David Seamands concludes, "The two major causes of most emotional problems among evangelical Christians are these: the failure to understand, receive and live out God's unconditional grace and forgiveness; and the failure to give out that unconditional love, forgiveness, and grace to other people."[12] Is this why we often approach the public with harsh rebukes rather than gracious freedom? We heap burdens upon others that threaten to bury us. Lightness of being is exchanged for a heavy load.

Grace seems to have been buried under good intentions. Parents want to protect their children from sin. They hope to spare them the painful insight gained through experience. Those who witnessed the libertine sixties wanted to avoid a reprise. Innocence was preserved through an elaborate system. A series of checks and balances was erected to keep kids from sin. Alternative music, videos, and curriculum were developed to promote "all Jesus, all the time." A steady diet of Christian entertainment provides protection from the MTV virus. A coterie of like-minded friends ensures a nurturing environment. The homeschool movement exploded in the wake of ever more permissive public schools.

As a parent, I understand the appeal. There are radically divergent truth claims within the marketplace of ideas. The proliferation of electronic communication increases the anxiety. Rather than allowing competing worldviews to have free reign within our children's minds, we can limit the sources. We control the content within our homes, our cars, and our computers. Unfortunately, we cannot squelch curiosity. The more fearful our faith, the more powerful and alluring our enemies become. Students obsess over sex simply because it seems so illicit. A Facebook group at Biola proclaimed, "I'm going to have crazy sex when I'm married." Parents pay a premium for Christian colleges in order to postpone the inevitable. Perhaps their children will find a mate without playing the field. Maybe they could share their first kiss with the only person they will ever kiss. It is so amazingly old-fashioned and romantic. Maybe four years of Christian college can postpone the age of accountability long enough to skip experimentation entirely. Given the complexities of today's dating games, married sex at age 21 looks quite attractive.

For a combination of reasons, the bubble that has been erected around the current generation of college students has resulted in prolonged adolescence. So while Christian students get married right out of college, the process of discerning their gifts, calling, and values is still underway. In some cases, newly married couples grow into adulthood together. In others, the sorting out that takes place in their twenties results in divergent paths. I have been honored to preside over the weddings of several incredibly cute couples. In several cases, they truly represent a first love. Their hormones are racing so strongly as they race to the altar.

Unfortunately, I have also sat down with devastated friends and former students going through a painful divorce. Just as they each were starting to define their career or calling, they woke up to the realization that they no longer recognized the person they married at age 21. In a few cases, a baby was caught in the middle of the messiness. I admire the goodness that drove them to the altar at an early age. And I believe God's grace can cover a multitude of sins. But what should a purple state of mind embrace? How much experience do we need to grasp God's forgiveness? How can we best fulfill the goodness that we're called to practice?

Whatever Is True

> **John:** You know what that album [Bruce Springsteen's *Nebraska*] suggested to me in a way that I couldn't have articulated then is that "you're blinding yourself with this whole religiosity thing that you got yourself into when you were sixteen years old."
>
> **Craig:** So blindness for you became seeing for me.
>
> **John:** Yeah, I think so. Here's the difference. For you, I think that Christ was in great part a liberation from where you came from.
>
> **Craig:** Yes.
>
> **John:** For me, it was slavery from where I came from.

My journey of faith is intimately connected to the R-rated films of Martin Scorsese, the punk rock of The Clash, and the songs of Bruce Springsteen. Their artistic cries for something genuine, real, and transforming resonated with me. They are restless truth seekers, willing to explore the darkest corners of human behavior in search of redemption. They told me things that I inherently suspected about schools, governments, and churches. "All is not as rosy as it appears." "Those who smile broadest may have the most to hide." "A healthy dose of skepticism will serve you well in life." "Sometimes there's just a meanness in this world." They proved to me that goodness and grace are both in short supply.

Shortly after I decided to follow Jesus, a Christian leader challenged me to throw away my Clash albums. Why do I need such angry music? Wouldn't I prefer the righteous anger of Petra to the rants of British punks? Actually, no. If The Clash instilled a hunger for truth within me, wouldn't that same hunger (and Spirit!) continue to draw me toward God?

I understand that some people need to turn away from their old habits to fully embrace a new life with Christ. They may need to exchange a destructive subculture for a supportive Christian community. Former alcoholics probably shouldn't be tending bar. But I am talking about holding on to the best of what spoke to you. Maybe Bruce Springsteen's music appealed to my best instincts. God may even like what it does to me, stirring up a longing for justice, a commitment to the greater good. Rather than focusing upon the anarchistic aspects of The Clash, I was drawn to the hope residing in their rants. Instead of giving up on social transformation, Joe Strummer sang with an intensity that demanded action. As Jesus galvanized his followers, so The Clash gave people a larger sense of purpose. We must fight, resist, and rebel against the forces of corruption. We shout in the face of cynicism. We crank our guitars up in an act of defiance, declaring that we will not be fooled (again).

Via Negativa

The *via negativa* is a time-honored means of achieving transcendence. As a pop culture commentator, almost every lecture I give to Christian audiences begins with questions about what we can watch. People want to achieve purity. They want to know what to avoid, what is permissible to consume in their pop cultural diet. If I will draw the lines, they will stay within them. If I will define it, they will adhere to it. The apostle Paul suggested we buffet our bodies and make them our slaves (1 Corinthians 9:27). He beseeched us to offer our bodies as living sacrifices, holy and acceptable to God (Romans 12:1). We deny ourselves the pleasures of the flesh in order to set our minds on things above (Colossians 3:2).

Christianity can be defined by what we give up, what we reject, what we deny. But we can also become slaves to suppression. Surely, the rise of eating disorders must alarm us. Elusive perfectionism can drive us toward an early grave. Jesus said our sins were not rooted in what we consume. He inverted the purification process: "What goes into a man's mouth does not make him 'unclean,' but what comes out of his mouth, that is what makes him 'unclean' " (Matthew 15:11). It is not a question of diet and discipline. Our problems arise from within us rather than outside us. Only grace can root it out.

Goodness also has an active component. We may not gossip, may not cheat, may not steal, but what difference do we make? I remember a friend who talked about obeying the speed limit as part of his Christian witness. But I couldn't figure out how people were supposed to connect the dots between his driving and his faith. Is that what those bumper stickers and fish symbols are for? Will they know we are Christians when we arrive at 55 miles per hour? Our understanding of goodness often stops at our privatized faith. But consider the actions of our global heroes. Dorothy Day modeled humble service to the poor at the Catholic Worker. Lech Walesa stood in solidarity with Polish workers against the Communist Party. Nelson Mandela went from prison to the presidency of South Africa through civil disobedience. Bono challenges us to reduce Third World debt by uniting as one (www.one.org). Aung San Suu Kyi won the Nobel Peace Prize for her nonviolent (but active!) protests against oppression in Myanmar. They demonstrated their deepest convictions through tangible actions in support of the poor, the oppressed, the downtrodden.

Our movie heroes are always acting on others' behalf. They get involved despite their best efforts to stay on the sidelines. Peter Parker intervenes, swooping in as Spiderman to rescue those who need a champion. In *Amelie,* the title character does random acts of kindness for others. She finds creative ways of delighting her friends and neighbors. In The Lord of the Rings, Frodo does more than resist temptation. He marches across kingdoms, accompanied by travel companions, in order to toss the ring in the molten Mount Doom. Rather than obsessing over personal purity, we must walk with community. We need our own fellowship of the ring, seeking the greater good for all. We need an immanent faith, rooted in this-world Christianity.

Via Positiva

What is the *via positiva?* The apostle Paul suggested, "Whatever is noble, whatever is right, whatever is pure, whatever is lovely, whatever is admirable—if anything is excellent or praiseworthy—think on these things" (Philippians 4:8). Paul's challenge to the Philippian church often serves as the starting point for Christian discernment. When we consider what movies to rent, what songs to listen to, or what television programs to watch, we question whether the particular artistic expression is noble, pure, and lovely. Far too often, the verse is misquoted. What is often left out of that equation is Paul's starting point: "Whatever is true."

How do we focus on Paul's important question of truth? We might ask, is the film realistic? Does the song reflect both the depravity and glory revealed in the Bible? Is the wisdom offered in the book in harmony or conflict with the wisdom literature of the Old Testament? From the garden of Eden to David's adulterous affair with Bathsheba, the Bible is fraught with sin. Jesus' family tree is loaded with fallen people. Jesus' church was founded upon Peter, a person who repeatedly denied him. The story is never how good we are but how God works through us anyway. We must tell the whole truth about foolish human decisions and the consequences of sin. We must depict the world as we see it—both tragic and glorious. *Raging Bull* demonstrates how we create our own hell. *The Lord of the Rings* illustrates how we resist it. We must celebrate what's possible—the power of Christ to redeem prostitutes, tax collectors, sinners…people like us.

One little overlooked Bible verse summarizes my cultural engagement. In 1 Corinthians 5:12, Paul encourages us to judge ourselves rather than the world. This shifts all my thinking about the letters of Paul. They are never to be applied to the general public. His admonitions are private correspondence, intended for our eyes only. To apply Christian standards to the culture at large is to invite judgment upon ourselves. It is misuse and abuse of scripture. It is why we're (rightly) perceived as un-Christian. It is far too easy for me to become pharisaical, to sort out others. We lash out at others when we're haunted by our own unsatisfied standards. When perfection becomes the goal, grace finds no place to rest.

When was fear substituted for faith? When was grace replaced by guilt? How did a forgiven people become such extensive record keepers? Grace is not an inoculation from the world but an invitation to enter the ring, to get dirty, bloody. Like Raging Bull, we may get hit, even beat up at times. But unlike Jake LaMotta, we turn the other cheek. We respond to anger with love, to frustration with patience. Life is not a battle but a ballet. It is not about overpowering others but standing in their corner and serving them. We welcome the bruised and bloody back to our corner. Our job is to provide comfort, to apply a cold compress, to offer a cup of cold water. When grace and goodness merge into a seamless whole, life gets powerful and poetic. That is the place where I want to live, the space I long to inhabit.

What is our goal? Far too often, we end up paralyzed, unable to move, a clean and fear-filled people. We want to rest in grace but walk in goodness. We want to see our children following Jesus within a gracious Christian community. Jobs, marriage, and grandchildren often follow. Such simple pleasures coincide with good citizenship. Societies are built upon self-sustaining economic engines. Democracies depend upon law-abiding taxpayers.

Nothing is wrong with raising kind people or responsible citizens. We need healthy families to sustain our systems. But we must remember that for us and for our children, following the way of the cross may involve hardship, turmoil, and self-sacrifice. Grace may get us into trouble, into situations that challenge established notions of goodness. Nice Christian kids may decide to serve God in ugly settings. They may choose to get dirty, digging wells in Africa or caring for prostitutes in Mumbai. Having a hedge of protection around us is wonderful, but we must allow grace to have room to roam. We need to test our theology, to take chances in ministry. We don't want to be reckless, but we do need to be adventurous. Goodness flows out of grace. Out of freedom comes a decision to make a difference.

The next wave of cultural warriors is learning to come alongside what God is already doing. Rather than condemning what we abhor, perhaps we can honor what we affirm. We can celebrate the right, the noble, and the lovely in entertainment, in journalism, in civic life. I am so encouraged by organizations like the Heartland Film Festival that honor the finest films rather than merely cursing the darkness. At the City of the Angels Film Festival, we hold up neglected cinematic classics for study and contemplation. We applaud grace when we see it. The Templeton Prize identifies the thinkers who have connected spirituality to public practices. How might theology and science be reconciled for social transformation? We cannot be satisfied with private morality. It must have a public component. Our public mission is to serve rather than to judge. We pursue personal purity and the public good. Only grace sustains us.

Our calls to personal holiness are often ineffective because they are too limited in their scope and application. The Old Testament always linked righteousness with justice. A series of do-not statements cannot transform a nation. But advocacy for the poor, the hungry, the hurting—that is real goodness, the grace of God in action. We are not called to lord our goodness or standards over others, but to give God's grace away. Transformation occurs not only by our personal purity but also from our public support of widows and orphans. It is not enough to oppose sex before marriage. We must surround children born with AIDS with love and support. When we advocate on behalf of the world's poorest citizens, we build bridges with humanitarian organizations around the globe. Eventually, they may know we are Christians by our love.

Creeds and Deeds

3

Uncertainty abounds. Plagues and catastrophes have caused insecurity. The church in the West worries about Islamic attacks from the Middle East. People are living in fear. Many cling to faith and tradition with greater fervency. Others cry out for massive change. Yet the church often seems more interested in consolidating power than serving people. Religious beliefs and nationalistic fervor have commingled in toxic ways. Walls between church and state have nearly collapsed. A wealthy church offers religious trinkets (Jesus junk!) instead of authentic faith. Belief has been reduced to a formula, a commodity to buy.

Scandals have made people question church authority. Rumors abound about cover-ups and conspiracies. New technologies enable people to disseminate information wider and faster than ever before. It is hard for pastors or priests to rein in people's beliefs. The growing gap between church creeds and Christian deeds has left the public confused. People are eager to go back to the original texts and decide for themselves who Jesus is, who God is, where salvation resides. What era am I describing? It is 1517. Martin Luther is about to post his complaints on the Wittenberg door.

We tend to think that the fundamental truths of the Protestant Reformation were handed down as a systematic theology. Luther, Calvin, and Zwingli had a couple of meetings, wrote up a document, and the Protestant faith was formed. Yet the discontent that drove the Reformation built for *years*. Questions of corruption and compromise dogged the Roman Catholic church. They were blinded by their power and influence. The sale of indulgences (a spiritual fire insurance!) drove Martin Luther to protest. When our beliefs fail to conform to our practices, something has got to give. Our experiences of faith (positive and negative) usually drive our doctrine.

Scripture arose out of a historical experience. Things were written down after the fact, looking back, finding God's fingerprints on the far side of trials and tribulations. Abraham didn't know where he was going when he headed for a promised land. Moses clearly lost the directions during the Hebrews' 40 years in the desert. Jesus' talk about the kingdom of God made people even more confused. It took the apostle Paul to explain what it all meant. A system of beliefs arose out of an experience of God. Divine actions force our hand, get us thinking, and cause us to write things down. God's deeds led to church creeds.

Are we living on the cusp of another reformation? Pastor Rick Warren of Saddleback Church has suggested that the first Reformation was about creeds. Luther reminded us that justification came by faith. We affirmed the authority of scripture and the priesthood of all believers. These pillars of orthodox Christian faith served as a beacon for the next 500 years. But may we have grown too comfortable in our beliefs? It is easy to assent to a statement of faith. Following Jesus is tough. Rick Warren believes that the church is ready for another reformation. People of faith and conscience are eager to make a difference. We want to turn our beliefs into actions.

A purple state of mind seeks to recover the connection between creeds and deeds. It recognizes the insecurities that leave us in search of a firm foundation. It upholds doctrine as more relevant than ever. But it emphasizes beliefs *and* practices, the recovery of creeds *and* deeds.

What is the most compelling proof of a risen Christ? A transformed people putting their faith into action, pouring grace upon all.

John: I'm going to start by asking you a pretty straightforward question that goes to the heart of our friendship, the times, and this project.

Craig: What do you want to know?

John: Do you believe Jesus is the Son of God?

Craig: Absolutely!

John: Why?

There are ample reasons to believe that Jesus is the Son of God. Numerous texts and scrolls have a veracity that suggests an esteemed teacher named Jesus walked the earth 2000 years ago. But are Jesus' miracles and resurrection an article of faith or a credible report based on eyewitness accounts? Massive and popular tomes have been written that suggest there is ample "evidence that demands a verdict."[1] Despite various high-profile efforts to discredit the reliability of the Bible, the four Gospels remain a compelling and authoritative narrative of Jesus of Nazareth. Exhaustive efforts have also been made to harmonize the Gospels, pointing out how the seemingly contradictory accounts can be reconciled into a consistent record of Jesus' birth, life, death, and resurrection. In a scientific era, the need for reliable defenses of the faith rose to considerable heights.[2] We're all indebted to the excellent research, archaeology, and historic reconstructions that have deepened our understanding of scripture and shored up our arguments for Christianity. We can make a compelling case for Christ using logic, facts, history, and science.

The postmodern era asks an entirely different set of questions. Discussions are often based on feelings and experiences rather than scientific methods. The contradictory passages in the Gospels can be embraced as alternative takes on the same person and events. The gaps between testimonies demonstrate a different kind of proof.[3] The Gospel writers offer *four distinct* takes on the person of Jesus. The Gospel of Matthew starts with a genealogy, emphasizing Jesus' continuity within the Jewish tradition. The Gospel of John appeals to a more Greek-speaking audience, describing Jesus as a more mystical Word. They are complementary versions rather than competing or contradicting histories. Only a conspiracy to cover up falsehood would result in Gospels that removed all differences. To postmoderns interested in acknowledging our "situatedness" ("from where I sit"), multiple perspectives are embraced as strengths rather than weaknesses.

Yet after I gave John Marks some reasons that support my faith, he immediately restated the question. He didn't want to know about the historical reliability of my beliefs, just *whether* I believed. What has experience taught me? What difference does it make? All too often, our debates separate beliefs from practices. People of faith have been trained to argue doctrine, when those on the outside want to know, does it work? We've focused on head games while people watched our bodies. How did we move? Where did we go? What did we do? For years, the Barna Group has published extensive surveys that measure the gap between what Christians believe and how they live. From mundane practices like the frequency of moviegoing to more haunting statistics like the prevalence of divorce, the Christian community in America has proven quite undistinguished from the general populace. While some may attribute that to wrong thinking—the dissolution of our beliefs—I will suggest it stems from an *overemphasis* on beliefs. We confess with our mouths, and then we do whatever we please. We have separated our faith from our practices, leaving us both empty-headed and ineffectual. A purple state of mind unites beliefs and practices, creeds and deeds, into an integrated whole.

Soul Meets Body

In their jaunty song, "Soul Meets Body," Death Cab for Cutie captures our quest for an integrated life. The Bellingham, Washington, band writes mid-tempo rock laden with personal memories emblematic of the emerging generation. Death Cab singer Ben Gibbard lets an anthropomorphized sun wrap its arms around him. He describes a kind of baptism, as cool and cleansing water bathes his skin. The song celebrates what it's like to be new, to feel whole. I want to join Death Cab in living where soul meets body. We may view our flesh as the enemy. Our women may engage in cutting or bulimia. Our young men may want to cut off their desire altogether. Even the apostle Paul finds himself at war within himself. He buffets his body, making it a slave. He struggles with the thorn in his side. He describes the division we all feel between our best intentions and our questionable actions. He admits, "I do not understand what I do. For what I want to do I do not do, but what I hate I do" (Romans 7:15). We struggle with compartmentalization.

For too long, I considered my love of movies a detriment to my spiritual life. I felt that I shouldn't like the things that consistently moved me. I was at war with my own sense of taste. Sure, certain films appealed to my worst instincts, feeding my tendencies toward rage, greed, or lust. But my favorite films took me to an exhilarating place, merging words and images, facts and feelings in transcendent ways. I emerged from the theater with my senses awakened and my spirit lifted, feeling strangely new. How can I cut off such an essential part of my spiritual journey? After all, Woody Allen explains in the movie *Love and Death,* "Only human beings are divided into mind and body. The mind embraces all the nobler aspirations, like poetry and philosophy, but the body has all the fun." How could I learn to live in my skin, to be at peace with myself rather than at war?

Theologian Nancey Murphy has helped me to push past the Greek philosophical categories of mind, body, and soul. Rather than viewing our lives as compartmentalized, Murphy suggests we return to the more holistic, Jewish roots of our faith. She finds no explicit biblical teaching on the metaphysical makeup of the human person. The biblical writers were "interested in the various dimensions of human life, in relationships, not in the philosophical question of how many parts are essential components of a human being."[4] Most of our notions of a separate and immortal soul come from Plato rather than the Bible.

She suggests we've been far too dualistic in our thinking. How do we push past either/or categories? Murphy encourages us to see ourselves as "spirited bodies."

Our mind-body split springs from the Greek philosophical influences on our faith. In the center of Raphael's massive Renaissance painting *School of Athens,* Plato and his student Aristotle engage in a vigorous dialogue. Plato points upward, to the realm of philosophy and idealized forms. He saw the body as imperfect and fallen, a source of evil and temptation. Matter was an illusion to deride, a hindrance to escape. In his famous cave analogy, the world we inhabit was depicted as a mere shadow on the wall. The things we see pale in comparison to the ultimate reality that resides elsewhere. The mind or spirit operated on a more transcendental plane, closer to the ultimate form of the good.

In Raphael's painting, Aristotle holds his hand out toward the world before us, toward things we can taste, touch, smell, and see. Aristotle affirmed the stuffness of life, encouraging artists to practice *mimesis,* or imitation. Good drama corresponded to our everyday surroundings. It imitated life. The poet's job was to put words into practice, to literally perform them in a tangible way. When the elements of comedy or drama fused together in an authentic manner, audiences experienced catharsis. Their fears were expunged, their sense of what matters reaffirmed. The early church fathers, like St. Augustine, drew upon Plato's philosophy more than Aristotle's. They taught us how to think about God.

The assumption that right thinking leads to right actions hasn't necessarily proven true. Philosopher Gerardus van der Leeuw noted that unfortunately,

> It is Christianity which has gone to school at the feet of Orphism and Neoplatonism, and has there forgotten its Jewish heritage. It is a Christianity, which, in an unfortunate hour, took over from the Greeks, along with the idea of the divinity and immortality of the soul, the idea of the evil of the

body. This is Christianity which almost replaced "good" and "evil" with the concepts "material" and "immaterial," and for which virginity was of more value than holiness.[5]

Rather than God's temple, the body was viewed as a prison, keeping our enduring spirit under wraps. To attain spiritual maturity, we were forced to buffet our bodies, subjugate our desires, and renounce our humanity. Van der Leeuw notes, "Almost from the very beginning, Christianity has been the outspoken enemy of the body and all sensual pleasures, which it never considers innocent. It seeks the secret of all guilt in the lust of the flesh, *concupiscentia*, which transmits sin as an inheritance from generation to generation."[6] Original sin was tied to sexuality and conception. Van der Leeuw calls us back to balance: "True Christianity knows that body and soul were both equally created by God, equally attacked by corruption, and equally saved by Christ."[7] The Jewish worldview concentrates upon ethics and practices more than beliefs.

Perhaps we have struggled to integrate body and soul because we have seen them as separate spheres, the physical *versus* the spiritual. Yet, Orthodox theologian Jim Forest suggests, "Nothing is more central to Christianity than its affirmation of the significance of material reality."[8] Orthodox faith is rooted in the incarnation, the life of Christ lived among us. He is Emmanuel, God with us. He was trained as a carpenter. Jesus knew plenty about hard work and sweat. He taught from everyday examples—sheep, mustard seeds, and water. Jesus practiced an immanent faith.

> Nearly all the miracles Jesus performed were physical healings. So important is the human body that most of the questions to be asked of us at the Last Judgment have to do with our merciful response to the physical needs of others: "I was hungry and you fed me, I was thirsty and you gave me drink, I was naked and you clothed me, I was homeless and you gave me shelter, I was sick and you cared for me" (Matthew 25:34-37).[9]

How we care for people's physical needs becomes the test and manifestation of our faith.

Jesus also experienced incalculable suffering on the cross. He bled and died. Yet we worship a risen Lord whose body proved incapable of destruction. We believe in a bodily resurrection. Lest we doubt, Thomas inspected his physical wounds. We remember Jesus' sacrifice in an equally dramatic, tangible way. So many memorable biblical moments took place around meals, amid the breaking of bread, the distribution of fish. In the Eucharist, we summon physical symbols of material and spiritual realities. Our faith is not an idea. The gospel is more than information. It reports on physical events, divine actions that occurred in space and time. It weds transcendent realities with our material world. It gets into our bones.

A disembodied faith allows us to wax philosophical about our beliefs without delving into our behavior. Beliefs tend to divide us. Martin Luther's revelatory in Romans 1:17 discovery of justification by faith led to a series of separations. He may not have intended to break away from his Catholic roots, but the protests that followed his 95 Theses fueled a series of religious wars centered on beliefs. The differences between transubstantiation and consubstantiation set off bloody battles. Anabaptists were martyred for this fervent faith. Now, 500 years later, we have a Christian community that often doesn't even know what it believes about the Lord's Supper (and is unwilling to fight over it!). Wars fought over doctrinal differences settled into practices we often take for granted.

The Hebraic roots of the Christian faith focus more upon practices. Our father Abraham serves as the original exemplar of faith, daring to start a family, found a people, and even sacrifice his son. He was a man on the move. The Jewish wisdom literature of the Bible emphasizes wise choices and the consequences of our actions. Proverbs suggests practical ways to avoid foolishness. Ecclesiastes suggests that our right actions may not always result in greater wealth or fame. Sometimes, the wicked prosper. The Teacher challenges his readers to enjoy their loved ones and to cherish family each and every miserable day. The

Jewish scriptural tradition affirms the gift of marriage. Song of Songs celebrates the body, reveling in physical love.

The Hebrew mind-set holds paradoxes in tension. Job tries to reconcile his unwavering faith with his lousy experience. He attempts to bring the text of life alongside what he has heard and believed about the Creator God. This wrestling with faith constitutes the core of discipleship. As theologian Karl Barth suggested, we walk with the Bible in one hand and the newspaper (or cell phone) in the other. The tension between the two is invigorating. Jewish Christian Marvin Wilson suggests, "Orthodoxy (correct or straight thinking) must lead to orthopraxy (right doing)...Christianity must be careful that it does not allow dogma (the way to believe, prescribed by creed) to overshadow *halakhah* (the way to walk or live). Both concepts must be held in balance."[10] While St. Paul emphasized right thinking, proper beliefs, and confessing our faith verbally, the letter of James suggests that faith without works is dead. James led the early Jewish church in Jerusalem. They focused upon demonstrating their beliefs with concrete acts of service and love. We need to recover the practical Hebraic roots of our faith.

Need for Creed

Our conversation in the film *Purple State of Mind* often centers on questions of belief. John and I start by defining ourselves, trying to find names or labels to describe the system we embrace. I readily acknowledge my allegiance to Jesus. John tries to pin me down as a particular type of Christian—an evangelical. I resist such labels. John confesses his inability to know the world, to have a set of boundaries that define human existence. He doesn't like to call himself an agnostic or an atheist. Beliefs and labels lead to frustrating limitations. The baggage and stereotypes that have sprung up around certain words and phrases create confusion. I want to define myself as "not that kind of Christian." John resists the label of atheist, finding it too limiting a system of disbelief. Perhaps we've both experienced too much mystery to reduce anything to a fixed set of beliefs. "Jesus loves me, this

I know, for the Bible tells me so" seems to suffice for most situations I encounter.

By labeling things, we're able to organize our world. We start to define and identify groups. Creeds helped to focus and define the early Christian community. As competing camps called themselves Christ-followers, it became important to sort out facts from fictions. The host of Gospels circulating throughout the ancient world made the person of Christ an elusive figure. Some early sects, like the Essenes, viewed the body as a prison, dragging down our soul. Others embraced the bread and the wine as important material embodiments of a transcendent faith. The formulation of creeds helped to clarify what happened. How do you explain the paradox of "fully God and fully human"? If asked, what would you say you believed?

To help unite a diverse community, the Nicene Creed boiled Christian faith into a succinct statement. It is a series of affirmations. At no point does it describe what we're against. Instead, it recounts the things we hold near, dear, and true. It affirms the Holy Trinity. "We believe in one God the Father almighty...and in one Lord Jesus Christ, the Son of God...and in the Holy Spirit, the Lord, the Giver of life." The life, death, and resurrection of Jesus serve as the central acts of history and the creed. The Council of Nicea concluded with an affirmation of the "one holy, catholic and apostolic Church." The creed is a remarkably compact and potent statement of faith.

I didn't grow up in a liturgical tradition. But now each Sunday morning, I relish the opportunity to connect with the founders of the faith across the centuries. They recited the creed to clarify the faith. We repeat the Council of Nicea's conclusions as a mnemonic device. The recitation and repetition burns it into my brain. We say it each Sunday so we do not stray too far from the path. It helps us stick to the essentials rather than being distracted by minutia. The creed doesn't list what we're against, but whom we worship and adore. The beautiful, Trinitarian object of our beliefs humbles us, inspires us, and renews us weekly. The creed unites us as a community. We don't have to engage in the petty disputes that the apostle Paul warns Timothy and Titus about. When the particulars of politics or practices threaten to divide us, the Nicene Creed emerges as essential.

But the need for creeds arose *out of* the reality of transformed lives. There was a need to explain what had happened both to Jesus and the early church. The letters of Paul arrived as the first Christian theology. He gave shape and concept to the God-given drama that had unfolded. Jesus served as the writer, director, and star of the Theo-drama.[11] Only after the curtain fell on his life did the buzz truly begin. People didn't necessarily understand what they had seen and heard. The apostles Paul and Peter and John served as the primary interpreters. Consider them theater directors, guiding the nascent church as it figured out which parts to play. We have recently rediscovered that theology arises *from within* the Christian community. Kevin Vanhoozer writes, "The-ology articulates the 'logic' inherent in the communal way of life—the culture—that is the Christian Church. *It is the form of the church's life that gives doctrines their substance and meaning.*"[12] Christian doctrines arose out of lived experiences. They made the gospel portable, easily translated across countries and cultures.

The explosive growth of the nascent Christian community under the Roman Empire was fueled more by fervency than clarity of belief. The proclamation of Jesus' resurrection power was usually accompanied by tangible demonstrations. Yale historian Ramsey MacMullen notes, "The manhandling of demons—humiliating them, making them howl, beg for mercy, tell their secrets, and depart in a hurry—served a purpose quite essential to the Christian definition of monotheism: it made physically (or dramatically) visible the superiority of the Chris-tian patron Power over all others. One and only one was God."[13]

Such power encounters remain commonplace in contemporary Africa, South America, and Asia, but Christians in the West (outside the Pentecostal tradition) are far removed from such practices. Yet in an ancient world comfortable with worshipping many gods, the monotheistic practices of Christians stood out (and brought them persecution). The Christians' renunciation of idols caused them to be branded—as *atheists!* Subsequent martyrdom would not seem to be a compelling strategy for church growth. Yet the early believers' willingness to suffer and even perish for the person of Christ captivated people. St. Basil wrote, "The blood of martyrs watered the churches and reared up many times as many champions of piety."[14]

Another distinguishing mark of the early church was generosity. To people fighting for economic survival, the shared wealth in the Christian community was a tangible attraction. Like today's prosperity gospel, such monetary rewards attract a crowd but may not engender deep faith commitments. Jesus' followers were not to hoard their faith as a sign of God's blessing. We give without premise of recompense on earth. Caring for the sick also distinguished the early Christian community. In an ancient world beset by health problems, the potential for Christ's healing power proved compelling. Even an avowed anti-Christian critic like Julian noted, "It is generosity towards non-members, care for the graves of the dead, and pretended holiness of life that have specially fostered the growth of atheism" (that is, Christianity).[15] Before the Council of Nicea, before Constantine embraced Christianity as an official state religion, the early believers distinguished themselves by sacrificial actions and uncommon grace. Vanhoozer reminds us that "doctrines arise not from speculative theories but from the core practices—baptism, the Eucharist, prayer, worship—that constitute the ongoing life and identity of the church."[16]

Digging out of a Hole

Unfortunately, our recent separation of creeds from deeds has left us digging out of a hole of our own making. In the twentieth century, we reduced salvation to a formula. In our valiant efforts to get people to confess with their mouths and believe in their hearts that Jesus is Lord, we limited discipleship to a statement rather than a long-term lifestyle. Many of us profess a faith in Christ, but our actions all too often betray our true beliefs.

Many have responded to the postmodern shift by clinging tightly to tradition. Going back to our roots could be a great thing. The creeds may take on added resonance. But our understanding of God (and our doctrines) may change as we move forward. We must not hold on to our doctrines as a static body of belief but rather put our convictions into practice. As Vanhoozer emphasizes, "For the way one lives *bodies forth* one's belief about the true, the good, and the beautiful, so much so that it becomes difficult to separate the person from the thesis or argument or doctrine uttered by the person."[17]

Having been raised within a culture of too many promises and not enough delivery, the next generation is obsessed with authenticity. Both products and people must pass a sniff test. Is this reliable, credible, and trustworthy? Do the advertised claims correspond to real-life experience? When what is preached fails to align with everyday practices, the next generation dismisses the source as unreliable and hypocritical. As the Barna Research group concluded, we have been far too *unChristian* in our behavior.[18] If Jesus is the Way, then we must walk in it.

My practices brought John Marks into the discussion. He knew what I came to believe in college. What shocked him was my continuing commitment to Christ. My entire adult life has involved some form of ministry or service. In college, I mentored rural high school students through Young Life. Our team of volunteers reached out to teen mothers and foster youth caught in the local system. The North Mecklenburg Young Life group included jocks and cheerleaders as well as stoners. We had black kids, white kids, poor kids, and rich kids gathering together every week to hear about a radical healer who proclaimed, "The kingdom of God is at hand." After graduation, I served as an English language teacher in Japan. I helped to plant a church that still gathers weekly as Tokorozawa Christian Fellowship.

After Japan, I started an Urban Young Life program in my hometown of Charlotte, North Carolina. I led a team of volunteers into the inner city to tutor the next generation of teenagers. We partnered with Reverend Mack and Progressive Baptist Church in providing opportunities for residents of public housing in Dalton Village. We took many kids on their first field trips, their first overnight camper experiences, their first climbs across ropes courses and zip lines. We attended as many funerals as graduations. But serving the urban community blessed and humbled us all. We caught a vision of the kingdom of God in action. Perhaps the most compelling evidence of the risen Christ comes from transformed lives. People will know we are Christians by our love, not by our beliefs. What we do demonstrates what we believe.

Unfortunately, it is tough to construct an argument based on our actions. We're specifically warned about calling attention to our service. We must not follow the example of those who perform: "Everything they do is done for men to see" (Matthew 23:5). Instead, Jesus suggested when we give to the needy, "do not let your left hand know what your right hand is doing, so that your giving may be in secret. Then your Father, who sees what is done in secret, will reward you" (Matthew 6:3-4).

We don't visit jails to earn God's favor. We don't serve the homeless because we want accolades. We care for foster kids because Jesus called the children to himself. He warned us not to hinder them in any way. We build houses with Habitat for Humanity because Jesus challenged us to care for widows and orphans. Our most compelling evidence is not supposed to be entered into the public record. People may notice. Newspaper reporters may write articles. Others may join us in our efforts. The goals of our beautiful actions are glorifying God and loving people. In his Sermon on the Mount, Jesus challenged us to "let your light shine before men, that they may see your good deeds and praise your Father in heaven" (Matthew 5:16). A purple state of mind doesn't do the right thing in order to gain attention. We must put our faith into practice regardless of the results, for love's sake.

Clear Cases

So, what do I believe? The most compelling case for Christ occurs when we serve the poor, the hungry, and the hurting. Jesus' solidarity with the suffering was made manifest on the cross. He understands what it means to be beaten, downcast, and defeated. People will continue to ask why God allows such suffering, but we must consider why we allow such suffering to continue. Jesus made our calling clear. "For I was hungry and you gave me something to eat, I was thirsty and you gave me something to drink, I was a stranger and you invited me in" (Matthew 25:35). When we come alongside the thirsty with a cup of cold water, we have an opportunity to serve (and represent) Jesus. Who can argue with such tangible acts of faith? Brian McLaren highlights the church's need:

> More and more Christian leaders are beginning to real-ize that for the millions of young adults who have recently dropped out of church, Christianity is a failed religion. Why? Because it has specialized in dealing with "spiritual needs" to the exclusion of physical and social needs. It has focused on "me" and "my eternal destiny," but it has failed to address the dominant societal and global realities of their lifetime: systemic injustice, poverty, and dysfunction.[19]

Mother Teresa of Calcutta's beliefs and values were quite clear.

> When a poor person dies of hunger, it has not happened because God did not take care of him or her. It has hap-pened because neither you nor I wanted to give that person what he or she needed. We have refused to be instruments of love in the hands of God to give the poor a piece of bread, to offer them a dress with which to ward off the cold. It has happened because we did not recognize Christ when, once more, he appeared under the guise of pain, identified with a man numb from the cold, dying of hunger, when he came in a lonely human being, in a lost child in search of a home.[20]

Her Home for the Dying reawakened the early Christian distinc-tive—caring for the sick and suffering. She invited us all to join her community, to discover the face of Jesus residing in her hospital beds. Thousands responded by serving alongside the Missionaries of Charity in over 450 centers around the world.

I still vividly recall the stench that arose when Westminster Pres-byterian Church in Charlotte opened up its basement to the homeless.

It had been a brutal winter. Twenty-five cots were set up as a satellite shelter. The men would start lining up for a bed well before dark. Our Young Life offices were upstairs, so every day we were reminded of the trying conditions below us. When I walked in the door, it stank. But after a while, I grew fond of the smell. It became the aroma of Christ to me, a tangible reminder of where Jesus could be found every night during a long winter in North Carolina. Spending a night in the basement serving my fellow Charlotteans became a privilege rather than a burden.

During my wife's battle against Hodgkin's lymphoma, we were on the receiving end of kindness and charity. It is humbling to receive gifts from strangers. A steady stream of friends and neighbors knocked on our door, bearing food, comfort, and clothing. Most of our friends are not part of any Christian community. But they poured out love in such compelling ways. A blanket was sewn together, each section reminding us of our children's classmates. A painting we hung on the wall became a visual symbol of hope. The love emanating from each brush stroke felt like a living prayer from the Jewish artist who gave it to Caroline. And the food! I never expected to gain weight during our family's greatest crisis. Yet working mothers would stop by to feed us on their way home from picking up their children. We got the best of everybody's cooking—a taste of the community.

I don't feel the need to preach Christ to my neighbors. They know what we believe. But I am curious about what drives them. They demonstrated God's love to us. I came away challenged to translate my faith into equally tangible actions. How many meals were cooked for us? In return, how many people can we care for? My strategy: act now, talk later.

Beliefs matter. They sharpen our thinking, focus our worship, and define our communities. Yet our practices communicate most clearly. We must recover the Jewish roots of the Christian faith. In a world divided by faith, practical, everyday ethics cut across our differences. How humbly we serve demonstrates how fervently we believe.

North Carolina

Davidson College is committed to the liberal arts and humanities. Founded by Presbyterians, Davidson promotes freethinking and vigorous Christian inquiry. Skepticism is a virtue. Professors also encourage cross-cultural plunges and public service. From Habitat for Humanity to the JET program in Japan, students are expected to build a better world through education, medicine, and business. For a small, Southern college, Davidson has graduated a disproportionate number of Rhodes scholars. The Wildcat basketball program also competes on a national level, turning contests against Duke or UCLA into a battle of Davidson versus Goliath. Davidson grads like being underestimated and surprising the competition. Their run behind the sharpshooting skills of Stephen Curry in the 2008 NCAA Basketball Tournament captivated the nation.

Davidson is located north of Charlotte, North Carolina, banking center of the New South. Charlotte is a gracious city of azaleas, dogwoods, and country clubs. It is also a religious hotspot, loaded with church steeples. Charlotte is the birthplace of Billy Graham and home to the Billy Graham Library. Growing up in Charlotte, I was invited to a plethora of church retreats, lock-ins, and vacation Bible schools. Yet religion never became personal until I attended my first Young Life club. The people I met there blended faith and fun into a relevant and revelatory experience.

Charlotte was also the ministry center for Jim and Tammy Faye Bakker's PTL Club. During the 1980s, their daily television show prospered. PTL stood for "Praise the Lord," but a series of investigative articles in *The Charlotte Observer* revealed that it might as well have meant "Pass the Loot." Jim Bakker turned Christianity into an enterprise, overselling timeshares in Heritage USA. His Christian theme park came tumbling down in a combination of financial fraud and sexual peccadilloes with a secretary. The PTL scandal turned Christianity into a laughingstock, the butt of cheap jokes.

These competing streams of religious experience filtered into our dorm room. John Marks and I were both raised in Southern cities populated by affluent Christians. Church attendance was a social expectation. We both made serious faith commitments through the ministry of Young Life. We were attracted by its authentic, alternative version of religious expression. Our classes at Davidson College forced us to question our faith, to consider its greatest critics. We wrestled with rigorous, demythologizing texts from Nietzsche to Bultmann. Hypocritical Christians paraded across the headlines made it even tougher to cling to our newfound faith. Was it foolish to follow Christ, to associate with such questionable behavior? John and I were shaken and stirred in all kinds of challenging ways.

At our twentieth Davidson class reunion, John and I arrived while the college was transitioning from its Presbyterian roots to something broader. The school was in an uproar over new, nonbinding faith statements for the trustees. The small, private Presbyterian school was dropping religious requirements among trustees, just as it had with professors a decade earlier. Some of Davidson's wealthiest donors, like John Belk, vowed to cease their support to protest such modernization. Angry editorials on both sides of the issue dominated *The Davidsonian* and *The Charlotte Observer*. This culture clash mirrored many of the issues central to our faith journey. Pluralism pushed its way onto the college while John took a few swings at my theology. We headed to our old room in Belk Dormitory. What buried memories might this place bring up?

Word and Image

4

Religion and art stand beside each other like
two friendly souls whose inner relationship,
if they suspect it, is still unknown to them.

FRIEDRICH SCHLEIERMACHER

We live in an era of abundant images. Television has expanded from the 13 channels of my childhood to the thousand choices of DirectTV. YouTube enables all of us to create our own network. We are inundated with advertising—even on our iPhones! NYU professor Mitchell Stevens, who believes the influence of electronic images has barely begun, wrote a book called *The Rise of the Image, the Fall of the Word*.[1] Protestant Christians committed to the word of God may be hesitant to enter such a visual era. If logic ruled the Enlightenment, then the postmodern moment is the era of artists. The right-brained thinkers are ascending. They are creative, intuitive, and visual. A quick review of the Mac-versus-PC commercials illustrates the tension. On the left, a pasty-faced, middle-aged man in an ill-fitting suit represents PCs. On the right, a casual dude in blue jeans kicks back with his Apple products. The choice is obvious. Would you rather be uptight or creative? Who wouldn't want to hang out with the earthy, artistic types in their Mac world? Far too often, our churches run like PCs, our worship laid out like a spreadsheet rather than an open-ended encounter with a living God.

How should people of faith respond to an imaginative era? This chapter will consider the church's rocky relationship with artists. It recalls how destructive ill-timed words against artists have been. It seeks to recover Christians' roles as patrons of the arts. A purple state of mind reconciles faith and art as complementary rather than competitive. It embraces the abundant experiences within God's beautiful creation. It recognizes all the variety and colors of the world as glorious and necessary. It seeks to recover the prophetic imagination. A purple state of mind celebrates logic *and* creativity. It is comfortable with questions and ambiguity. It lifts up Jesus as both the Word of God and the image of the invisible God.

> **Craig:** In high school, I was, like, straight-up jock. Didn't care a bit about poetry, art, drama...anything other than raw power. Coming to Jesus totally woke up my creative spirit. The other thing that woke up my creative spirit was rooming with you.

John Marks was the first person I ever met who wanted to be a writer. The career aspirations within my high school leaned toward the practical—doctors, bankers, and coaches. But a writer? What does that look like? And how can an 18-year-old declare such a lofty intention? Doesn't that take years of practice? How would you know what to write? How would you know if you were finished? A writer?

The concept intrigued me. Such seriousness of purpose challenged me. John had found a calling, but I hadn't even decided on a major. Politics interested me, but political science seemed too abstract. History sounded too musty. I had aced classes in economics, computer science, and philosophy. My worst grade came in British literature. Clearly, I had plenty to learn about the basics of reading and writing. If I really wanted an education, maybe I should major in my weakest subject—English. Rooming with a writer like John might sharpen my skills in analyzing texts and composing essays.

While searching for a major, I entered into an evangelical movement that disdained art. We were past the days of record burning, but as I mentioned earlier, an early Christian mentor still encouraged me to throw away my Clash albums. Although I couldn't have come to faith without the music of The Clash or the films of Martin Scorsese, such secular sources were viewed as distractions from or even destructions of my embrionic faith. I adopted the anti-art, anti-culture trappings of my new community (while clinging tightly to the artists who pushed me toward transcendence).

My humanities classes at Davidson affirmed the sacred roots of art. We studied images emerging from the cultic practices of the ancient world. Fertility gods, animal sacrifices, and flood narratives sacralized the prehistoric cosmos. In a pantheistic society, gods resided behind or within every bush, tree, or river. Life was organized around crops and seasons, with nature deities responsible for rainfalls and harvests. Efforts to curry the gods' favor resulted in all kinds of creative expressions. The Egyptians developed a complex symbology that connected particular animals to particular gods. A hawk symbolized the sky god, Horus. A cow head denoted the goddess Hathor. The pharaohs' divinity proceeded from these gods. At the end of their earthly reign, Egyptian pharaohs would return to nature in a cycle of life and death, fertility and fallow.[2]

Greco-Roman art put humanity on a pedestal. Gods and goddesses bore striking similarities to muscular human models. The Greeks celebrated human achievement in statuary that depicted the human body with reverent detail. Maybe eternity was within our reach, fame only a glorious Olympic victory away. The lines between celebrity and divinity blurred. Despite their beautiful forms, the pantheon of Greco-Roman gods often seemed as petty as everyday citizens, prone to power moves and backstabbing deceits. Human aspiration began to meet eternity, and the gap between human and divine slowly collapsed.

In pre-Christian cultures, art and religion were inseparable. All image making and songwriting had a sacred character. Gerardus van der Leeuw suggests, "There was a period—and for the so called primitive peoples this period still exists—when art and religion stood so close to each other that they could almost be equated. Song was prayer; drama was divine performance; dance was cult."[3] St. Augustine suggested that signs, words, and gestures have always been means of worship, ways of connecting our story to a sacred story. Van der Leeuw notes, "Throughout the world, drama arose from a holy play whose purpose was to assure the cycle of life."[4] To some degree, the arts have been falling from their sacred purpose ever since.

Jewish, Christian, and Islamic monotheism shifted the emphasis from the means of worship to *the object* of worship. The question became, who is the one true God among competing gods? Elijah's power encounter on Mount Carmel illustrated how dramatic the competition could become. The Bible sets up a theatrical scene, loaded with tension. Elijah asks the people, "How long will you waver between two opinions? If the LORD is God, follow him; but if Baal is God, follow him" (1 Kings 18:21).

Two bulls were prepared for ritual sacrifice. Firewood was placed beneath each one. The priests whose deity produced fire would be declared the winner. The priests of Baal asked their god for an answer all morning. Elijah mocked their techniques, suggesting Baal might be asleep or even going to the bathroom. The priests cut themselves, shedding their blood for no results. On his turn, Elijah builds an altar dedicated to God. He raised the stakes by adding water. Like a master magician, he doused his wood three times, making the appearance of fire even more improbable. Yet when Elijah asks God for an answer, the fire of the Lord falls down, consuming the bull, the wood, and the water. Talk about dramatic timing! The God of Israel delivered a crushing blow to the pagan opposition. This was divine theater. Faith in Yahweh undercut the prehistoric, pagan gods as false; it thereby nullified the arts attached to their worship. A dramatic way of invoking gods like Baal is folly if the gods are merely powerless, stone idols.

Eventually, Christian liturgy became its own drama, the locus of a new work of the people. Plenty of sacred art dedicated to Christ (and funded by the Christian church) followed. Church patronage underwrote much of Western art history. Altarpieces, frescoes, and sculptures decorated churches and cathedrals. The Christian faith expanded through visual representations of Jesus' life. The Gospels were retold in stained glass windows and illuminated manuscripts. The liturgy offered a dramatic representation. The Lord's Supper was reenacted each week through tangible, tactile symbols: bread and wine.

A nonreading people learned the faith through the senses: the word painted, the word proclaimed, the word eaten. Seeing inspired believing. Hearing led to understanding. Eating and drinking served as regular reminders of Jesus' life and death. Street theater like the English Mystery cycles took Jesus to the masses. The church reenacted the dramatic aspects of the faith with pageantry and panache. Artists had a valuable place within the worshipping community. Priests, actors, and paintings all communicated their faith in visual ways.

Over time, the Renaissance reached back to Greco-Roman models, celebrating the human body within the Christian story. Leonardo da Vinci and Raphael painted exquisite portraits of Madonna and her child. Michelangelo sculpted the boyish David as the giant slayer of colossal dimensions. But such a glorious, embodied artistic center could not hold. As humanity increasingly became the focus of our artistic intentions, art fell from sacred purposes to profane ends. Rather than a free, communal gift to God, painting and sculpture became a craft motivated by profit. Love or devotion took a backseat to practical matters of paying the bills.

Van der Leeuw traces the decline in theater: "The drama emerged from the church to the church square, from the temple into the marketplace. The history of the drama is the history of secularization."[5] Mystery plays coinciding with the church calendar gave way to satires mocking clerical hypocrisy. Painting followed a similar path. Francisco Goya depicted Catholic priests as empty suits in his satirical engravings, *Los Caprichos* (1799). By the twentieth century, art for art's sake celebrated color on a canvas as an end unto itself. Art historian Robert Hughes famously referred to the decline of meaning and debasement of painting as "The Shock of the New."[6] Controversies pitted Christians against artists and included accusations of blasphemy. Churches went from serving as the patron of the arts to being the enemy of artists. Arts became divorced from worship, to the impoverishment of both the faith community and the artists.

Were John Marks' artistic aspirations incompatible with his faith? Should we both major in something more useful, like medicine? From an eternal perspective, isn't art disposable?

Idols or Icons?

John: You remember when we were talking about being a stumbling block?

Craig: Yeah.

John: Well, you were. And do you remember the conversation?

Craig: No.

John: Because there was one conversation and there was a moment. You said, "God doesn't like artists because they ask too many questions." You said that...

Craig: Really?

John: Shortly afterward, I wrote it down. I think that really made a deep impression on me. It was sort of like, "Oh, well you know what? I think I've chosen my side."

Have you ever said something you regret? Would you want to hear unequivocal assertions you made at age 18? Unfortunately, John Marks replayed one of my most shortsighted declarations. When we returned to Davidson College for our class reunion, John and I took a tour around campus. Belk Dormitory was unchanged. Our room was intact. Outside the window, he brought up some unfinished business.

In our dorm room, in a moment of heated debate, I once insisted that he must choose between faith and art. As an impressionable person, trying to figure out his calling, John accepted it as fact rather than foolishness.

I forced a false choice upon John. I was too ignorant of the profound religious contributions to art history. Why didn't I cite literary examples like Flannery O'Connor or Walker Percy? Writers like Anne Lamott and Frederick Buechner are great because they explore life's deepest questions in their art. They find humor amid our tragic condition. Twenty-five years ago, I was operating under a modernist paradigm that put art and religion at odds. The glorious marriage between church patronage and artistic endeavor had ended in a bitter divorce. Both sides claimed to be sacred, denigrating the other as profane. Such a false either/or choice may have pushed a creative person like John away from the Creator. Our ill-chosen words can have consequences.

It is too easy to send conflicting signals. We do it when we ask aspiring Christian filmmakers if they're going to make good, clean movies. We might joke with young Christian painters about when they're going to get real jobs. Perhaps we deride our children for playing video games when they may someday forge their experiences to become game designers. How many artists have longed to bring their gifts before God, only to be rejected by the Christian community? Could the separation of art from worship have been predicted (or even avoided)? What does the Bible have to say about the creative process? How have we navigated the creative tension between worshipping God through icons and the construction of false idols?

We often focus on the biblical warnings against images. The Ten Commandments arose in response to an idol-making people. Historic sculptures of Ashtoreh and Baal demonstrate rampant idolatry in the ancient Near East. Yet on their exodus out of Egypt, even God's people created a golden calf. Exodus 20:4 makes the prohibition quite explicit: "You shall not make for yourself an idol." Is art so corrupting that pictorial representations of God are forbidden? Our hunger for tangible manifestations of gods is so great that images are a grave temptation. Our eyes get caught up in gold, rubies, and jewels. We will get confused, embracing the representation rather than the living Lord.

Yet just five chapters later, God is offering specific instructions about the iconography on the ark of the covenant. God says, "There I will meet with you; and from above the mercy seat, from between the two cherubim which are upon the ark of the testimony, I will speak to you about all that I will give you in commandment for the sons of Israel" (Exodus 25:22 NASB). After forbidding graven images, God connects his commandments to a particular physical space marked by visual splendor. Commandments forbidding images are followed by specific designs and commandments to *create images*. The book of Exodus concludes with long passages about God's vision for the tabernacle. We are called to worship God with eyes wide open. Images can lead to idolatry. They can also enhance true worship. The challenge resides within us.

It has always been easy to confuse creation and the Creator. Psalm 19 affirms the glory of creation, the ability of the stars to celebrate Elohim's handiwork. The skies proclaim God's majesty, serving as a form of preaching, a general revelation available to all. Yet the psalmist also warns against sun worship. He takes great pains to separate the creation from the Creator and to offer a reminder of who put the sun and stars in place. The divine production designer deserves sole credit for setting such beautiful bodies in motion. Yet humanity has a tremendous capacity for missing the Creator amid created splendor. How can we develop eyes to recognize divine handiwork?

The early Christian church was divided on the use of images within worship. Eusebius documents the practices of the fourth-century Christians in his *History of the Church*. He notes, "I have seen a great many portraits of the Savior, and of Peter and Paul, which have been preserved up to our time."[7] Icons were clearly produced for and incorporated within the early Christian community. Yet Eusebius associated religious images more with pagan practices than Christian worship. Could the cultic practices of an image-saturated culture be co-opted for Christ by means of icons? Or should people of faith oppose pagan rituals by pursuing a more ascetic, imageless faith? Early critics of icons included Tertullian, Clement of Alexandria, and Lactantius.[8] Cultural pressures connected to the rise of Islam and its strict prohibitions of images led to a banning of images within Christian worship. Hoping to bring Christianity closer to the rising tide of Islam, Emperor Leo III ignored the wishes of both the (Orthodox) Patriarch of Constantinople and the (Catholic) Pope in Rome. Orders were issued to remove icons from churches and destroy them. Iconographers fled to Italy with their brushes and their cherished icons.

St. John of Damascus found a theological defense of icons in the incarnation of Christ:

> Since the invisible one became visible by taking on flesh, you can fashion the image of him whom you saw...he, being of divine nature, took on the condition of a slave and reduced himself to quantity and quality by clothing himself in human features. Therefore, paint on wood and present for contemplation him who desired to become visible.[9]

St. John's articulate defense of religious imagery found champions at the Seventh Ecumenical Council of 787. Empress Irene insisted that reverence and veneration of images is not only permissible but also obligatory; actual worship was reserved for God alone.

A second wave of iconoclasm followed, led by Emperor Leo V in 813. Monks took to the streets, bearing their beloved icons in protest. Thirty years later, another woman, Empress Theodora, defended icons and affirmed the teaching from 787. Gerardus van der Leeuw notes the two different religious sensibilities battling each other: "the rational, exalted deistic religion of the emperors under Mohammadan influence, and the primitive but strongly Christian religion of the women and monks."[10] Should we only *talk* about God, or can we also paint and portray the Almighty? The resulting recovery of images is still celebrated with the Feast of Orthodoxy, a sacred day on the liturgical calendar that recreates the monk parade by bringing personal icons from home back into the church.

While the Orthodox and Catholic churches retained a robust appreciation of images in worship, the Protestant Reformation set off a new wave of iconoclasm. In the medieval Catholic church, lines had undoubtedly blurred between worshipping *through* images and the worshipping *of* images. The Old Testament warnings against graven images rose in relevance. Too much magic was associated with saints, too much indulgence attached to spending. For reformers like John Calvin, the prohibition of images within the church was absolute. A purging of images coincided with the purification of the church. An emphasis on *sola scriptura* allowed the word to triumph over the image.

The austere sanctuaries of American Protestantism reflect Calvin's lasting influence. Protestant churches are often stripped of iconography except for a bare (disembodied) cross. Theological emphasis falls upon the resurrected Christ rather than the suffering Savior. More of a disembodied, otherworldly faith followed. An immanent Orthodox and Catholic faith was replaced by more transcendent worship, "not of this world." Some Protestants focused on the glory to come rather than our contemporary surroundings. We came to worship through our minds rather than our senses.

However, the warnings against graven images still apply within an anti-pictorial tradition. What is to keep us from worshipping the word made manifest—the Bible? Bibliolatry is clearly idol worship. How often do televangelists reduce the Bible to a magic formula, a book with instant answers to complex problems? We may recite Bible verses as incantations, thinking the words themselves will call God to action on our terms and timetable. Aren't words just as limited as images in capturing the divine and the eternal? Orthodox thinker Leonid Ouspensky comments on this:

> In this sense both theology and iconography are always fail-ures. Precisely in this failure lies the value of both alike; for this

value results from the fact that both theology and iconography both reach the limit of human possibilities and prove insufficient. Therefore the methods used by iconography for pointing to the kingdom of God can only be figurative, symbolical, like the language of parables in the Holy Scriptures.[11]

Both words and images fall short in their quest to approximate the glory of God. The apocalyptic language of Ezekiel or Daniel fails to capture the wonder of God. The Apocalypse of John attempts to describe eternal battles to come. It evokes images of a new heaven and a new earth with potent word pictures. No painting or description can contain all the splendor of the Almighty. Our finest words and images can only suggest the grandeur of our God, the beauty of the risen Christ, the power of the Holy Spirit. Given their limitations, don't we desperately need both words *and* images to approximate the wonder of the Creator and the splendor of creation?

Recovering an Artistic Tradition

John: We got into this discussion. And the upshot in the end was, you said, "God doesn't like artists because they ask too many questions." You don't even remember the conversation.

Craig: No, but I'll tell you what, you know what I do for a living? Convince young Christian people to ask questions if they want to be serious about being artists. That's what I do. That's all I've been doing. So if I said that your choice was between faith and art, I apologize.

To move forward, we must apologize for our recent past. We need to say, "We're sorry we discouraged artists." We apologize for making it even more difficult for them to pursue their calling. We must make room for creative types to practice their craft. We need their gifts, their visions, and their passion within the Christian community. As a professor, I train aspiring artists to reconcile their faith with their craft. I also equip tomorrow's pastors to incorporate creativity into their congregational worship. We study art history in an effort to recover our profound Christian heritage. More and more churches are buying projectors, setting up cameras, and encouraging worship leaders to create original content. We are on the cusp of a rebirth of art within worship. We must merge past and present, Catholic and Protestant, red and blue in order to create a complex shade of purple—to accurately portray Christ our king.

So what does our anti-art, anti-image Protestant heritage have to do with this present moment? Our immaterial theology is a real handicap in an era of abundant images. I appreciate the ascetic calls offered by Shane Claiborne of the Simple Way.[12] His *Irresistible Revolution* seeks to restore the radical nature of the Christian faith. We need to simplify our lives by resisting consumerist culture. But that doesn't mean disdaining art as worldly, superficial, or nonessential. Claiborne actually urges us to recover the prophetic side of art. Painters and poets practically assume a vow of poverty to pursue their craft. Artists are comfortable living on the margins, challenging notions that comfort equals happiness. They also understand the power of observation, of stillness, of learning to see God in nature and everyday life. A visual faith can simplify our lives and deepen our discipleship.

An embrace of images may be necessary to subvert our overabundance of entertainment. That doesn't mean more images, but a deeper respect for their positive potential. We need a greater understanding of the theology behind icons and their incorporation into our devotional lives. To a bigger, louder, and faster world, I propose a smaller, softer, slower religion. Icons are the ultimate silent sermon. In a superficial world, they dare us to go deeper with them and with ourselves. In a culture saturated with stimulation, the icon invites us to sit down. To catch our breath. To rest. To sit in silence. The icon doesn't beg for our attention but waits patiently upon us to get focused. It meets us more than halfway, offering a focal point within our space. When we settle down, the Holy Spirit settles in.

Unfortunately, the 200 Christian film students at Biola University are penalized by their Protestant roots. They do not start even with their filmmaking competition; they start in an anti-image hole.

A heavy emphasis upon the word can create great screenplays, but aspiring Protestant filmmakers must reach beyond their theological heritage in order to create memorable moving pictures. Thankfully, the sacramental side of Christian faith maintained an appreciation of images. The abundance of Catholic and Orthodox images remains a treasure trove for us to explore. We have titans of visual faith to draw upon— from Giotto to Rembrandt, from Caspar David Friedrich to George Rouault.[13] Even the celebrity portraits of Andy Warhol were rooted in his Byzantine Orthodox upbringing. In the last years of his life, Warhol repeatedly returned to images of the Last Supper, updating da Vinci's work with postmodern commentary.[14] Future filmmakers need not fear. The greatest visual art was often rooted in the greatest story ever told—of Jesus' life, death, and resurrection.

Film scholar Richard Blake has noted how a Catholic imagination fueled the classic films of John Ford, Frank Capra, Alfred Hitchcock, Francis Ford Coppola, and Martin Scorsese.[15] A Catholic upbringing surrounded by images of saints, candles, and crucifixes gave them permission to make extravagant movies. John Ford defined the western with classics starring John Wayne like *Stagecoach* (1939), *She Wore a Yellow Ribbon* (1949), and *The Searchers* (1956). Frank Capra's films clarified the American dream of a humble man rising up and prospering against the system. Audiences continue to love the positive portraits of *Mr. Deeds Goes to Town* (1936), *Mr. Smith Goes to Washington* (1939), and the Christmas classic *It's a Wonderful Life* (1946). Alfred Hitchcock's name became synonymous with thrillers like *North by Northwest* (1959) and *Psycho* (1960). Francis Coppola and Martin Scorsese drew upon their Italian Catholic heritage to redefine the gangster film from *The Godfather* (1972) to *The Departed* (2006). They placed their sinful characters within church settings, contrasting the sacred rites of baptism with cold-blooded contract killings.

These films may not announce themselves as inherently religious or specifically Catholic. They may even disdain church practices. Yet Richard Blake suggests an "afterimage" of their Catholic roots remains in how they film the physical world. The sacramentality of their upbringing results in a comfort with sets, props, and actors. Hitchcock's films are loaded with telling close-ups and attention to detail. His plots revolve around desirable objects—the MacGuffins—that drive the plot. The seven sacraments practiced by Catholics offer filmmakers an understanding of signs, symbols, and gestures. The ritual actions inherent in bowing, kneeling, and making the sign of the cross are transferred to scenes of preparation for battle. Soldiers, cowboys, and crooks check their equipment before proceeding. A film like *The Godfather* takes its time, giving proper respect to the ceremonies and rituals surrounding a wedding or a murder. John Ford's westerns are communal in their outlook, whether John Wayne is leading a cattle drive or a cavalry into battle. Mr. Smith and Mr. Deeds take up the cause of the common man, fighting on behalf of the community.

Having grown up listening to priests, these Catholic filmmakers depict a masculine world. The greatest tragedies arise when individuals cannot join the community. Memorable moments include Ethan Edwards walking away from civilization in *The Searchers* or Travis Bickle failing to find a calling beyond assassin in *Taxi Driver*. Cinematic antiheroes like Michael Corleone wrestle with the dark side, struggling to find redemption. Such struggles are the heartbeat of enduring drama.

Of course, such dramatic imagery is not exclusive to Catholic filmmakers. I recall the poetic, Protestant vision of Robert Benton that informs the end of *Places in the Heart* (1984). For a community torn apart by murder and revenge, Benton suggests a heavenly reunion. Characters who have been brutally judged gather together in church, united in communion. Time and history collapse into a sacred space where all wait in the pews for the blessed sacrament of the Lord's Supper.

Steven Spielberg incorporated Catholic rituals for a memorable sequence from *Amistad* (1997). While a judge purifies himself with water and prayer, slaves under arrest discuss their connections to Jesus. They see a picture of Jesus walking on the water. They conclude that he came across the water—just as they did. Though innocent, he was arrested and put on trial—just as they were. Could his glorious resurrection offer them a tangible hope en route to sentencing? Spielberg finishes the sequence with close-ups of crosses. In a ship's mast, the slaves find comfort. They are not alone in their persecution. Christ also suffered for crimes he did not commit.

The history of Hollywood is often described as Jewish moguls hiring Catholic directors to create films for Protestant audiences. Movies animate a visual imagination that is often starved in church. Catholic filmmakers provide an example for how religious faith may enhance the creation of art. A visual faith is baptized by possibilities, embracing a world pregnant with dramatic potential.

Yet, another aspect of Richard Blake's observations disturbs me. Blake draws upon the work of sociologist and priest Andrew Greeley, who discovers that church attendance enhances the artistic imagination and appreciation of Catholics.[16] In Protestant settings, regular church attendance *discourages* artistic pursuit. The most faithful Protestant churchgoers are less likely to attend concerts, patronize museums, and appreciate beauty. The Catholic imagination fuels creativity; the Protestant imagination squelches it. To a professor training aspiring Protestant artists, this is a problem.

Asking Questions

> I can produce no drama, administer no sacrament,
> without depending on hearing and sight. In this
> respect, religion and art are fully alike.[17]
>
> GERARDUS VAN DER LEEUW

Perhaps the false choice I presented to John Marks was rooted in tragic realities. If John hoped to pursue his dream of becoming a writer, God (as presented in certain Protestant settings) could prove to be a stumbling block. I am left wondering whether God does discourage questions. Would the Almighty prefer a compliant people? Certainly, the grumbling of God's people during the exodus in the desert tested divine patience. How could they fail to remember how far they'd come? Why were divine interventions met with such short-lived appreciation? Does God get tired of artists' questions?

As we survey scripture, we find a surprising array of questions.[18] God confronts Adam with the question, "Who told you that you were naked?" When Adam blames Eve, God expresses the full gravity of Eve's choice and his own shocked amazement in the question, "What is this you have done?"

When Cain slaughters his brother Abel, God asks a simple question that still resonates today: "Where is your brother?" Cain responds to God with his own question, "Am I my brother's keeper?" Like Cain, we try to escape responsibility, to see ourselves as isolated from other's struggles. Yet God listens to the cries of Abel's blood calling out for justice. Are we our brothers' and sisters' keepers? God makes clear that the answer is yes by responding to Cain's question with yet another question—the same one he asked Eve—"What have you done?"

Abraham is shocked when God suggests he will found a people through him. Abraham wonders, "What can you give me since I remain childless?" His question is rooted in a seemingly unchangeable reality. Our doubts arise when we cannot imagine another way. Moses looked at the travail besetting the Hebrews in Egypt and asked, "Why have you brought trouble upon this people? Is this why you sent me?" David was overwhelmed by the strength of his enemies. He couldn't imagine a way out, and he asked God a bold question: "Why are you so far from saving me?" When Job experiences a series of setbacks, losing beloved members of his family, he asks God, "Why have you made me your target?" Job's friends encourage him to bury his complaints and questions, but God proves capable of answering valid questions. The Old Testament chronicles the history of a people wrestling with God.

Jesus' compelling teaching and dramatic miracles were also met with skepticism (and resistance!). From prison, John the Baptist sends his followers to find Jesus. After years of waiting for the Messiah, John sends the message, "Are you the one who was to come, or should we expect someone else?" Jesus was often confronted by such ultimate questions. Having grasped the grandeur of Christ's claims, the Samaritan woman at the well wondered, "Where can you get this living water?" The rich young ruler gets to the core of discipleship by asking, "What must I do to inherit eternal life?" Jesus offers a challenging response: "Sell everything you have and give to the poor." Such a call to sacrificial action makes most of us shudder. Could Jesus be serious about his radical demands? (New monastics like Shane Claiborne think so!) A Pharisee boiled down our incredulity: "Who is my neighbor?" Doesn't discipleship end with my family, those I agree with, or those who serve the same God? As Cain attempted to evade responsibility for Abel, so the Pharisees tried to bracket their benevolence. To those counting the cost, Jesus asked, "What good is it for a man to gain the whole world, yet forfeit his soul?"

Jesus also asked his audience basic questions. To those suffering from sickness, he asked, "Do you want to get well?" To disciples who were shaken by a violent storm, Jesus asked, "Why are you so afraid?" When questions of his lordship arose, Jesus flipped the question around, asking his disciples, "Who do you say I am?" In his most vulnerable moments, Jesus expressed the hurts we all bring to God. When his closest friends abandon him in a time of crisis, Jesus asks, "You do not want to leave me too, do you?" To his false accusers, he wonders, "Why are you trying to kill me?" He stares into the human heart of darkness but gets no satisfying answer. At his lowest point, naked, stripped, and abused, Jesus utters the core question we've all addressed to God, "My God, my God, why have you forsaken me?" This guttural question baptizes all complaints we may utter to God. Where were you when I needed you? How could you allow my wife, father, and daughter to die? Have you heard my cries? Where is the answer I sought? Why are you so slow, so silent, so asleep on the job?

Great art begins with enduring questions. The most haunting dramas often begin where our logic ends—trying to make sense of senseless acts of violence and suffering. Out of grief arises the raw material for timeless books and movies. Dostoyevsky's *The Brothers*

Karamazov is a form of protest theology, a shaking of our fist at God.[19] As such, it coincides with the biblical psalms. Asking questions, filing complaints, putting God on trial—this is the task of artists and Christians. No one willingly enters into such dark places. We don't invite such suffering. But when it arrives, we wrestle with God, trying to find meaning within seemingly random circumstances. Thank God for artists who attempt to find light within darkness, who force us to stare at the question for longer than we're used to contemplating.

The darkest event in Old Testament history was the fall of Jerusalem. The faith of the Hebrew community was shattered. It birthed a haunting series of questions. How could God have failed to defend us in our time of need? How can an idolatrous Babylonian people conquer us? How can evil men bring down our glorious temple?

The poignant Psalm 137 begins by the waters of Babylon, in exile. Behind the words we hear the confused cry, how is this possible? It is a prayer for revenge and expresses Israel's longing to see judgment and disaster befall their Babylonian conquerors. How could they ever dig out of such a horribly dark hole? We asked the same questions after the World Trade Center collapsed. In Bruce Springsteen's mournful "My City in Ruins," he sings of his lost soul and wonders how he begins again.

Artists are often blessed with an ability to imagine a better world. The prophetic imagination in the Old Testament painted a picture of a rebuilt Jerusalem (even while they were in exile).[20] Isaiah and Jeremiah used words laden with loaded images to reawaken faith in a fallen people. They talked of rebuilding broken walls and inspired people to return to a city in ruins. Bruce Springsteen finishes his song with a hopeful prayer for strength to carry on. He almost wills the city into restoration, shouting, "Rise up!" After the fall of the Twin Towers, Springsteen dares to title his album *The Rising.* The prophetic imagination paints a bright future that no one can picture—yet.

A purple state of mind recognizes art as a handmaiden to faith. They arise from the same muscle. Imagination is an act of faith, an ability to see a world of possibilities despite distractions and destructions. When screenwriters type, "Fade in," they are engaging in an act of faith. They believe that a producer will come along and pour $100 million into realizing their dream. That is an absurd level of hope. And yet every day, people in Hollywood see their dreams come true. Faith is rewarded with investment, with a team of supporters coming alongside the dreamer and turning a vision into a dramatic reality. Can we practice the same kind of faith within the church? Can we summon new language to rally people to action?

I cherish Jesus' metaphors about the kingdom of God. But to a culture that has only known democracy, such imaginative historical metaphors may not communicate. What if we talked about God's extended network? Can we invite the next generation to put God atop their friends' list? What if we invited people to join God's Facebook group, where everyone is a favorite?

As we push past the rhetoric that has divided us, we desperately need new pictures of possibilities. What kind of society can we erect from the ashes of post-9/11 America? What artists and leaders will help us paint a new image of ourselves? What kind of rising do we need? The religious satirist Reverend Billy (www.revbilly.com) challenged our assumptions about consumption. His Stop Shopping Choir made audiences rethink their Christmas spending. The provocative documentary about Reverend Billy, *What Would Jesus Buy?* (2007), makes us laugh and think about our purchases at the same time. He took his countercultural message into Wal-Mart, Starbucks, and Disneyland. This kind of street theater harkens back to the Old Testament prophets. Such comedic imagination disarms people.

California artist Lynn Aldrich takes common everyday objects and infuses them with new meanings.[21] She arranged slices of bread across a gallery like edible dominoes. Her installation included 45 loaves of bread, from white to dark pumpernickel. Thirty-five feet of bread seemed like quite a waste. But the title of her piece, *Bread Line* (1991), highlighted the homelessness that continues to beset our cities. Both white people and dark people are forced to line up every single day for a meal. To what degree are those lives wasted because of our indifference?

Aldrich's recent work has focused on the environment. She stood up a swath of blue and green garden hoses to resemble a dynamic ocean wave. The work connects the over-watering of our lawns to the water shortages around the globe. In *Clean Water Act* (2003), cross sections of colorful PVC pipes and hoses look like ocean bubbles from afar. It can also be seen as coral, the vital core for undersea life. For *Sea Change* (2003), Aldrich arranged bright scouring pads and dishwashing accessories into an unlikely aquarium. Her playful art makes me think about what I wash down the drain. How does my (mis)use of water drain the oceans we allegedly value? Lynn Aldrich's prophetic vision makes me laugh and think at the same time.

Barack Obama stands out as an image of hope. His speeches may have skimped on substance or practical policies, but his words of change resonated with alienated voters. His presence as a person of mixed race, growing up both within and outside America, made him a global citizen. Obama emerged as a symbol of hope to a weary people. He is a living political icon of possibilities, awakening our best intentions. Can we push past racial divisions? Can we cross the red/blue divide? Can anybody still grow up to be president?

How do we empower the next generation to reclaim the prophetic imagination of the Old Testament? We must allow people to color with all the crayons of God's kingdom. We must draw upon the riches of our Protestant heritage, celebrating the word of God. But we must also reclaim the storehouse of visual icons preserved by our Catholic and Orthodox partners. We need to unite word and image for an era saturated by sales techniques. We must speak more slowly, and see more clearly in order to calm weary postmodern pilgrims inundated by images. Jesus, the original Word and image, will gradually draw us to God as we become reacquainted with the beauty of worship through the arts.

Doubt and Laughter

5

Times are tough. Hope is in short supply. People have heard the bad news. They've even forwarded it to their friends. As much as we may like to avoid tragedy or heartache, it inevitably confronts us. For people of faith who have been taught to consider themselves "more than conquerors through him who loved us," such gritty realities can be unsettling. We try to reconcile a resurrection faith with a mundane existence. In such times of crisis a "name it and claim it" faith can sometimes serve as an impediment to healing. We cannot get to the other side of a mountain by avoiding it. Sometimes it is simply a rough, uphill climb.

Our communities of faith are founded on the fallibility of their members. Only broken people may join. Yet far too often, we feel alone in our struggles. We mask our true feelings for the sake of appearances. We feel that a deadly perfectionism is required. Christians must learn how to air their questions, acknowledge their doubts, and confess their darkest thoughts. By surfacing our struggles, we discover we are not alone. A purple state of mind experiences periods of doubt and depression, dark nights of the soul. It endures serious, unexpected tests. But rather than escape from pain, a purple state of mind confronts death and dying with confidence, knowing Jesus overcame our greatest fears. A purple state of mind embraces doubt and depression as natural parts of life. It seeks out the hidden passages of scripture that discuss the dark aspects of the human journey. It finds healing laughter even amid pain.

> **Craig:** [My sister, Dixie, died in a car wreck at age twenty-one.] That's a close encounter with death, that was a living reality that put everything I believed into test mode. If this is the randomness of this universe, if God is in charge of a universe that works this randomly, then what kind of control is that? What kind of God is that? And I think I came close to saying, "If that's what you've got for us, God, then I don't know if I want a piece of that action."

We all dread the phone call. Nothing can prepare us for the volcanic force that follows. A wave of confusion threatens to overwhelm us. How? Why? It can't be. Life-changing news of death, divorce, or destruction arrives when we least expect it. For parents of teenagers, it may be a wake-up call after midnight. A phone call can bring assurance or horror. In my case, the phone rang while I was out of town.

I was in Chicago, visiting my girlfriend's grandmother. Grandma Pickett was not expected to live long. She had enjoyed a full life, but now she was ensconced in a nursing facility, and her body was withering away. This was my first and perhaps only opportunity to meet Grandma Pickett. She wanted to see me before she passed—to have a better grasp of the man who would marry her granddaughter. It is tough to enjoy such weighty moments. The reasons for entering are so obvious to all involved that it is hard to act naturally. The gravitas of final meetings ensures either an awkward silence or superficial small talk. But I was glad to shake Grandma's hand, to stare into her eyes, to connect with this fading generation prior to our joyous engagement.

I was resting easy with the test seemingly behind me when the phone rang. I was upstairs in the guest bedroom. "Your brother is on the phone." What time is it? Why is Drew calling me here? Why so early? I was totally disoriented. Drew broke the news before my head had cleared: "Dixie was in a car accident. And she's dead."

Now I was even more confused. "How? When?"

No amount of detail can make sense of such horrifying news. Drew pieced together a probable timeline. "She was on her way to work. She stopped to get breakfast. She had just been through the drive-through window..." As more details emerged, the painful ironies multiplied.

Dixie was on her way to the hospital. My sister helped people, checking patients in as they sought treatment. As a senior in college, she was hoping to go to pharmacy school, to ensure that people got the medicine they needed. She was the most safety-conscious person in our family of five. She always wore her seat belt and regularly reminded us to put ours on. So why on this morning was she driving without a seat belt? Dixie was slightly short. She unhooked her seat belt to reach her order at the drive-through window. Ouch.

"So who hit her? What happened?"

It was a single-car accident. Her car got over on the side of the road and flipped.

"Why was she on the berm?"

She had swerved to miss a dog in the road. Dixie had always been an animal lover. But it turned out that the dog was already dead. It had been lying in the road for a while. She lost her life trying to save a dead dog. What an ugly array of catastrophic coincidences.

I hung up the phone, still in shock. My sweet Caroline walked into the room. She sensed something grave had occurred. I muttered simply, "My sister, Dixie, is dead." Caroline sat down beside me on the bed. Before she could even hug me, the bed collapsed. We hit the floor in a slapstick moment straight out of a Three Stooges cartoon—*splat.* We had a brief chuckle, and then we sank into tears. Death and laughter met in the same haunting moment.

Death challenges us. It reminds how few guarantees we're given. It forces us to face our mortality. It is a rite of passage that none of us escapes. Death can be physical, emotional, or spiritual. We may lose a loved one. We may suffer through painful breakups and divorce. We may lose our job and our sense of security. But sooner or later, our (false) sense of security will be threatened. Our faith will be tested.

Has death confronted you? Have you been shocked by sudden reversals? How many stages of grief have you experienced? Did you hold on to hope within desperate circumstances? Or did you fold under the weight of tragedy? A purple state of mind experiences periods of doubt and depression, dark nights of the soul. It endures serious, unexpected tests—shocks to our system. It may not fear the worst, but it anticipates troubles. Rather than escape from pain, a purple state of mind merges faith and doubt. As Jesus endured the isolation of the cross, so we may walk through periods of loneliness. We may ask God, *Why have you abandoned and forsaken me?* The desperation of Psalm 22 is answered in the comfort found in Psalm 23. The road to hope is paved with despair. A purple state of mind may walk through the valley of the shadow of death, yet it does not fear. This chapter will look at the roots of doubt. We will also wrestle with death and depression—dark periods that can overwhelm us. How do we confront our worst fears and retain our faith? How do we rediscover the gift of laughter?

Doubt

To you, I'm an atheist. To God, I'm the loyal opposition.

WOODY ALLEN, *Stardust Memories*

John: I am someone who wanted to believe. I wanted to believe in the big world or the big spirit or the big idea. And Nietzsche came along and said, "God is dead and we killed him." Do we understand yet what that means? Do we understand yet the nature of this murder we committed? Because it is immense. It is so huge that we are too frightened to confront it.

Craig: That's actually sad.

John: Yes, there is a sadness. There's a sense that "It's done."

Craig: It's a tragedy. It's not a pronouncement. It's not a triumphalist statement.

John: It's not a triumphalist statement at all. Nietzsche grappled with the meaning of what it means for us to have killed God in our culture and our world. What he's saying is, "Okay, you've done this. The body is dead. It's decomposing." I think those are his exact words. But you have to do something about this now. Because there is no bringing that body back to life.

Craig: Like clean up the mess...

John: No, I don't think it's clean up the mess.

Craig: Or sweep it off from the stage.

John: I don't think he believed you could do either. Because I think he says, "You have to now come up with an idea to replace that one."

Nietzsche was right. We killed God. We put Jesus to death for undercutting the purity codes of ancient Israel. We crucified Christ for defying the self-deification practiced by ancient Rome. An innocent man was murdered by well-intentioned, law-abiding citizens. Religious and political leaders pooled their resources to take out a mutual threat. Two thousand years later, similar conflations of church and state threaten to strangle God's Spirit. In Nazi Germany, too many Christians refused to confront the Holocaust. Patriotism robbed them of perspective. South Africa enforced apartheid as God-ordained. The Janjaweed seek to purge Darfur of non-Muslims. To what degree has the United States used religious language to justify war in Iraq? Sincere defenders of the state crucify Jesus again and again.

In Nietzsche's Europe, Christian ethics had become just as rote and uninspired as the religious culture Jesus undercut in Judea. And like Jesus, Nietzsche earned plenty of enemies. Anyone who points out how hollow our moral precepts have become is no friend of politicians, pastors, or parents. How will we get people to follow the rules if people like Jesus continue to redefine them? What do we do with dangerous doubters like Nietzsche (and Jesus)?

Religious doubt has an extensive history. In *Doubt: A History,* Jennifer Michael Hecht traces its lineage back to Greco-Roman skeptics. Doubters in Hindu and Buddhist traditions demonstrate that it is not a Western phenomena. The questions may shift slightly. For example, the Japanese do not struggle as much with why bad things happen to good people. In Buddhist thought, suffering is to be expected. The absence of suffering raises far more questions. Why do good things happen? That is an equally vexing question. Though not a Christian, Jennifer Hecht considers Jesus a doubter in a biblical line begun by Job and the author of Ecclesiastes. His soul-searching in the garden of Gethsemane and his faltering utterances on the cross are important affirmations of pain. Hecht suggests, "The only thing such doubters really need, that believers have, is a sense that people like themselves have always been around, that they are part of a grand history. I hope it is clear now that doubt has such a history of its own, and that to be a doubter is a great old allegiance, deserving quiet respect and open pride."[1]

In the film *Purple State of Mind,* I am confronted by John Marks' reasoned objections to the faith. He wants to know why the innocent suffer, how I can continue to believe in a loving God amid so much human suffering. In many cases, I don't offer an answer (much to Christians' frustration!). Perhaps that is because I secretly share his doubts. In listening to his hard questions, I am processing my own. German theologian Jürgen Moltmann asks the humbling question, "Is not every unbeliever who has a reason for his atheism and his decision not to believe a theologian too?"[2]

Perhaps atheists offer Christians a great gift, some much-needed perspective. We can be strengthened and even encouraged by the loyal opposition. Moltmann suggests, "Nietzsche's book *The Antichrist* has a lot to teach us about true Christianity, and the modern criticism of religion put forward by Feuerbach, Marx, and Freud is still theological in its anti-theology."[3] We must learn to affirm the biblical roots of protest theology, rooted in the hard questions found in Lamentations, Ecclesiastes, and Job. This requires patient listening and honesty about our own struggles.

When atheists point out how much evil has been done in the name of religion, I tend to agree. I've read most of the sordid histories of the Inquisition. I am familiar with the atrocities associated with the Crusades. I followed the Native Americans' trail of tears. Like rock band Rage Against the Machine, I get angry about "killing in the name of God." What is the crucifixion besides the ultimate misguided mission? Sincere followers of God murdered God. Surely Jesus struggled to wrap his head around such a twisted scenario. He may have been willing to die, but did it have to include the betrayal of a close friend under payoffs from local religious leaders? For some, such tragic histories fuel doubt and lead to despair. For others, the mistakes of the past cause us to redouble our efforts, to stop such abuses before they recur. Can we learn our lesson?

Today's atheists continue Nietzsche's important idol-smashing work. They rightly expose toxic expressions of faith. They decry abuses of power and resistance to scientific progress, places where organized religion brought death rather than life.[4] Just as ancient Israel needed correction, so the Christian community needs such critics. It is far too easy for us to get defensive.

Depression

Craig: That's a heart of darkness you don't want to go to ever again. But if God isn't in that, I don't know how you get through it. I have so much respect for those who would go through death without a faith. How do you do that? How do you go serve in Iraq without a faith in God? How do you go watch your friend or your buddy die without a faith? That I don't understand. So I had to find God in the midst of that ugliest of situations because I don't know if I would have survived it otherwise...

It takes a while to simply overcome the shock. The emotions at a funeral are so high that almost none of the reality sinks in until after the departed are buried. But as a whirlwind week of weeping concludes, the real struggle begins. After friends and family have gone, after the gifts of food and hospitality have been consumed, the silence begins. It rages from an empty bedroom. It roars from phone calls that cease. It shouts from a future cut short. Mail addressed to the deceased continues to trickle in. Credit card companies try to collect debts. Not much grace or understanding is offered.

The mind games commence. Internal monologues attempt to create a rationale for an absurd situation. You retrace the steps leading up to the accident. You consider alternative scenarios, a series of "what ifs." You replay final conversations in your mind. Regret creeps in. *If only I'd told her... If I could just see her again.* But there is almost nothing you can do about it. Heaven is a distant comfort. You have to live with this new bracing reality. Long periods of darkness follow.

Depression is a tunnel with no light in sight. It kicks in when we're far enough from the event that it is not in our face. Yet it is far enough from the past that we can't get away from it. Life seems pointless, cruel, and absurd. Each morning becomes a test. *Why bother? Why try? What is the point?* My midlife crisis hit at age 27. I couldn't remember why I was working. How could I offer hope to impressionable young people? It was tough to minister to teenagers in such a state of mind. I wasn't suffering from a purple state of mind but from a deep, dark blue.

It is somewhat comforting to discover saints like Mother Teresa suffered from the same dry spells. In private letters to Reverend Michael van der Peet, she wrote, "Jesus has a very special love for you. As for me, the silence and the emptiness is so great that I look and do not see, listen and do not hear."[5] She continued to care for the poor, even while wondering why God seemed so silent, so distant. What makes life seem so unfair?

We try to sort it out theologically. The specter of 9/11 raised so many questions of theodicy. Three films that followed that cataclysmic event illustrated the creeping effects of depression. We see Mel Gibson's priest struggle with his wife's death in *Signs* (2002). We see a grieving father refusing to join his surviving children in prayer in the touching film *In America* (2002). Benecio del Toro accidentally runs over a little girl after he has dedicated his life to Christ in *21 Grams* (2003). Each of the characters asks God, *What was that about? What kind of divine plan could result in such abject suffering? And if God wouldn't intervene, then why was I praying?* Following Dixie's death, my whole spiritual scaffolding was in danger of tumbling down. When our preexisting assumptions bump up against new realities, something has got to give. I've known people who've endured such crisis points. Many emerge with their faith strengthened. Others drop religion altogether.

Theologian Don Browning describes this crisis point as the place where the outer envelope of experience bumps up against the inner envelope of conviction. How can we make our experience and beliefs work together? Browning offers a "fundamental practical theology" that fills in the gaps. He encourages us to make the adjustments necessary with a supportive community. We can't do it alone. Most often that involves a shift in our thinking. Browning suggests, "The community must examine the sacred texts and events that constitute the source of the norms and ideals that guide its practices. It brings its questions to these normative texts and has a conversation between its questions and these texts."[6] Our beliefs may take a holiday, but they are more likely to simply be altered. A new set of biblical promises may take precedence. Forgotten sections of scripture may emerge as profoundly relevant. Our previous set of assumptions may be set aside as we enter a new season. A practical theology works for us rather than against us. It brings head and heart, beliefs and practices into alignment.

The simplicity of Proverbs may be chastened by the world-weariness of Ecclesiastes. Both books of the Bible offer enduring truths about life. Proverbs offers a series of couplets. Most follow an if-then formula rooted in likely scenarios. If you cheat in business, you will likely be found out. If you cheat on your spouse, you will likely be discovered. If you choose wisely, you will likely prosper. Ecclesiastes deals with the exceptions to the rules. What happens when the wicked prosper?

What if our faith is not rewarded? How do you deal with a justice system that doesn't add up? Sometimes wisdom involves doing the right thing. But a different kind of wisdom arises when bad things happen to good people. The contrasts between these two biblical collections demonstrate the situational nature of biblical wisdom. Our circumstances determine what we need to read. Proverbs provides a road map. Ecclesiastes offers comfort when we're derailed.

We may also find the proximity of Psalm 22 to Psalm 23 instructive. Abject despair is followed by poetic comfort in the canon of scripture. We should expect periods of highs *and* lows. Jesus was well acquainted with both. His painful prayers of resignation in the garden of Gethsemane echo David's complaints in Psalm 22. Why must I endure this? Why do my enemies prosper? Why does God allow such injustice to continue? Jesus understands what it feels like to be forsaken. He desperately needed green pastures at the end of his life. What still waters did he turn to on the cross? When soldiers offered him bitter wormwood as a false salve, did he pray, *Your rod and your staff, they comfort me*?

Some will attempt to snap us out of our funk. They will suggest we get over it or get on with it. But how can galvanizing memories be shrugged off? Our experiences can't be discarded. They must be processed, rolled around in our psyche as we search for clues. If the grieving parts of scripture do not suffice, the depressed may need a doctor. There is no shame in seeking a physician for anything. It would be lovely if our social networks provided the sympathetic ears we need. Friends can be important sounding boards. Pastors will sometimes have the gift of counseling. Sometimes professional help is well worth the money.

As I wrestled with Dixie's death, a Christian therapist proved to be a lifesaver. She provided a safe place to air the depths of my pain. I had some serious shouting matches with God in her office. She helped me identify the false assumptions I carried through life. Her well-timed questions punctured my self-centeredness. Why did I think I would escape death? Was my faith supposed to make me indestructible?

Where was it written that following God guaranteed a life of comfort? In memorizing Psalm 23, I skipped over Psalm 22. In claiming the truths of Proverbs, I avoided the messier conclusions of Ecclesiastes. My selective applications of scripture had resulted in the worship of a false god. My sister's death assaulted my idols.

In *A Grief Observed*, C.S. Lewis described how the death of his wife, Joy Gresham, altered his conceptions of God. He noted how "images of the Holy easily become holy images—sacrosanct. My idea of God is not a divine idea. It has to be shattered time after time. He shatters it himself. He is the great iconoclast. Could we not almost say that this shattering is one of the marks of his presence? The incarnation is the supreme example; it leaves all previous ideas of the Messiah in ruins."[7] We must be willing to let go of our images of God. If life experience does not shatter them, the Great Iconoclast will. This is not cruelty, but a severe mercy.

The Hebrews had to learn what God's favor entailed. They thought it was a blanket protection plan. Yet the arrival of the Babylonians on their sacred soil shattered their conception of what it meant to be a chosen people. By the waters of Babylon, they sat down and wept when they remembered their homeland. In Psalm 137, they ask, "How could our God allow this to happen to us?" They were forced to reread and in some cases rewrite their history. The outer envelope of their experience bumped up against their inner convictions. Something had to give.

The biblical prophets offered a different version of Jewish history. They flipped the script on Israel's assumptions. "Yes, you are chosen. But with that special status came significant responsibility. You were blessed to be a blessing. Your prosperity was intended to translate into generosity toward others. Your faithfulness is measured by the health of your widows and orphans. Have you been just toward the least among you? If not, then perhaps you can spend your era in exile rethinking your faith. By the time you understand what it means to be God's people, you will probably find yourselves back in Jerusalem."

We should never be surprised when we miss God's intentions.

That is the human story. Hoarding our prosperity. Privatizing a public God. Missing the Savior in our midst. If the disciples misunderstood Jesus' message, aren't we capable of the same error? Doubt and depression can be great companions to faith. They force us to challenge our assumptions. Have we rested on false laurels, banked on foolish notions? We do not seek out death. We do not feed our doubt. We never relish depression. But we recognize how faith is forged out of ashes, out of folly. Trials produce character. A faith that is tested is a faith that is refined. "Although the Lord gives you the bread of adversity and the water of affliction, your teachers will be hidden no more; with your own eyes you will see them. Whether you turn to the right or to the left, your ears will hear a voice behind you, saying, 'This is the way; walk in it'" (Isaiah 30:20-21).

Laughter

> Comedy equals tragedy plus time.
>
> WOODY ALLEN, *Crimes and Misdemeanors*

Woody Allen is the most theological comedian. His finest films are rooted in life's toughest quandaries. They poke fun at our pettiness and expose the folly found in our independence. Allen says, "If you want to make God laugh, tell him your plans." He represents a celebrated tradition: the Jewish comedian. He manages to look at the worst aspects of human behavior and still find humor in them. How do a people so familiar with suffering become known for the most robust sense of humor? From a persecuted people emerged the most self-deprecating, life-sustaining humor.

After Dixie's death, I honestly wondered, *Will I ever smile again?* Amid depression, nothing seemed hopeful and bright. Everything appeared a dull gray. A decade later, I was writing comedies as a career. In the teen road movie *Extreme Days,* two brothers surf, skate, and joke despite the loss of their sister. Her death doesn't keep them from living. It actually makes them love life more. The jokes in my screenplay for *Extreme Days* counterbalances the brothers' trying circumstances. The bitter accompanies the sweet. When laughs are rare, you relish them. When life is tough, you hunger for a joke. Humor emerges as a healing agent. Hasn't humor always played a significant role among God's people? It is one of our most attractive features-retaining a sense of humor amid sorrow. It is God's gift amid horrific circumstances. He grafted it into his people through Isaac. His name means "he laughs."

The biblical book of Hebrews famously defined faith as "being sure of what we hope for and certain of what we do not see" (Hebrews 11:1). It celebrates the heroes of faith from Abel to Abraham. Enoch is remembered as "one who pleased God." Noah gets recognition for the holy fear he exhibited in building an ark. Abraham emerges as the father of faith through obedience to God's call. When called to set out for a foreign country, Abram pulled up stakes. Then, as a childless man in his seventies, he had given up hope for an heir. In Genesis 15, God challenges Abram to look up, for his descendents are to be as plentiful as the stars in the sky. Abram responds to this far-fetched notion with faith. God responds by establishing a covenant with Abram.

Astute author Frederick Buechner describes faith as a verb rather than a noun: "It is an on-again-off-again rather than once-and-for-all. Faith is not being sure where you're going but going anyway. A journey without maps."[8]

The reciprocal relationship between our faith and God's action is demonstrated in Abraham's late-in-life fatherhood. He and his wife struggled with infertility. Hebrews 11:11 indicates that, "Abraham... was enabled to become a father because he considered him faithful who had made the promise." God says it, Abraham believes it, and that settles it. Or rather starts it. A long waiting period followed God's promise in Genesis 15. Twenty-five years pass before the long-awaited heir arrives and Abram becomes Abraham, "father of many." A prosperous line of Hebrews follows. Would God have withdrawn his blessing if Abraham had faltered? Does our faith in God prompt him to act? These are messy questions connected to prayer, providence, and free will.

Abraham's initial reaction to the news of his impending fatherhood does not fit neatly into our definitions of faith. In Genesis 17:15-16, God tells Abraham that his barren wife, Sarah, will give birth to a son. Abraham falls facedown, doubled over with laughter. Is that a sign of delight or disbelief? Probably a bit of both. It may have been a sense of comic relief. After years of waiting, God finally delivers. We get a glimpse into Abraham's mind-set. He says to himself, "Will a son be born to a man a hundred years old? Will Sarah bear a child at the age of ninety?" (Genesis 17:17). Abraham realizes how far-fetched such possibilities sounded.

When Sarah hears about her due date, she also laughs. Having waited on God for a quarter century, she doesn't necessarily leap at the possibilities. Having given up on childbirth, she cannot imagine such a late-in-life surprise. Husband and wife both think God's promise sounds ridiculous. Yet God doesn't look upon her laughter as a sign of delight but as a questioning of divine ability: "Is anything too hard for the LORD?" (Genesis 18:14). Her laughter veers toward scoffing.

Perhaps after all the pain and disappointment she'd dealt with, such a promise sounded like too much, too late. Where was God when she was desperate to become a mother? Any couple that has struggled with infertility knows how heartbreaking each month can be. Imagine 25 years of waiting and wondering and hoping, only to receive nothing. Her laughter may have been rooted more in relief than belief.

Laughter arises from the unexpected. It is often connected to absurd juxtapositions. The image of an aged couple with a newborn baby is bound to get a reaction. The long odds against Abraham and Sarah's paternity made God's miraculous intervention that much clearer. This wasn't a modest gesture, but a major test of God's providence. As that son is born, Abraham names him Isaac, "he laughs" (Genesis 21:3,6).

But is that laughter *for* Sarah's blessing or laughter *at* Sarah's predicament? Does she recognize her child as a divine delight? Or is she worried about becoming a public laughingstock? Are people laughing with the elderly parents or talking behind their backs? Isaac's birth is both miraculous and scandalous. Sarah and Abraham may not have felt capable of handling such a blessing. Who wants to be a mother at age 90? My wife and I wonder why we waited so long to have kids. Caroline was only 29, but I was a step slower at 35. It requires serious energy to keep up with a child. This gift of laughter may have over-whelmed these elderly parents. God laughs at their best-laid plans.

How encouraging that Abraham and Sarah, the most faithful role models, began their parenting full of disbelief. For parents struggling with infertility, their story suggests that regardless of how much frustration and disappointment we have experienced, God never gives up on us. Even after we've abandoned our dreams, God may still deliver. After all, "Is anything too hard for the LORD?" Abraham and Sarah do not answer his question. The same question stands before us. Given the absurd aspects of life, it is easy to lose faith, to consider our case closed. Yet God demonstrates that he is never finished with us. Periods of doubt have always accompanied faith. They are not rivals but old friends accompanying us on a journey.

Death is often sudden. Healing takes time. We cannot expect to speed through grief. Depression can also set in when our dreams are deferred. We may have a timetable erected in our brain that God refuses to follow. It is easy to despair. We cannot change our attitude overnight. It takes time. But fear not, the gift of laughter is ours, provided by a compassionate God who sees how painful our circum-stances can be. Abraham and Sarah waited a long time to see their prayers come to fruition. But God proved faithful. Isaac arrived with healing laughter—a gift to us all.

Texas

Dallas is John Marks' hometown. It is marked by a preponderance of megachurches. For 50 years, W.A. Criswell pastored First Baptist in Dallas, the largest church in the Southern Baptist Convention. John was raised near the equally massive Highland Park Presbyterian Church. Among the more recent suburban incarnations are Prestonwood Baptist Church in Plano and Fellowship Church, pastored by the dynamic Ed Young. It is a remarkably Protestant city.

What other structures dominate Dallas? Oil wells undergird the economy. The excesses of Nieman Marcus testify to a surplus of oil money. The Cotton Bowl stands as a fading testament to the place that football plays in the public consciousness. But what dominates the spaces between churches? Strip clubs. Open at all hours, ready for a "business lunch." Is there a relationship between denying the pleasures of the flesh on Sunday and indulging them on Monday? Dallas mixes the sacred and the profane in all kinds of strange ways.

The Council for Christian Colleges and Universities invited me to Dallas. They are the lobbyists for Christian colleges that seek to protect their religious freedoms. They also are committed to creative forms of cultural engagement. The CCCU sponsors acclaimed study abroad programs in Egypt, Oxford, China, and Costa Rica. They also offer semesters immersed in the arts. Music majors can attend the Contemporary Music Center on Martha's Vineyard. Fledgling journalists spend a semester in Washington DC at the American Studies Program.

For students interested in movies, the CCCU offers a semester in Hollywood at the Los Angeles Film Studies Center.

The CCCU hosted over a thousand presidents, administrators, and professors in Dallas. We came together for a series of "Significant Conversations." I gave a plenary address regarding pop culture. How should Christian educators respond to the onslaught of electronic entertainment? What do we do with this postmodern moment when outside forces threaten a fading Christendom? It was a timely topic of growing importance.

While I was speaking, Soulforce's Equality Ride was driving in. Soulforce is a lobbying and advocacy group founded by Mel White. Soulforce had decided to protest at Christian colleges with policies that excluded or disciplined gay students and professors. Inspired by the Freedom Riders of the Civil Rights Movement, Soulforce sent a busload of gay, lesbian, bisexual, and transgendered students to Christian colleges across America. The CCCU conference provided a great one-stop location to make their point.

Unfortunately, the Gaylord Resort Hotel and Convention Center forbade the Equality Ride from entering. (The irony of the hotel's name provided some comic relief.) So any cultural engagement with the gay community would have to take place outside the convention. When I concluded my address, John Marks and I headed to the entrance of the Gaylord Resort to meet the equality riders. I told them what I told the attendees—about the first cross-cultural missionary in the Bible, Philip. As an early Christian faced with persecution and death threats, Philip sought refuge amid people well-acquainted with suffering and rejection, the Samaritans. Along the way, Philip encountered an Ethiopian eunuch reading the book of Isaiah. Together, they discovered that God wants to build a house of worship for all peoples, where none shall be cut off, not even a eunuch. How might this surprising Bible story of race, sex, and spirituality reflect on our conversation? What issues remain unresolved in Texas and within the Christian community? What differences continue to divide us?

Love and Disappoint- ment

6

Britney Spears kissed Madonna on MTV. Janet Jackson stripped at the Super Bowl. Paris Hilton launched her career as a celebutante with a sex tape. And to all three events, young people let out a collective sigh. Justin Timberlake vowed to "Bring Sexy Back" (even though most of us didn't think it went away). Such blatant attempts at titillation largely failed to (a)rouse the next generation. In the words of the power-pop band Weezer, they have grown "Tired of Sex." Is that good news? How should we respond to such a highly sexualized culture? Love may have been reduced to sex in popular parlance, but that doesn't mean we abandon it. In fact, the confusion surrounding a word like *love* may offer more opportunities than ever to redefine it.

Issues of love and sexuality are quite loaded. Who can love whom? Where? And under what conditions? Christians have gotten remarkably involved in monitoring the sexual habits of others. Statistics in the book *unChristian* indicate that young people increasingly perceive Christians as judgmental. David Kinnaman from the Barna Group writes, "In our research, the perceptions that Christians are 'against' gays and lesbians—not only objecting to their lifestyles but also harboring irrational fear and unmerited scorn toward them—has reached critical mass. The gay issue has become the 'big one,' the negative image most likely to be intertwined with Christianity's reputation."[1] At a time when Christians are nervous about an overly sexualized culture, we've focused in on one form of sexual expression as the most repugnant to God. Rather than getting our own house in order, we've insisted that others cease and desist. How could Jesus, the great lover of others, have become associated with such isolating, unloving behavior? We've applied standards meant for us to society at large. Biblical verses intended to provoke introspection have been turned into deadly weapons in the culture war. Our actions parallel those of Jesus' enemies in scripture—the sincere followers of God who sought to preserve their fading cultural power. My fear is that the Christian community may end up on the wrong side of history. How can we reverse such perceptions? We can start by practicing what we preach—that God is love.

A purple state of mind receives love and extends love. It acts as a constant companion, cheering others on, comforting them in times of crisis. It affirms the gift of marriage but deals with people where they are. It acknowledges the disappointment that accompanies our romantic fantasies. Genuine love endures during many shifting seasons of life. A purple state of mind loves throughout, even those we disagree with—especially fellow Christians.

Silly Love Songs

John: I can talk all I want about how to believe what I believe, but I think in the end, my philosophy is her. My wife and my son, they have provided the shape of my life and I think in ways that I can't even comprehend.

The hyperkinetic movie musical *Moulin Rouge!* (2001) revolves around a surprising musical theme. The opening song is a remake of Nat "King" Cole's chart-topping hit from 1948, "Nature Boy." It spins a "once upon a time" type of setting. The fantastic sets, the garish costumes, and the vibrant colors all suggest that we are entering a fairy tale. In *Moulin Rouge!* that enchanted boy is a struggling artist played by Ewan McGregor. Christian (McGregor's character) demonstrates a remarkable faith in the bohemian virtues of courage, truth, beauty, and love. The musical lesson we all will learn? *Moulin Rouge!* reminds us that the greatest thing we'll ever learn is to love and to be loved in return.

Christian's object of affection is Satine (Nicole Kidman), a highly paid consort in the Moulin Rouge nightclub. She is cynical toward love, seeing it as a transaction rather than a lived reality. Having sold herself too many times, she can no longer envision true love. Satine's notion of love has been buried by disappointment. But Christian continues to woo her, singing "Silly Love Songs" atop an elephant. He offers promises from the KISS song, "I Was Made for Loving You." He summons Dolly Parton's hit, "I Will Always Love You." Christian dares to suggest that love can transform them into "heroes—just for one day."

Satine rejects his overtures. She doesn't want to be disappointed again, "You will be mean, and I'll drink all the time." But Christian keeps singing. Satine comes to understand the implications of this radical love Christian proposes. If she gives him a chance, if she dares to love, it will be "bad for business." Christian's extravagant love will alter her behavior (even though he never mentioned her questionable profession).

It is easy to dismiss the "Elephant Love Medley" as a simple seduction scene. Yet I remain so moved by Christian's tireless efforts. In his winsome wooing, I hear God singing to us, pushing past our cynicism. To a world "Tired of Sex," God sings a silly love song. Despite our promiscuity, our obsession with bodies, our short-changing of ourselves, God still loves us. He longs to dance with us atop an elephant under the Parisian stars. Ridiculous? Certainly. Essential? Absolutely!

I doubt that the director of *Moulin Rouge!* Baz Luhrmann or the songwriter of "Nature Boy," eden ahbez, were consciously striving for gospel allusions. Luhrmann attributes his inspiration to the Greek myth of Orpheus going underground to rescue Eurydice and bring her back to life. Orpheus's musical abilities charmed Eurydice's captors, Hades and Persephone, allowing her another lease on life. The author of "Nature Boy" embodied his song title by adopting a hippie lifestyle and allegedly resorting to a diet of fruit and nuts. In changing his given name to eden ahbez, he refused to use capital letters, insisting only God deserved such attention. However ancient or obscure their motivations, the artists behind *Moulin Rouge!* tapped into a *natural, universal* longing, a song we all sing. The hunger to love and be loved animates ancient and contemporary pop culture.

The religious community has gone to great lengths to distinguish between romantic love and godly love. Countless sermons have explained the four types of love described in Greek during biblical times. Affection, or *storge,* is love rooted in familiarity, extended to those in our family. We never chose this affection. It arrives naturally. The word *erotic* comes from *eros,* the passionate, physical love associated with sex. *Philia* love is about the ties that bind us together as friends through common interests. Such bonds form the basis for pursuing a common good in society. It is commemorated in the name of Philadelphia, or the city of brotherly love. *Agape* is the pure love embodied in Jesus' life and death: "This is love: not that we loved God, but that he loved us and sent his Son as an atoning sacrifice for our sins" (1 John 4:10).

In *The Four Loves,* C.S. Lewis points out the difference between the love we need (like a child dependent upon a mother for survival) and the love we receive as a gift (like God's grace).[2] How should we respond to such unexpected, sacrificial love? "Since God so loved us, we also ought to love one another" (1 John 4:11). We respond with appreciative love. We extend what we've experienced to others. *Moulin Rouge!* failed to acknowledge God as the initiator of life's greatest lesson—to love and be loved in return. (All creators deserve credit for the things they've invented!) But that doesn't make it any less true. We have a prime opportunity to redefine love in God's terms.

We've all made the mistake of demanding love. Our hunger can grow so great that we insist that others satisfy our needs. We remain childish, dependent, clinging. Love becomes our end goal, an elusive idol we long to possess. We construct fantasies about movie stars and musicians. We picture ourselves performing before adoring crowds, basking in their approval. We fixate upon the approval of a parent. We believe that when we're married, we shall be complete. C.S. Lewis suggests, "Love begins to be a demon the moment he begins to be a god." We expect love to deliver things that it cannot.

We're so accustomed to a transactional world. We're used to shopping, buying, and consuming. We turn sex into a commodity, something we cherish in our hearts, a possession we unwrap with our eyes. The Christian community has numerous reasons to associate sex with seduction. We can easily turn love into an obsession, an orgasm into the ultimate high. In the film *Purple State of Mind,* John Marks admits that his first experience of sexual intercourse was on his to-do list: "This must get done, today." Attaching such significance to a single act is bound to end up underwhelming. Like Satine, we may end up disappointed, bitter, and alone.

Yet Christians' efforts to separate *agape* from *eros* may have resulted in missed opportunities. We may have inadvertently squelched the love song of God. My deepest understanding of God's love arose *within* relationship. In falling in love and experiencing a grace-filled marriage, I started to grasp the mystery of God's *agape.* My wife, Caroline, serves as my angel of grace. John Marks also describes his wife in equally rapturous term. He told me, "I think in the end, my philosophy is her." When the person who knows us best, who has been hurt and disappointed by us, still manages to love, forgive, and honor us, we have experienced a sneak preview of God's grace. Caroline stuck around even when it may have been easier to bail on me (and us). She stood by me during tough times of death and depression. She celebrated my proudest moments of exhilaration. She walked through my darkest periods of desperation. Caroline is a living witness to what I've seen, done, and become. Through her extravagant love and support, I've slowed down, taken risks, treasured the gift of life. A purple state of mind receives love and extends love. It acts as a constant companion, cheering others on, comforting them in times of crisis. A purple state of mind is a conduit for God, enabling us to love and be loved in return.

Erotic Poetry (in the Bible)

The Song of Songs merges the erotic and the spiritual. It affirms the human body as beautiful, attractive, and alluring. The Canticles are about sexual desire. Solomon's Song celebrates young love. It alludes to sneaking out, secret trysts, and an anxious rendezvous. The protagonists are clearly not married, yet they actively pine for each other's body. To teenagers, this biblical book is welcome relief. Raging hormones are nothing new. To parents, the Song of Songs confirms their worst fears. Young men and women have long been driven by desire. Instead of repressing these tensions, the Song of Songs expresses them in lush terms. It is loaded with poetic images of mountains, springs, gardens, and vineyards. Physical love is celebrated in vivid terms.

To contemporary ears, the ancient metaphors in Song of Songs come across as strange rather than romantic. A lover's hair is compared to a flock of goats. Paeans to breasts like fawns, ears like does, and a nose like a tower were much more apt in the biblical era. Obviously, our standards and associations with beauty shift with time. Ancient audiences must have blushed when Song of Songs was read in synagogues. My wife and I had a recently married couple read it responsively at our wedding. To hear the verses alternate between the lover and the beloved was a powerful reclamation of the author's intent. (It was also smoking hot!)

Many interpreters have tried to read the Song of Songs as an allegory for Christ and his bride, the church. Yet it includes minimal references to a bride or marriage. Most of the meetings take place at night, in secret hideaways and gardens. Attempts to reduce the Song of Songs to allegory are misguided. It may be both erotic love poetry and a song about Christ's passionate affection for his bride, the church, but only the former is abundantly clear. Canticles operates as both poetry about falling in love and a metaphor for godly love. Both are burning with desire, fueled by an eagerness to embrace each other.

The Song also stands out as one of the few books of the Bible written in a feminine voice. The heroine of the story is remarkably active, pursuing her beloved, anticipating a reunion. Since the church has struggled with accusations of patriarchy, the Song of Songs offers a welcome corrective. The lover pursues her beloved with considerable passion. Their relationship is rooted in mutual attraction. Even their passion is shared: "My lover is mine and I am his" (Song of Songs 2:16), and "I am my lover's and my lover is mine" (Song of Songs 6:3). Old Testament scholar Elizabeth Huwiler notes that "the Song presents a view of male-female sexuality which is neither exploitative or hierarchic. Both the man and woman act on their own initiative as well as in response to one another."[3] Men and women are made to be together, to enjoy each other's bodies, to consider lovemaking as a God-given sacrament.

While the Song of Songs may be interpreted as an affirmation of fidelity and a celebration of marriage, it stops short of identifying the lovers as a wedded couple. The lovers revel in the moment. They embrace physical pleasure, celebrating the splendor of our bodies in motion. Rather than emphasizing the distance between spiritual and sexual love, maybe we need to reinforce their proximity. To a sexualized society, we can embrace an earthy physical faith that affirms the body, upholds attraction, and associates both with the Divine. Love is both *eros* and *agape*.

Choosing Sides

John: So let me ask you this, point blank: Gay marriage—you got a problem with it?

Craig: Do I have a problem with it?

I enrolled at USC film school right after graduating from Fuller Theological Seminary. I had no time to think through the people I might meet or the issues I'd be forced to consider. My class at USC was filled with the best and brightest aspiring filmmakers on the planet. I was making movies alongside Turks, Greeks, Lebanese,

Chinese, Bengalis. Their faith and politics were literally all over the map. Most had formed their opinions of evangelical Christians from the televangelists who buy airtime around the world. It was not a pretty sight.

We made five short films in our first 15 weeks. Every Tuesday and Thursday, we'd premiere our three-minute movies. With so little time to prepare, the student filmmakers went for the gut, straight out of the personal experience. Many of their short films dealt with sexuality and spirituality. The films grew more extreme during the semester as the students attempted to distinguish themselves from the competition. I saw scenes of Bibles being trashed, run over, and burned. (Evidently, people had a few issues with institutionalized religion!) As the semester continued, the films also became more sexualized. How amazing to see filmmakers willing to expose themselves in such literally naked ways. They put their bodies on display. They outed themselves as gay, lesbian, and bi-sexual. My modest, romantic comedies about heterosexuals in love seemed positively countercultural at USC. My classmates would ask, "Where do you find such normal people to act in your movies?"

Amid all the shocking mini-movies, one classmate emerged as a more humane filmmaker. Robert was interested in digging slightly deeper, into dreams and nightmares, the mysterious parts of existence. While classmates ripped each other in critique, Robert tried to be positive and constructive in his comments. Through casual conversations, I discovered that Robert was an agnostic. His parents left their Mormon roots behind. Robert grew up in the heady atmosphere of Stanford University. He could readily talk about faith, politics, art, and literature. We bonded over a mutual disdain for atrocities committed in the name of God. Robert also had a sharp sense of humor, making him a perfect creative foil for my comedies.

For our second semester, we had to find a filmmaking partner. Robert and I agreed to collaborate. We made a good team, both of us interested in keeping things simple and attainable. While our overly ambitious classmates made each other miserable, we stayed on task and under budget. Only after we'd worked on several films together did Robert propose a more personal script about a young student who is seduced by a slightly older, more experienced man. The story was quite chaste, reduced to a single kiss, a fleeting first homosexual encounter. Like all of Robert's short films, *The Good Son* was filled with longing, regret, and frustration. I was proud to produce Robert's poetic and heartfelt "coming out" film.

The Good Son played at more than 25 gay and lesbian film festivals around the world. It won the jury prize for Best Short at the Philadelphia International Gay and Lesbian Film Festival. It was also a finalist for the Best Breakout Film at the Outfest in Los Angeles. I was in the audience gathered at the Los Angeles Gay and Lesbian Center for the awards presentation. Robert was nervous about the screening, but I was feeling slightly anxious about being outed as the token heterosexual in the audience. West Hollywood is the gathering place for Southern California's homosexual community. I wasn't just at the Outfest in WeHo, I was at *the* center for the gay, lesbian, bi-sexual, and transgendered community!

How humbling to become a minority—whatever the setting. It immediately expands one's capacity for empathy. Stepping into other people's shoes enables us to grasp why they feel so self-conscious, why they speak with hesitation, why they lash out in frustration, why they feel misunderstood and beg for representation in Congress, on city councils, on school boards. Who will speak for them? Who will defend their rights? This is the plight of all minorities in all cultures.

Before the screenings began, the Outfest director made a grave announcement. Evidently, a young man had been murdered in Wyoming. The crowd grew quite still. Matthew Shepard, a student at the University of Wyoming, had been beaten up and left for dead outside Laramie. The audience gasped. Details were still arriving, but this cold-blooded act may have been connected to Matthew's homosexuality. A palpable sense of outrage erupted: "Noooo!" There were cries of "Not again!" There was wailing and introspection—"Why? Why? Why?" I was swept up in a wave of grief that stretched across hundreds of years and thousands of Matthew Shepards. The festival proceeded with the knowledge that the painful stories we were about to watch were not merely fictional but a defiant act of determination. Despite threats and even attacks, these gay and lesbian filmmakers would tell their stories to whoever would listen. I left the evening shaken by the news of Matthew's death, humbled by the strong sense of solidarity I witnessed.

When I saw the photo in the paper, I couldn't believe it. Reverend Fred Phelps held a sign with Matthew Shepard's picture on it that said, "Matt's in Hell." How could Christians picket a funeral? Basic decency insists that friends and family be allowed to grieve in peace. Surely, the youth group at the Episcopal church that Matthew grew up in deserved some space to remember him. My friend Robert said, "Even the most primitive cultures have a basic code about an enemy's right to a proper burial." But evidently Rev. Phelps and his Westboro Bible Church are beyond primitive. How could a pastor dare to declare "Matt's in Hell" at a Christian funeral? What kind of faith announces to the world that a murder victim is condemned? Even worse, how can parents arm their children with placards that proclaim, "God Hates Fags"? Such twisted actions stood in marked contrast with the genuine community I witnessed at the Gay and Lesbian Center. I felt compelled to take action. I had to say something, to stand up for those who were still in shock. Under such a brazen declaration of war, I chose sides.

For my church's Sunday bulletin, under the headline, "Newsflash: War Is Over," I wrote this:

> Matthew Shepard's funeral will go down in history as the culture war's "D-Day." The Christian Right may continue strategizing, protesting, and fighting, but the war is over. And the church lost. Why? Because silence=death. Why did the Christian right lose the culture war? Because as any military strategist will attest, when you surrender the high ground (especially the moral high ground), you are doomed to defeat.

Beatings, lynchings, snipings. These are the reckless acts of the defeated. Desperate men fighting desperately to hold their ground at a distant battle line. Somebody needs to tell them the war is over. Before more civilians are mowed down in the name of Jesus. So why haven't the "generals" of the Christian right announced a cease-fire? Admitting we've lost is Jesus' only chance of winning.

Matthew's death shook me. Deeply. After years of trying to mediate between my leftist humanistic friends and my rightist Christian brothers, I have given up. I will ride out the last days of the culture war in silence. Holding onto Jesus. Because our shame is too great. Our complicity too obvious. Our self-anointed leaders' silence too deafening. Call me crazy. Call me chicken. Call me liberal, communist, or gay. But please, please, do not call me Christian.

I didn't really choose sides. They were chosen for me. My decision was forged in Jesus' first public reading of scripture in Luke 4:18-19. When Jesus announced good news for the poor, freedom for prisoners, release for the oppressed, I found a calling. When Jesus was accused of being a friend of sinners, I discovered my role model (Matthew 11:19). My choice was made in passages where Jesus talked about being neighborly, stopping long enough to care for the beaten and bruised traveler (Luke 10:25-37). Passages about caring for lepers, comforting widows, and loving orphans made my loyalties a foregone conclusion. But they didn't make my commitment any easier to live out.

Thankfully, key architects of the rise of the religious right began to notice that their methods were failing to reform America. Cal Thomas and Ed Dobson suggested that in adopting Caesar's methods of fighting power with power, the Christian political movement might have sacrificed its soul. In *Blinded by Might*, they cling to their conservative Christian beliefs but beg their fellow believers to stop placing their faith in politics to solve religious problems. They do not suggest that Christians abandon the public sphere. Rather, "Religious conservatives, no matter how well organized, can't save

America. Only God can. But he will only consider doing it if God's people get out of the way and give him room."[4] *Christianity Today* offered an extensive cover story asking the question, "Is the Religious Right Finished?"[5] After so much grandstanding and grasping for power, I sensed a surprising humility. Under pressure from Mel White and Soulforce, even Jerry Falwell vowed to tone down his rhetoric. Eight years under Democratic President Clinton appeared to chasten the virulent strains of Christian faith that contributed to Matthew Shepard's death. I breathed a massive sigh of relief. Unfortunately, some hostile tendencies of the Christian right proved to be dormant rather than dead.

Against this backdrop, I started teaching aspiring Christian filmmakers. I tried to help my students understand why they entered Hollywood with so much baggage. They were viewed as a judgmental, hypocritical threat before they even entered the studios' gates. To understand the roots of the culture war, I showed films from each decade in cinematic history. We talked about the central issues of each era. The first half of the class covered ideologies—from Darwinism to Communism. We tracked how Americans united to defeat Fascism and Nazism. We watched *Invasion of the Body Snatchers* from 1956 and traced how a fear of Communism led to the abuses of McCarthyism. We came to understand why the entertainment industry feared Christians' attempts to clean up Hollywood. When Christians said *protest,* the Jewish studio moguls heard *pogrom.*

The struggles shifted in the sixties from nations to individuals. The Cold War against Communism raged in places like Vietnam. But back in the States, a battle over civil rights was brewing. Racism was a form of ideology, but it had quite a personal connection to black residents of the South. Under the leadership of Rev. Dr. Martin Luther King, civil rights became an argument on behalf of all people that was rooted in scripture and upheld by the Constitution. The stakes were literally black and white. Could people be discriminated against because of the color of their skin? The Civil Rights Act of 1964 and the Voting Rights Act of 1965 ensured equal rights for all. It was a victory started by Christian churches, fueled by a biblical understanding of God-given dignity of every life.

The ideologies on trial in the second half of the twentieth century were racism, sexism, and homophobia. We watched tough films like *Do the Right Thing* (1989) and *Boys Don't Cry* (1999). The battleground shifted from the ground beneath us to the humanity within us. Whether we were debating civil rights, women's rights, abortion rights, or gay rights, each argument revolved around our bodies. Who decides what we can do with whom? Can my boss discriminate against me? No. Can I sit where I want? Yes. Can I live in any neighborhood? Absolutely. As the hypothetical scenarios took shape, so did the resistance. Can a black man marry a white woman? Can a teen get an abortion without parental knowledge or consent? Can two lesbians be united in matrimony? These questions pushed many Americans beyond their comfort levels. We watched how filmmakers responded to the timely issues of their era. Having chronicled the march of human rights, I asked my students to consider where we would stand as a community of faith. How would Jesus respond to these challenges?

As I finished each semester, a pattern emerged. Days before graduation, the quiet students sitting in the back would offer to buy me a cup of coffee in exchange for an open ear. They'd heard my take on cinematic history. Now they wanted to offer a personal history. I talked to John, Michelle, Pablo, and Drew. They each sought a safe place to be themselves, to admit their fears, to process their faith. They struggled with doubt, wondering whether they could be true to themselves and remain within a faith that attacked them. Where was God amid all the mudslinging on both sides?

I did not choose to become a friend of homosexuals. They chose me. It happened mostly by accident. As I befriended people and led Bible studies, people began to take what I was teaching seriously. I don't recall saying anything directly about homosexuality. We were probably studying passages about Jesus' solidarity with the suffering, his embrace of the marginalized. They would ask to talk to me privately, afterward, in hushed tones. They'd confess their painful secrets. They'd weep from a combination of grief and relief. The conversations were almost never about what they should do, how they could change, when it would go away. They simply wanted to know they were not alone. Jesus' attitude toward homosexuals remains the same: You are loved—without caveats or conditions.

Forgiving the Christians

I started taking film students to the Sundance Film Festival so they could see the competitive stakes of independent cinema for themselves. They were expected to see a dozen films in one week and to write about the movies that most impacted them. At Sundance, virtually all the films are world premieres. We bought advance tickets to sold-out screenings with only minimal ideas of what the films might contain. Occasionally, we encountered amateur acting and awkward scripts. Sometimes the material was offensive. But most of the time, the profoundly personal Sundance films provoked massive food for thought. The festival became a time for theological reflection and spiritual searching. We called our Spirit-led conversations The WindRider Forum.

Forgiving the Franklins sounded interesting. It follows a Southern Baptist family who are killed in a car wreck on their way to a church potluck. Ushered into heaven, they encounter Jesus, portrayed as a black man who is chopping down a cross. The verdant hillsides are covered in crosses. Jesus complains about being sick of these things: "I need a new symbol." Perhaps he doesn't like being reminded of the most painful moment in his life. Jesus reaches into the back of the Franklin family's heads and plucks out a bloody apple. He sends them back to earth, offering them a new lease on life. The Franklins return to their small town with no sense of guilt or shame. Jesus removed their original sin.

The Franklins live quite guilelessly, walking around their house naked, even going out to pick up the newspaper in their birthday suits. When they return to church, they find it quite boring. In their newfound freedom, they simply walk out, never to return. A frolic in the park provides the Sabbath they seek. Mom and Dad start to enjoy sex and don't mind sharing their new techniques with friends and neighbors. They sing the Song of Songs a little too loudly. Their son falls in love with his high school football coach. The Franklins are totally supportive. Their church community freaks out, asking, "What can we do about the Franklins?" The Franklins are too frightening, too free. At a Bible study, the community agrees to send the Franklins an apple pie—laced with poison. Sincere, God-fearing Christians murder the Franklin family.

The Sundance audience howled with laughter throughout the film. This savage satire portrays churchgoers who are repressed, joyless, and even murderous. *Forgiving the Franklins* suggests we'd all be better off without the guilt and shame emanating from religion. At the conclusion of the screening, filmmaker Jay Floyd received a rapturous standing ovation. While the filmgoers celebrated this assault on the religious right, I shed a tear, depressed and convicted by the depiction of Christians as judgmental and vindictive. It was painful to watch sincere Christian characters shun (and then kill!) their neighbors. My heart ached, my pulse raced. As Jay answered the audience's questions, I felt the Spirit bearing down upon me, urging to say something.

Evidently, Jay grew up in North Carolina. His father taught Sunday school until an elder told him to stop because his classes were too humorous. As a homosexual, Jay clearly felt condemned by the faith he grew up in. Somebody asked if any conservative Christians had seen the film. Jay proclaimed he was ready for a fight. The audience applauded. When the moderator said we had time for only two more question, I spoke up.

I struggled to compose my words. My voice cracked slightly. I eked out, "Jay, thank you for this film. As a native of North Carolina, a fellow filmmaker, and an evangelical Christian..."

I never use the word *evangelical*. It is so loaded with negative baggage that I usually attempt to distance myself from such associations. But in this instance, it seemed quite right. I was speaking for my community, responding to a particular stance we'd staked out for ourselves. Jay stepped back, ready for that fight. He tensed up, preparing to launch a counterattack. The crowd sensed that things were about to get ugly. My next words caught them off guard:

"Jay, I apologize for anything ever done to you in the name of God."

The entire tenor in the room shifted. Audience members turned around. "Did I hear that correctly?" They craned their necks. "Who said that?" Jay fumbled for words, not knowing how to respond. He was ready to be attacked. He was not prepared for an apology. He offered a modest, "Thank you." The audience was literally disarmed. It had instantly transformed from a lynch mob to a love fest. The Holy Spirit swooped in, surprising us all. The moderator concluded the conversation. Audience members approached me afterward with hugs. A lesbian couple thanked me. Gay men kissed me. One person said, "If that is true, I might consider giving Christianity another chance." Tears were shed far and wide. All it took were two little words: "I apologize."

My students leaped at the occasion, talking to the cast and crew, inviting them to join us for further conversation. Our "enemies" became fast friends, joining us for lunch. The cast came to our class the next day, answering questions for an hour. An actor admitted how scared he was to enter our church meeting place. Onstage, he confided, "Coming into this building, my heart was beating more than at any audition I've ever had." The producer said, "This was the most significant moment of our week." A simple apology set off a series of conversations and exchanges about our faith and how we live it.

Sundance films reveal the dark side of the Christian faith. They are profoundly political and overt in their messages. My students and I saw how judgmental, exclusive, and unloving we've been. We could have easily responded to the anger of the filmmakers by launching defensive tirades or aggressive counterarguments. For one brief moment, we had an opportunity to challenge the stereotypes and epithets we've earned.

We did not script that moment. An opportunity was thrust before us. The Spirit moved. One loving statement undercut years of judgment and disappointment. That is much more than movie magic. We rode on God's wind.

A Sexually Ambiguous Black Man

I told my *Franklins* story to the Council for Christian Colleges and Universities in Dallas. My assignment was to discuss cultural engagement. I talked about where television, digital entertainment, and the Internet were headed. But I also spoke about what is possible. When we love, we may be loved in return. A thousand professors and college presidents measured my words. While I talked about coming alongside our neighbors, joining them in their struggles, a busload of gay teenagers stood on the street. The Soulforce Equality Ride had been banished by the Gaylord Resort, rejected by the CCCU Convention. I understand that their presence would have been distracting. Attendees didn't want signs of protest in their face. But to talk about the importance of cultural engagement, to dedicate a conference to significant conversation, and to ignore people knocking on the door is a travesty. Did Jesus erect barriers or tear them down?

The same Spirit who washed over our discussion of *Forgiving the Franklins* was unleashed when Philip baptized an Ethiopian eunuch in the biblical book of Acts (chapter 8). The eunuch was a religious seeker who had come to Jerusalem to worship. He served in the court of Candace, the queen of Egypt. As a eunuch, he could work in close proximity to the queen without any threat of sexual hijinks. He was returning to Egypt discouraged. He had been shunned at the Jewish temple. Imagine his disappointment when confronted by the limits imposed by the purity laws. His sexual alteration kept him from entering the most sacred part of the temple in Jerusalem. As a black man, he may not have been overly welcomed either. Purity laws designed to keep the temple holy kept him from converting to Judaism. He was excluded. Yet the book of Isaiah seemed to offer a different story. In Isaiah 56:7, God clearly wants his temple to be a house of prayer for all peoples. The eunuch was eager to join. Philip, led by the Spirit, entered into this loaded scenario.

Notice Philip's approach. It starts by listening to God and to what the eunuch was reading. Philip figures out the questions before he proffers an answer. He asks, "Do you understand what you are reading?" The Greek phrase is *Genoskeis ha anagenoskeis?* It is a playful rhyme. The eunuch, intrigued by Philip's timing, invites him into his chariot. Surely, this is an evangelistic moment. We long to have someone say, "Please, explain the meaning of the scriptures to me!" This is the opportunity discussed in 1 Peter 3:15—being ready to give an answer when asked.

Unfortunately, not many of our friends and neighbors are reading the Bible in their spare time. We are more likely to be reading the Bible in public and hoping someone will ask us, "What are you reading?" But they are reading *The Da Vinci Code, Harry Potter,* and *The Secret.* Those bestselling books are loaded with opportunities for conversation. Films like *Moulin Rouge!* The Lord of the Rings trilogy, and *The Matrix* are loaded with layers of meaning. They provide ample opportunities to listen in to the spiritual questions swirling around pop culture. We can ask, "Do you understand what you're seeing on television shows like *Lost, Heroes,* or *Saving Grace?*"

Philip fills in the details about Jesus, how he embodies the promises found in Isaiah. The eunuch is overcome with interest. When he spots a pool of water, the eunuch stops his chariot. He's eager to be baptized. But notice the question he asks: "What prevents me from being baptized?" (Acts 8:36 NASB). Having heard the glorious possibilities available in Christ, he stops short. Why? The eunuch has had his spiritual search cut off at the temple. Like Satine in *Moulin Rouge!* he's already experienced his fair share of disappointment. She considers Christian's silly love songs. Are they reliable? What makes Jesus any different from all the promises the eunuch has heard before?

Does Philip offer a series of preconditions? Does he indicate the changes that the eunuch must make before deciding to follow Jesus? Philip breaks social, cultural, racial, and sexual barriers by baptizing the Ethiopian eunuch. One of the first non-Jewish believers in the Bible is a sexually ambiguous black man. Upon this brokenness, Christ expands his church. And what happens as a result of this ridiculous act of love? The Spirit of God is unleashed. Philip is swept up in a whirlwind, whisked away to a higher plain. The book of Acts uses allusive language to describe an elusive event. God breaks through human history!

The barriers torn down in Acts 8 continued in Peter's trance in Acts 10. He develops a vision that pushes past preconceived notions of clean and unclean. In Acts 15, at the first Council in Jerusalem, Peter points to the presence of the Holy Spirit as sufficient proof for accepting Gentiles into Christian fellowship. Peter says, "God, who knows the heart, testified to them giving them the Holy Spirit, just as He did to us; and He made no distinction between us and them, cleansing their hearts by faith" (15:8-9 NASB). Without Peter's argument before the council, most white Anglo-Saxon Protestants would be deemed unworthy of the name Christian. Will we join the church in Jerusalem in surrendering our preconceived notions of who can be saved? Like Peter, will we push past our ideas about clean and unclean, worthy and unworthy? If so, a powerful gust of the Holy Spirit awaits us.

I was caught up in a similar whirlwind at the Sundance Film Festival. God longs to pour grace upon grace upon us. But we have withheld love and poured out judgment instead. We have disappointed people desperate to be included. If we want to be surprised by the Spirit of God, we need to engage in deep listening. Like Philip, we must get on God's frequency. Who has questions about God? Who eagerly desires to receive the love of God yet feels excluded by purity laws? How many lives might be transformed if we remove preconditions for people to receive our love? How much transformation might Christ unleash?

In *Moulin Rouge!* Satine realizes, "Love is bad for business." It will take us out of our comfort zones. It will blow past the limits of our grace. It will unleash the power of the Spirit in ways we cannot explain.

How do we incorporate God's grace into our lives? We must allow God's love to penetrate our every fiber. We must ask, seek, and knock on God's forgiving door. We must be reformed by the love of God. It is easy to be cynical, not to bother. We can disqualify people from relationship based on their appearance, their culture, and their behavior. Yet God continues to sing a silly love song. Can we hear it?

Revealed
and
Revealing

7

Postmodernism makes many people nervous. We've invested heavily in a scientific era in which truths were built upon objectivity and reason. Christians are used to building a case on the authority of scripture. We've grown comfortable with first principles rather than multiple perspectives. But what happens in a pluralistic context that forces us to consider others' stories? What if people consider the Bible inadmissible evidence or, even worse, a chronicle of questionable actions authored by a violent God? Such relative truths seem to undercut the timeless nature of scripture. What role does the Bible play for people focused on today rather than eternity?

Scripture is still authoritative but in a deeper way. We're rediscovering scripture as story, a dynamic drama rooted in a series of divine revelations. We're invited by the Holy Spirit into a process of discovery as he comes alongside us. We're not as interested in facts as we are in the *interpretation* of facts. We want to apply what we've studied. We long for wisdom rather than just knowledge. We're recovering a more holistic approach to scripture. Gerhard Maier suggests, "At work here is a personal knowing reminiscent of what the Hebrew *yada* (to know) conveys: entering a relationship, experiencing through practice, confirming through involvement."[1] A purple state of mind embraces the Bible as God's timeless living word, still speaking into our lives today. It stresses the importance of dual listening, balancing what we see with what God says. A purple state of mind reaches into the past in an effort to grapple with the present. It searches the ancient scriptures for contemporary wisdom, following the Spirit's lead into progressive revelation. Such a journey requires faith, humility, and patience.

> **Craig:** I'm wondering, what are our differences?
>
> **John:** Here's what I think is the difference between you and me, if I may.
>
> **Craig:** Uh oh. [John picks up a large black Bible and holds it in front of his face.]
>
> **John:** This is the big difference. I don't have this walking around in front of my eyes.
>
> **Craig:** Are you saying I'm blocking the world out with the Bible?
>
> **John:** You would admit, this is not a pair of binoculars. It's not a telescope. It's not a pair of bifocals...The thing that separates us most deeply is this book. As far as I can tell, this book for you is everything.

I love the Bible. It unfolds in such dramatic fashion. From the creation of the world to the formation of a people, God is so active. God is the writer, the director, and the star of the story.[2] Humanity grasps God's grandeur through a series of revelations. God parcels out his presence gradually, giving out as much information as we can handle. Despite his best efforts to communicate clearly, his people consistently fail to understand the full implications of his call.

God speaks through multiple sources throughout the Bible—through nature, through angels, through dreams, through kings, through prophets. Dramatic flourishes capture Israel's attention. The blood that covered Israel's sons at Passover is quite striking. The parting of the Red Sea makes an indelible impression. But the collective memory often dims. God's people are called to remember the exodus, to tell the story, to celebrate all that the Lord has done. Some are blessed with the ability to hear and remember. Others seem deaf to even the loudest divine ovations. God's clearest statement arrives in a person, Jesus Christ, God incarnate. And yet even Jesus is rejected by a large segment of ancient Israel.

I am humbled by God's gracious self-revelations. The Bible demonstrates how God longs for relationship with his people. It is a torturous love story, full of twists and turns. As we try to grasp the enormity of the biblical vision, we continue to struggle in our understanding. Reading does not equal receiving. Despite the seeming clarity of scripture, we still depend on the Spirit to reveal God's truth to us.

We can all agree that the Bible is a groundbreaking compendium of ancient literature. It contains an astounding variety of formats, from the history of Israel to the poetry of Psalms. The wisdom contained in Proverbs offers a glimpse into the values of the ancient world. Books like Job contain innovative storytelling devices—a cosmic drama. The accounts of Matthew, Mark, Luke, and John represent a new literary genre—Gospel, intended to be received as good news. The letters of Peter and Paul make an interesting historical puzzle. They represent only half of a historical correspondence, so scholars attempt to fill in the gaps in our understanding of the early Christian church. The apocalyptic literature of Daniel, Ezekiel, and the Revelation of John can be read in multiple ways. Their creative visions have resulted in more speculation and misunderstanding than any other section of the Bible. Such speculation can grow offensive to people critical of the faith like John Marks. The Bible can raise just as many problematic questions as it answers.

As a professional writer, John Marks respects the Bible. He appreciates the use of metaphor, the poetic allusions. He recognizes its importance as a historical window. But he is disturbed by some of that historical record. In Deuteronomy 7, God orders the destruction of seven nations, including the Hittites, Amorites, and Canaanites. Later, God sends the Hebrews on a mission to destroy the Amalekites:

"Make war on them until you wipe them out" (1 Samuel 15:18). A study of these cultures may reveal plenty of vile practices and human rights abuses. The world may have become a better place without them. But we all wonder how a God who slays rival armies in the Old Testament is reconciled with the sacrificial actions of Jesus. Mark Twain humorously noted the apparent discrepancies: "The two Testaments are interesting, each in its own way. The Old one gives us a picture of these people's Deity as he was before he got religion, the other one gives us a picture of him as he appeared afterward."[3] How do we understand the relationship between vengeance and love? Is the Bible responsible for slavery, for genocide, for oppression? John Marks asks valid questions of scripture, raising objections that we must take seriously.

What do we do with passages of scripture that challenge our notions of divinity? What about historical episodes that make us blush, that we refuse to read to our children? Can the Bible be both God-breathed and R-rated? We are often selective in our acceptance of scripture. Thomas Jefferson attempted to separate Jesus' ethical teaching from any supernatural phenomena.[4] More recently, scholars like Albert Schweitzer have gone on a rigorous and helpful quest for the historical Jesus. Rudolph Bultmann demythologized the Bible as a means of making it more palatable for a scientific era.

Bultmann's form criticism inspired contemporary efforts like the Jesus Seminar, in which biblical scholars led by Robert Funk and John Dominic Crossan employed a bead system to vote on the authority of certain texts and passages from the Gospels. The options went from red beads (Jesus said it) to black beads (Jesus didn't say it) with pink (Jesus probably said it) and gray (it captures Jesus' idea) in between.

It is easy to mock the Jesus Seminar for presuming too much, standing in judgment over scripture. Yet we all engage in some form of editing. We may gloss over the stickier passages of scripture, upholding certain sections that are easier to digest. Our children's Bibles hit the highlights, avoiding the thornier aspects of scripture that create theological conundrums. What's the difference between Jefferson's

Bible and our children's Bibles? Don't they both pick and choose what makes them comfortable? How do we affirm the inspiration of scripture while acknowledging disturbing biblical episodes? Can our heads and our hearts align? Gerhard Maier recommends a more lived approach to the scholarly enterprise:

> It is nonetheless impossible to present the unity of Scripture as an abstract doctrinal system. Scripture itself, is after all, not put together as an arrangement of proof texts. It rather gives a step-by-step description of God's activity in a historical progression. At each stage God reveals himself in the specific manner fitting for that time. We are dealing then with a "progressive revelation."[5]

I consider the Bible much more than a book. It is a divinely inspired, living document. Second Timothy 3:16 describes it as "God-breathed." The same Spirit who animates us brought forth the word of God. Consequently, we ascribe power to the words contained within the Bible. We call it holy. It is not merely a recounting of ancient history, but a dynamic chronicle of God's story. We do not read the Bible for information, but for inspiration and reformation. We invite the Holy Spirit into the process. We turn to familiar passages for wisdom, comfort, and understanding. We submit ourselves to scripture, reading with a humility that invites correction. As we immerse ourselves in scripture, we gradually internalize the stories. God's word eventually becomes the ground of our being. It bubbles up from within us without prompting. God's words and actions are then not just second nature, but first instinct. The Bible becomes a lamp, a signpost, and a daily guide applicable to all manner of settings.

We still avail ourselves of the best scholarship available. We are informed by recent discoveries that shed light on the ancient biblical texts. Archaeology deepens our understanding of both the text and its context. We must engage in careful exegesis before we start interpreting and applying biblical truths. New Testament scholar Gordon Fee suggests that "good exegetical questions fall into two basic categories:

questions of *content* (what is said) and of *context* (why it is said)."[6] It is important to understand the historical context that informs the biblical writers' occasions for writing. The more we know about ancient Judea or the Roman Empire, the more we grasp how revolutionary God's promises appeared. As we understand the threatening circumstances surrounding the kingdom of Israel, we appreciate how much good news is contained in the Bible. As we understand the Jews' struggles, we can better connect our story to their story.

Yet these exegetical skills can be applied to virtually any ancient document. We must understand the historical context to fully appreciate *The Iliad, The Odyssey,* or *The Tales of Genji.* All great art deserves a close reading. So what makes the Bible different?

The canon of scripture is closed, but the truths captured within it are still being revealed. The history of God's relationship to humanity is still being written. As the early church wrestled with the implications of Jesus' life, death, and resurrection, so the Christian community continues to work them out in our contemporary setting. We wonder how God could be pleased with the slaughter of women and children. Consider the bloody plight of the Midianites in Numbers 31. We question why God would slay Uzzah when Uzzah attempts to protect the ark of the covenant from falling in 2 Samuel 6. We struggle to understand why God allows Satan to ruin Job's life. The tests of the faithful in scripture make us reflect on the hurdles we all face. We try to follow Jesus in a twenty-first-century context. As new technologies introduce new possibilities and problems, we turn to an ancient text in search of timely answers. We believe that a resurrected Jesus is still alive, still speaking into our lives. The Bible serves as our most reliable starting point.

But scripture isn't the only tool God uses to communicate to us. Anticipating his death, Jesus tells his disciples, "I have much more to say to you, more than you can now bear. But when he, the Spirit of truth, comes, he will guide you into all truth" (John 16:12-13). In the book of Acts, the Holy Spirit arrives as a comforter to lead, guide, and direct the nascent church. The same Spirit leads, guides, and directs us today. We study the Bible, we pray, we share the collective wisdom gathered in our communities. God may speak through history, through experience, through dreams, through angels, through kings, through prophets.

The Bible reminds us how tenuous divine discernment can be. We are warned not to speak too confidently for God lest we condemn ourselves. The Bible both humbles and empowers us.

I cannot expect friends like John Marks to accept the authority of scripture. Although there is plenty of evidence to support the historicity of its accounts, no amount of proof will make it more authoritative to John. A dedicated rationalist will still stumble over miracle stories in the Old and New Testament. Even eyewitnesses within the Bible struggled to reconcile their experience with their beliefs. For many, faith remains elusive.

How do we develop eyes to see divine actions clearly? How do we develop an ear that is tuned to the voice of God? We can remove as many barriers as possible. We can meditate on the scriptures. We can engage in rigorous scholarship. Yet only the Spirit can offer the whisper of reassurance. We make space for God to engage in self-revelation, to surprise us with joy.

Rereading History

A survey of biblical history demonstrates how veiled divine revelation can be. The apostle Paul received a blinding light, but the majority of biblical characters wander in the dark. They make mistakes, stumble, and get restored through God's mercy. Their understanding of God shifts across time. An initial cockiness toward or about God may morph into a more measured, mature faith. History is reread in light of more recent revelations. Acquiring wisdom takes aeons.

The Bible begins with *Elohim,* the Creator God. Divine fingerprints are found in the sky, in the stars, in the natural world. The Bible begins with beauty we all can behold. God makes a covenant with Abraham, promising to make him patriarch over a people as numerous as the stars. When those people are enslaved in Egypt, God calls Moses to lead them back to their promised land. When Moses asks for more clarification,

God reveals his holy name, *Yahweh*—"I am that I am." The exodus out of Egypt is a long, arduous, character-forming journey. The Ten Commandments and subsequent laws provide a behavioral code for the nascent Hebraic nation. They are learning about God's character and his expectations of a people. They are becoming a community.

The kingdoms of Israel and Judah vacillate between periods of profound prosperity and abject despair. They wrestle with their calling, alternating between eras of social justice and irresponsibility. The vision of their kings usually determines the health of the kingdom. When particularly hardheaded kings preside, God raises up prophets to provide correction. They paint a picture of the upside-down kingdom God longs to establish. Israel is blessed to be a blessing. God pours out abundance on his people but expects them to be open-handed with others in response (Deuteronomy 15:6-8). They are to operate under a different set of standards than their idol-worshipping neighbors use. God reminds them, "You are to love those who are aliens, for you yourselves were aliens in Egypt" (Deuteronomy 10:19). Despite the dramatic words and images provided by the prophets, the Israelites fail to implement God's vision. The Old Testament reads like a torturous love story. God woos his wayward people back into relationship again and again.

God's ultimate revelation arrived with the Incarnation. Intimations of an anointed one were scattered across Israel's history. The prophet Isaiah envisioned a virgin bearing a son named Immanuel, "God with us" (Isaiah 7:14). Additional names or adjectives attached to the messiah include "Wonderful Counselor, Mighty God, Everlasting Father, Prince of Peace" (Isaiah 9:6). Jesus embodies both the word and the image of God. He comes to usher in God's kingdom. He inaugurates his ministry in Nazareth by reaching back to Isaiah 61, proclaiming freedom for prisoners, recovery of sight for the blind, and release for the oppressed (Luke 4:18-19).

The Gospels of Matthew, Mark, Luke, and John offer compelling portraits of Jesus. He is portrayed as kind, witty, and subversive. Jesus preaches, teaches, and heals. Yet he does not conform to all messianic expectations. He shuns power rather than claiming it. He builds a movement upon social outcasts rather than political acumen. Isaiah's prophetic description proves accurate: "A bruised reed will he not break, and a smoking wick he will not snuff out" (Isaiah 42:1-3).

Jesus' contemporaries wrestle with his message. He rearranges their conventional thinking, offering a much more gracious, inclusive, and empowering vision of God. In the Gospel of John, Jesus speaks of the Father in warm and personal terms. It is disarming to a religious community used to trying much harder to reach the divine. Jesus challenges the purity laws, expanding our understanding of Sabbath (Mark 2:23–3:5). The Gospels reveal just how misunderstood Jesus was even among his closest friends. Only after his death did they begin to grasp his sacrificial leadership. Jesus offered a new understanding of Moses and the prophets to his disciples on the road to Emmaus (Luke 24:27). History was reread in light of the resurrection.

The limited vision of Jesus' closest friends encourages me. I appreciate the colorful cast of characters. The disciples' flaws remind me on my own. They're full of fear. They scheme, collude, and jostle for position. All too often, their best-laid plans are thwarted. Jesus' disciples strike me as profoundly human. They provide a perfect foil for divine intervention. Their radical transformation in the book of Acts provides a compelling case for the resurrection. Would such small-minded people have engaged in such risky behavior to cover up a ruse? They witnessed something that caused them to grow up fast. They abandoned their old ways with remarkable quickness. Even when confronted with prison, they refused to recant. The blood of biblical martyrs fueled early church growth.

For those of us not necessarily attracted to martyrdom, the letters of the apostles offer reassuring comfort. Acts of courage are followed by petty infighting. The bold faith of the apostles helped spread the nascent Christian faith, but the squabbles within the early church suggest that following Jesus is never a straight path. It is negotiated. In the letters of Peter, Paul, and John, Christians struggle to get along. They bicker and fight. Doctrine divides them into rival camps.

Following Jesus takes on particular forms dependent upon local customs. To the church in Jerusalem, James stresses ethics, putting faith into practice. Paul's letters to the libertine Corinthian church emphasize personal purity. In Peter's letters, he encourages a persecuted people to hold on. Through a decidedly messy process, God still manages to mold us into something resembling a people. Grace sustains us despite our weakness.

I am awed by the grandeur of the biblical vision. It is intended to humble us, to put us in our place within the universe. Sometimes we need to be knocked off our high horse. We are the fallen, reprobates, prodigal, and broken. At other times, we need a pat on the back or a warm embrace. We are a little lower than angels; sons and daughters of the Most High God (Psalm 8). Regardless of the perspective, God's word consistently rearranges my thinking. It is my norm, the baseline that I return to again and again to renew my focus. This external source of insight has slowly become internalized. Years of study, shelves full of reference books, annual immersions in God's story are all intended to free me from the words themselves. It is an opportunity to make it the ground of my very being. It offers a mental Rolodex that no longer needs the numbers to identify the verse. The truth of God emerges at moments when I need it. Like carbo-loading before a marathon, we feast on God's word for a long journey. We're not sure when or where we'll need it, but we trust that we'll summon the resources in that moment when we feel we cannot continue.

Unfortunately, God's word was suppressed for several centuries. Illiterate believers were forced to rely on public readings of scripture. The Bible was deemed too sacred for everyday people to handle. It remained rarified in Latin. The Protestant Reformation unleashed the power of the people to read (and decide) for themselves. It emphasized the importance of *sola scriptura,* recovering the word of God as the final arbiter in church life. Rigorous translation work put the Bible into common parlance. With the printing press, God's word became widely available. The power of interpretation no longer presided with the priests, but potentially with all believers. Such freedom also sparked unprecedented fissures within the Christian community. With the newfound ability to think for ourselves, we've been fracturing into smaller bits and more denominations ever since.

Are we getting further from the orthodox roots of our faith? Or is the Spirit in that process? The answer is yes. We splintered into smaller sects but with more conviction than ever. Bible translators have put God's word into countless native tongues. The new faces of Christianity look much more colorful and inclusive than those in the previous era.[7] We are approaching a truly global Christianity. We are just starting to get African, Asian, and Latin American readings of scripture.[8] Black theology helps us to read the Exodus stories of freedom for the captives anew. Theologies of liberation in Latin America enabled us to find God serving the poor and fighting against injustice. Feminist theology pushed past the patriarchy of the Bible to find role models in Ruth, Elizabeth, and Mary. There is still much to discover, plenty to be revealed. God has spoken. God is speaking. We are part of a great chain of being and engaged in a crucial historical moment.

So where are our understandings of scripture being challenged? What historical blind spots are under reexamination? "The aim of good interpretation is not uniqueness; one is not trying to discover what no else has ever seen before."[9] Rather, we walk forward as a community of believers on our knees, desperately seeking the Spirit of wisdom and discernment. What new revelations does the Spirit have in store?

Too Much, Too Little, or Just Right?

Craig: You can make that book say whatever you want.

John: Well, then what good is it?

Craig: You can justify slavery with it, and we have. You can justify oppression of homosexuals in it, and we have. You can justify war, killing all manner of things with it, and we have.

John: Then why do you bother, Craig? Why bother?

Craig: Because the reality of Jesus revealed in there is not a dead issue. That is a living issue. This book, I call it the word of God. It is active. But I don't think it is finished. God is still active.

John: How does that work? I don't even know what you're talking about.

Have you ever attempted to read the Bible to children? The stories get pretty grisly pretty quickly. I don't necessarily want to explain to my five-year-old why Cain killed Abel. "Daddy, how does blood cry out from the ground?" It may be fun to imagine all the animals loading onto Noah's ark, but the flood that follows paints a disturbing picture of God. To those overcome by the waters, the olive branch arrived a little too late. By the time we get to Genesis 38 and Onan's condemned *coitus interruptus,* I am usually ready to abandon biblical bedtime stories altogether. Children's Bibles are edited to present a rosy picture of God and a kinder portrait of humanity.

We all engage in some form of editing, underlining the passages that comfort us, avoiding those that may disturb our status quo. We end up building our faith upon *selections* from the Bible rather than the whole word of God. But over the course of our lifetime, we make space for forgotten passages to speak. We seek out obscure corners of scripture in an effort to shine light on the darker corners of our being. Our relationship with God and scripture is one of progressive revelation.

The interpretation of sacred texts is both an art and a science. It involves careful study. A well-trained ear helps, but we can still be surprised. Hermeneutics requires great humility. Without it, our sacred texts can become dangerous weapons. We can misuse scripture to justify our actions and oppress others. A way of love can be turned into a power play. People can end up threatened, hurt, and even murdered in the name of God. How can we build enough silence into our lives to hear God? How do we deal with periods when the Bible stops speaking? How do we make sure we don't mishear or even misspeak for God?

When I first decided to follow Jesus, I bought a devotional guide called *This Morning with God.*[10] It outlined an ambitious four-year plan to study the entire Bible. As a college freshman, four years sounded just about right. I got a notebook and got busy answering questions about one passage per day. I mimicked David, who prayed, "In the morning, I lay my requests before you and wait in expectation" (Psalm 5:3). In three months, I had already filled my first notebook. Unfortunately, I couldn't sustain my fast start. My on-again, off-again project continued through college and on into my teaching in Japan. Four years stretched toward eight years. Months of sustained interest were followed by comparative indifference. But I studied on, eventually accomplishing my goal. It wasn't merely a badge of honor, but an honest attempt to make sure I was well acquainted with God's word. I was glad to know I'd turned every page, inviting the Spirit to surprise me.

Sections of profound interest and applicability were often followed by arcane or seemingly irrelevant genealogies. In the Bible, God seemed to alternate periods of profound revelations with epochs of comparative silence. My shifting moods toward my study reflected the evolving circumstances of God's people. Intimacy was often followed by indifference. At times, I attended to the Bible for the right reasons. Sometimes, I restarted due to guilt. Some mornings were meaningful. Others were merely routine. Bible reading can descend into monotony. Yet sustained exposure to God's word is preferable to ignorance and hearsay. Simply by showing up, poring over the passages, we invite the Spirit to speak. The revelatory process begins with a listening posture, making space for God.

I mustered a fair amount of enthusiasm my first time through the Bible. Yet I must also confess that the Bible often feels silent. At times, God doesn't seem to communicate loudly or clearly. What happens after we've heard one too many sermons? When particular passages have been exegeted and explicated excessively, they can start to sound familiar. We respond to the good news as if it were old news. Like drug addicts, we need stronger hits to evoke the same high. Instead of pressing on, we may give up on the Bible, consigning it to ancient history. Writer Annie Dillard wonders how we can become so inoculated.

Does anyone have the foggiest idea of what sort of power we so blithely invoke? Or, as I suspect, does no one believe a word of it? The churches are children playing on the floor with their chemistry sets, mixing up a batch of TNT to kill a Sunday morning. It is madness to wear ladies' straw hats and velvet hats to church; we should all be wearing crash helmets. Ushers should issue life preservers and signal flares; they should lash us to our pews.[11]

The Bible is a dangerous book, loaded with possibilities. So how do the powerful words of life fall silent?

Perhaps we need time in the desert to appreciate the bounty before us. We can take God's riches for granted. We may have overindulged our appetite, ingesting more than we could digest. We may be in over our heads, trying to read beyond our wisdom or experience. God's word may fall silent because we cannot hear it at this time. Scholar John Goldingay suggests that "God accommodates the revelation to the limitations of those to whom it is given."[12] Parents sometimes withhold info from their children, knowing that their kids will come to appreciate their wisdom in hindsight. We can frustrate our children by telling them more than they need to know. We allow things to bubble up over time. Passages I flew past at age 21 may be waiting to be unwrapped at age 51. I desperately need a whole new set of filters to apply Leviticus or Numbers to today. I want God to reveal hidden gems. Who knew that Lamentations would prove so comforting? How come no one bothers to preach out of Ecclesiastes? We need time to let the words speak.

I've found the ancient practice of *lectio divina* an effective hearing aid. As early as AD 220, Origen turned the reading of scripture into an act of prayer. In poring over the words of God slowly, we change our pace. This ancient monastic practice allows our heart and mind to adopt a different rhythm. We digest the word of God as a daily sustenance.[13] Psalm 1 talks about meditating on God's word day and night. In *lectio divina,* we inhale the God-breathed words with our every breath. We stop searching for facts and become aware of impressions. A particular word or phrase may captivate us. *Wait. Watch. Lift. Depths. Wilderness.* Such loaded words offer something to meditate on, to search for or embody throughout our day. While we wait for sparks to fly, we make do with the intimations that have been revealed to us so far.

Sometimes we make the Bible say more than was intended. We can so worship the book that we miss God's message entirely. Instead of approaching the Bible with humility, we may search the scriptures with a vital agenda. We extract verses from their context in order to create a comprehensive statement on a particular issue. Such isogesis often twists the scriptures to serve our purposes. The Bible can become a crutch or a weapon. It can be co-opted for political purposes. We can bend it into our image. Selective applications of scripture can be conjured to justify almost any form of idolatry or abuse. New Testament professor James D.G. Dunn suggests, "Evangelicalism alone without scholarship can easily become lopsided…individual presuppositions can easily bracket out what one doesn't want to hear. Or a meaning can be heard in a text which is quite divorced from its original or scriptural sense. A text can become a pretext."[14]

Dunn reminds us that the devil can cite scripture for his purpose too. We spew judgment far and wide because we are called to "preach the Word." We beat our children because God said, "He who spares the rod hates his son." We do not listen to our wives because God said, "Women should remain silent." We can use the Bible to evade responsibility. We can blame God for our foolish decisions. We can grow bitter when things don't work out on our timetable. The Bible is not magic. It does not contain scientific formulas. It does not provide instant relief. God, speaking through scripture, might. But without the illumination of the Holy Spirit, the Bible can become a dangerous book.

Progressive Revelation

Once upon a time, we used the Bible to justify slavery. God-fearing Christians bought and sold slaves without a crisis of conscience. In the Sundance Film Festival documentary *Traces of the Trade* (2008), Katrina Browne examines her family tree. She discovers that her ancestors, the DeWolf family of Bristol, Rhode Island, were the largest slave traders in U.S. history. The DeWolfs were pillars of their Episcopal church, donating funds for stained glass windows and memorial chapels. Katrina leads nine family members back to Ghana, to the cells where captured Africans were held. The Africans were baptized as Christians, stripped of their names and their heritage, before being herded onto slave ships bound for the Americas. The documentary makes us wonder how seemingly faithful Christians could engage in such barbarous practices. What seems so egregious today was viewed as a biblically sanctioned reality in its day.

Were the scriptures contorted to justify the slave trade? Not by much. Leviticus offers instructions about who can be bought and sold: "You may purchase male and female slaves from among the nations around you. You may also purchase the children of temporary residents who live among you, including those who have been born in your land. You may treat them as your property, passing them on to your children as a permanent inheritance" (Leviticus 25:44-46 NLT). In Exodus, God's law allows the Hebrews to sell their children, apparently as sex slaves. "When a man sells his daughter as a slave, she will not be freed at the end of six years as the men are. If she does not satisfy her owner, he must allow her to be bought back again" (Exodus 21:7-8 NLT). Even the coming of Jesus doesn't abolish the slave trade. The apostle Paul exhorts, "Slaves, obey your earthly masters with deep respect and fear. Serve them sincerely as you would serve Christ" (Ephesians 6:5 NLT). Paul's instructions about master-slave relationships were seen as sufficient proof that God condones slavery as part of a natural order.

Less than 200 years ago, serious Christian discipleship required masters only to treat their slaves well. Baptists in the South were so convinced of their ministers' rights to own slaves that they formed their own denomination. The Reverend R. Furman of South Carolina argued, "The right of holding slaves is clearly established in the Holy Scriptures, both by precept and example."[15] The Southern Baptist Convention was founded in Augusta, Georgia, in May 1845. Civil war eventually followed. Selective interpretation of scripture fueled a tragic chapter in American history.

Over time, an alternative reading of the Bible held sway. We discovered overlooked passages about freedom in Christ, about setting captives free, about our new reality: "There is neither Jew nor Greek, slave nor free man, male nor female, for you are all one in Christ Jesus" (Galatians 3:28). Such revelations were always available, but people either refused or were unable to listen. As recently as 1968, a survey by the Home Mission Board of the Southern Baptist Convention found that only 11 percent of their churches would admit African Americans as members. Despite their high view of scripture, most Southern Baptist churches were still grounded in racism. One hundred fifty years after the denomination formed for racist reasons, the Southern Baptist Convention of 1995 adopted a resolution apologizing for its past defense of slavery. We still have much work ahead, with Sunday mornings among the most segregated moments in America.[16]

God blessed the SBC despite its lamentable heritage. The Spirit can work through our sinful ways, slowly calling us toward wholeness and integration. It takes time, but we eventually discover where we have erred. Scholars call this process *progressive revelation*. Ben Witherington notes how the biblical letter to the Hebrews "enunciates a hermeneutic of progressive revelation from the very beginning of the book. He [the author] says that God revealed himself in various times and ways, or partially or piecemeal in the past, but now God has revealed himself fully and finally in the person of his Son."[17] Jesus may be the crown of creation, but God revealed himself throughout the Bible. Only a few people were privileged to grasp the full breadth and depth of what they were experiencing. Those with ears to hear and eyes to see were blessed.

To extend the notion of progressive revelation into our contemporary context can make people nervous. After all, couldn't the Book of Mormon be an example of progressive revelation, a late-breaking message from God? The Baha'i community sees their inclusive beliefs as the logical progression of all religious faiths. Orthodox Christianity insists that the canon is closed. But the Spirit of God that inspired the scriptures is still revealing the truth contained therein.

Scholar Walter Henrichsen distinguishes between our evolving comprehension and God's unchanging nature: "God does progressively reveal himself as history unfolds. But this does not mean that God's standards become progressively higher or that God changes along the way. Rather it is our understanding of God and His revelation that progresses. God never changes."[18] Hermeneutics, the art of biblical interpretation, resides in the ongoing conversation between scripture, the Spirit, and God's people. What the Southern Baptists couldn't see in their cultural context was gradually revealed to them. As they got in step with the Spirit, their hearts changed. They repented of their racist roots.

How many foolish stances have I taken for God? How many of my nonnegotiables have eventually been altered? As we follow God, we open ourselves up to refinement and correction. In the movie *Purple State of Mind,* John Marks points out several regrettable things I said. There are plenty of moments in the film that I'd like to change or edit. Instead, I offer ample proof of just how fallible I am and we are, even with our best intentions. God works through us despite our foibles. What issues that we hold as essential today will be revealed as folly? We must walk humbly, with eyes wide open, ready to receive the Spirit's revelation.

And so we work out our salvation with fear and trembling. Our burning issues may not cross over to the next generation. What we consider nonnegotiable, they may consider nonessential. In the meantime, God's progressive revelation continues. The Bible has been written, but our story is not complete. We make space for God to speak. We read the Bible as a community, eager to interpret it for today. Should we need correction, I am confident Christ will provide it. Our greatest danger arises from talking so much that we fail to listen. And so we pause, to allow the Spirit to speak.

In and Out

8

Where do bad folks go when they die?
They don't go to heaven where the angels fly.
Go to a lake of fire and fry.
Won't see them again till the Fourth of July.

THE MEAT PUPPETS, "LAKE OF FIRE"

Will you be left behind? Are you saved? Have you been washed in the blood? We have some strange language to describe our deepest convictions. Much of it distances those we aspire to draw near. We hope to attract people to the love of Jesus by demonstrating how far they are from his grace. Wouldn't it be easier to emphasize Jesus' proximity to our suffering? Jesus consistently sides with those who are broken, confused, and excluded. But to those who erect barriers between God and his people, Jesus levels stinging criticism. He reserved his harshest judgments for those most convinced of the purity of their positions. A purple state of mind does not stand in judgment over friends, family, or neighbors. It heeds Jesus' warnings. Who's in danger of hell? The most sincere, well-intentioned defenders of the faith—people like me. Consequently, a purple state of mind approaches others with gentleness, respect, and humility.

Our affluent era has indulged in so many comforts that we no longer long for a mansion in the sky. Despite the robust sales of the speculative Left Behind fiction series, interest in the afterlife seems to have waned. Cemeteries are rare reminders of the reality of death. Perhaps we need to recover forgotten metaphors for heavenly rewards. What type of eternal perspective can we offer people interested in this side of paradise? We are called to tend the garden, to prepare the heavenly country to come. Surprisingly, eternity culminates in a city. In the New Jerusalem, there will be no death, no sorrow, and no tears. The divine comedy ends with a wedding. Unfortunately, we've neglected to extend an invitation. We have been too busy deciding who's off the guest list, when we should have been welcoming people in.

Craig: I am regularly disturbed by my reading of scripture. Everything I read about Jesus and his reactions to people indicates that the people he had the biggest problem with were the most sincere defenders of God. And so when I read the Bible, I see who is in danger of hell. Me. Not you. And when I read the Gospels, I see if you're outside the kingdom, then Jesus says, "You're in." And if I think I'm in, then I'm probably out.

I came home to celebrate my eighteenth birthday. It was a modest occasion including just my parents, my brother, Drew, and my sister, Dixie. I seized the opportunity to bring along my new girlfriend. It also seemed like a natural place to talk about my newfound faith. After 17 years of living in a certain kind of stupor, trapped in my self-interest, I finally felt free from sin. As I talked about the love of God that had invaded my heart, my little brother, Drew, scoffed. He always had a gift for taking the air out of my tires. Younger brothers are supposed to snipe at siblings in effective ways. But when he called me judgmental, I started to reel. How could he attack me on my birthday? And how could he call me judgmental when I had just been forgiven of such folly? If anything, I felt more gracious and loving than ever! How did such a gap form between my intention and how I was perceived? Following Christ gave me a new set of lenses for seeing the world. Yet my brother suggested that my vision was still skewed. Three months into my born-again experience, I already needed a different prescription.

This chapter is about our dangerous desire to sort others out. In celebrating my forgiveness, I was already distancing myself from others. Rather than attracting my family to the love of God, I was turning them off to my allegedly pristine state. My salvation left them feeling rejected rather than loved. I was communicating condemnation when I thought I was offering reconciliation. Somehow, my notion of justification by faith veered toward justification of self. Baptizing such self-deception in God's name is dangerous for everybody. In fact, it led the religious leaders of Jesus' day to kill him.

God's most faithful followers condemned Jesus to death. His radical grace was a threat to the religion that had been handed down. By taking his message directly to the people, Jesus undercut the religious hierarchy. He offered unmediated access to his loving Father. What would happen if people were freed from their religious obligations? If Sabbath laws were not enforced, the public would no longer be able to distinguish the righteous from the unholy. People may end up thinking for themselves. And that could undermine a long, revered religion tradition. The rabbi from Nazareth had to be stopped.

Jesus' inversion of the power structure was also a threat to Caesar. By suggesting that only God was worthy of honor, Jesus sounded positively atheistic. What about fealty to the king and all the other Roman gods who preceded him? The religious leaders found it preferable to compromise with the state, to preserve the power of both institutions. In turning Jesus over to the Roman authorities, they could ensure their own future. It was a practical cost-benefit question. Who wouldn't have considered the death of one man a small price to pay for the salvation of many? But such logical solutions can get us all in trouble. A purple state of mind learns not to stand in judgment over friends, neighbors, or siblings.

My brother's pronouncement forced me to rethink my righteous posturing. Maybe the cross I was wearing around my neck was communicating the wrong message. I wore it as a badge of honor, yet it was received as a symbol of judgment. Maybe praying in the college cafeteria before meals wasn't sending the signal I intended either. When I stopped conversations to offer thanks, my friends weren't compelled to follow Christ. They felt excluded from the holy huddle I formed with my God. Maybe I didn't need to announce to my fraternity that I wasn't drinking. People could decide for themselves whether to down another beer without my help. "Knowing when to say when" could evidently be applied to alcohol consumption or self-righteous behavior.

Feeling broken and bruised by my birthday, I retreated to scripture. Maybe all those verses I memorized weren't intended for public consumption. Just because I recently grasped that "all have sinned and fall short of the glory of God" (Romans 3:23), that wasn't necessarily breaking news for my hall mates. They understood their sinful status. If I understood that "therefore, there is now no condemnation for those who are in Christ Jesus" (Romans 8:1), why did my classmates feel condemned by my presence? Shouldn't they have felt remarkably loved? If I really understood that "we are more than conquerors through him who loved us" (Romans 8:37), did that mandate that others feel defeated? The Roman road of Bible verses was intended to lift people's spirits, not add to their burden. Yet I turned it into a yoke for those I attempted to love.

My first inclination was to slough off the burden. I concluded that they felt condemned because they were condemned. The Holy Spirit was clearly convicting them of personal sin. I should feel good when I made people feel bad. After all, it moved them that much closer to repentance. Killing their buzz was a prerequisite to their acceptance of Christ. How could they receive the good news without first acknowledging the bad news? One whiff of the hell they'd created should be sufficient to draw them toward heaven, right?

Once upon a time, threats of hellfire and damnation were effective. The promises on this side of paradise were so meager that people longed for something much richer—life after death. To a medieval world battling the plague, death was right around the corner. Getting your eternal house in order made sense. Disaster could strike at any minute. An entire village could be wiped out in one month. The artistic depictions from the Middle Ages tell the story. Hieronymus Bosch painted a triptych called *The Garden of Earthly Delights* (1504). What begins as bliss in the garden of Eden descends into a monstrous version of hell in the third panel. We were subject to so many snares. So many demons threatened to drag us down. Unseen forces literally consumed us. The hellish grip of death needed a heavenly reward. Beyond the church, who else had the words of life?

When did hell lose its fear factor? Maybe modern medicine defanged our demons. The discovery of bacteria turned sickness from a Satanic attack into a scientific problem. The mold in Dr. Florey's coat turned penicillin rather than faith into the panacea.[1] Inoculations were now medical rather than spiritual. Make no mistake; modern science is a good thing. The ability to cure diseases and to prevent pestilence is a great gift to humanity. Most scientific advances were inspired by theological rationale. The Bible gave us permission to study nature, to treat it as a created thing rather than the locus of a sacred god.

In the pagan world, nature was mysterious, a force to be feared. Christianity suggested that the natural world was not animated by spirits, but created by God. It was subject to humanity, at our disposal.[2] We need not live in fear of the unknown, but scientists should venture out like explorers to conquer foreign lands. Death and disease became problems to be solved rather than mysteries to be dreaded.

Yet in reducing the world to physicalist terms, science eventually undermined both paganism and Christianity. Spirits or demons no longer did it. Notions of hell seemed increasingly onerous. Why did people of faith seek to spiritualize everything? Hell was put on trial.

The Question of Hell

John: You once apologized to me for driving me out of the kingdom. That implies to me that you think I am going to hell. I'm lost. Do you believe that?

Craig: I think the bigger question is, do you believe that?

One of the most excruciating experiences of my life occurred on camera. At the Council for Christian Colleges and Universities international convention in Dallas, John Marks and I sat down for a third round of talks. He picked up where he had left off in Los Angeles. The question of whether he will be "left behind" continued to bother him—maybe not out of fear but out of revulsion. John couldn't believe that godly people were consigning him to hell. It was a personal affront. And so he decided to pin me down, to put my convictions to the test. "Do you think I am going to hell?" John desperately wanted to know.

Jesus' warnings against spiritual overconfidence are legion. He repeatedly lambastes those who stand in judgment of others. He slams those who heap religious burdens on the lowly. He chastises the whitewashed tombs that put on a righteous front but store animosity in their hearts (Matthew 23:27). His entire life was spent in solidarity with those on the margins. Jesus was born under exclusion. His parents were on the road. There was no room at the inn. He entered a world full of muck and mire. As a baby, he became a refugee, on the run from the political violence of Herod the (not so) Great. In his public ministry, Jesus continued to threaten the established order. He sided with the outsider, offering solidarity with the condemned. When a woman was caught in adultery, Jesus protected her from her accusers (John 8). When a Samaritan was left for dead on the side of the road, Jesus challenged his followers to treat the ceremonially unclean Samaritan as their neighbor (Luke 10:25-37). Jesus' judgment consistently upended assumptions about who was in and who was out.

So when John asked me to assess his mortal soul, I absolutely resisted his ovations. Why would I pour condemnation on myself by judging John? How could I presume to play God with his life? I only felt comfortable answering his questions of hell with more questions. After all, Jesus consistently got to the heart of people's objections with a well-timed word. He cut through the smoke screens people erected and got to the heart of their matter. Why was John so hung up on the question of hell? Was he truly worried about eternal torment? Did he fear that God might grandfather him into heaven while condemning John's Jewish wife to hell?

While I danced around John's hunger for judgment, a small crowd formed. Most of the delegates to the Council for Christian Colleges and Universities conference were professors and upper-level administrators. These Christian leaders were intrigued by our interaction occurring in such a public place. The cameras recording the conversation only added to the drama. This was live, high-stakes theologizing. When we paused to change tapes in the cameras, the crowd started shouting, "Answer the question!" Clearly, I was frustrating my fellow Christians. The judgment directed my way was quite palpable. They yelled, "Tell him! Tell him he's going to hell!" Wow. That was one haunting moment. I got a glimpse of how a lynch mob forms. There will be blood indeed.

Where do I stand in relation to my friend John and the larger Christian community? If they've already condemned John, why are we even talking? Does God have no room for legitimate beefs? If so, maybe I'm being condemned by the same system. Are John *and* I going to hell? In the moment, I felt what it was like to stand condemned. As the crowd once begged Pilate to free Barabbas, so this gathering wanted a simple answer—send him to hell. I paused. I prayed. I begged for the Spirit to send me wisdom. How should we answer the question of hell? Who is in and who is out?

Questions for God

Craig: Everybody will be judged. Everybody. I am not going to stand in judgment of you. That's not my call. I don't know what's in your heart. I don't know what will be in your heart. I don't know that everybody doesn't get a second chance. I don't know that everybody doesn't get a seventh chance. Seventy times seven chances. But you will have a moment, I have no idea how long it even lasts, when you will stand before your maker and give an account. We all will.

John: You know what I might say to God if that happens? "Why should I allow you, who have been the head of a church that has persecuted untold numbers of people throughout the centuries, you, who led armies into battle and killed others— why should I allow you to make me answer that question?" Maybe the only moral choice I have, should that day ever come, is to say, "Based upon what your son taught, the only option that I had was to say no. I will not believe. I do not believe because I will not believe. I will not believe that you, the God who has led that story, have a right to put that question to me."

Craig: What you just described there—I could see God easily saying, "Thank you, my son. Thank you for that courage. The church makes me weep. The things done in my name make me weep. Your tears are my tears. I share your pain; I embrace your question. Come on in, and let's talk about it."

Is God an accountant? In the parable of the talents (Matthew 25:14-30), the story of the ten minas (Luke 19:11-27), and the parable of the laborers (Matthew 20:1-16), Jesus suggests that we will be judged according to the gifts we've been given. Have we invested our talents wisely or buried them to little profit or purpose? The time to prepare our résumé is now. Yet despite these parables of warning, the biblical God strikes me as remarkably patient. He deals with rejection, with blame, with a stiff-necked people. And still he extends grace. How many opportunities are we given to straighten up and fly right? How many glimpses of glory do we take for granted? How longsuffering is the Almighty? Jesus asks us to follow God's example. We're called to forgive not just one time or seven times, but seventy times seven times (Matthew 18:22). That is quite a dollop of grace. I can't be that patient with others *or* myself! I don't want people to betray me even once. I keep long accounts, remembering what critics have said or written about me and my work. God, on the other hand, can handle our most petty accusations or tired questions.

John Marks dares to take God to task. Like Job, he demands an answer to all the suffering in the world. How much anger can God handle? Will John be given an opportunity to ask God his questions? How long will they talk about the mysterious and painful aspects of life? Will we all get a private audience with the Almighty? So much speculation; so few ways of knowing. We know that the biblical book of Psalms arose from the pain of the people. David complains about his enemies, about God's bad timing, about so much silence in the face of crises. He wonders what takes God so long to show up. Where is God when I need him to fight on my behalf?

The greatest questions of God are lobbed in the biblical book of Job. God allows Satan, the accuser, to strip Job of his wealth and family. Job's sons and daughters, his house, his sheep, his camels, his servants are all swept away. Yet Job never charges God with wrong-doing. Satan afflicts Job with a skin disease, but Job still refuses to curse God or die. Such extreme suffering prompts questions in the community. What has Job done to deserve this? Job's friends put the blame squarely at his feet. Eliphaz advises Job to turn from his unrighteousness, to confess his resentment toward God (Job 4–5). Job refuses to accept his friends' bad theological advice. He holds his tongue as long as possible.

Finally, at the end of extended suffering, Job blurts out, "Oh, that I had someone to hear me! I sign now my defense—let the Almighty answer me" (Job 31:35). God arrives in a whirlwind, and the effect is chilling. The Lord says, "I will question you, and you shall answer me. Where were you when I laid the earth's foundation?" (Job 38:3-4). As God recounts the glory of his creation, Job buries his face, repenting in dust and ashes (Job 42:6). Humbled by a close encounter with the Almighty, Job shuts up for a good long time. God ultimately restores him, making him twice as wealthy, blessing him with seven more sons and three daughters.

The book of Job offers a cold comfort. It suggests that God is willing to put us to the test. The Lord allows Satan to chip away at our prosperity to demonstrate our righteousness. Job is held up as a role model for us all. When bad things happen, we may be tempted to curse God. But hold on. God will come, in a whirlwind, to answer your questions. The presence of God may be so overwhelming that we will fall silent. Our questions will cease. But we may need to be prepared to squeeze out some bumbling answers.

God is absolutely not afraid of our questions. Most of them aren't new. They are variations upon ancient themes. Why so much suffering? Why so much silence? Why is life so difficult? The letters from skeptics will continue on this side of eternity.[3] We may not grasp why bad things happen to good people until we see God face-to-face.[4]

The enduring questions of theodicy do not haunt the Japanese. The Buddhist mind-set expects suffering. Pain is a given. So Buddhists do not ask why a just God can allow such suffering to continue. It is the unique nature of the Judeo-Christian tradition that creates certain theological problems. How do we reconcile an all-loving, all-powerful God with so many travesties that surround us? And how can a gracious God consign people to hell?

Why is Christianity so exclusive? Does it have a right to condemn others or claim an exclusive corner on the truth? The rise of pluralism and proximity to others' religion has reawakened this objection to Christian belief. We want to believe there are many routes to God. We are not comfortable with notions of heaven and hell. Doesn't God make room for everyone?

Perhaps people take umbrage at a God who condemns people to hell because they feel like they're already there. It is tough to scare people who would say they are quite familiar with hell. As a high school senior, I sensed how hellish my day-to-day existence had become. Living in Japan, I watched the salary men cram onto the subway six days a week. They endured a deadly mix of psychic torture and mundane dreariness. Suicide becomes quite an attractive option in Japan. I remember walking home one night and finding police gathered at the railroad tracks. A body was covered; definitely not the victim of an accident. This was an intentional exit from a living hell.

Some consider suicide a selfish act. We can become so fixated on our problems that we lose all perspective. Life seems pointless and absurd. We exit this mortal coil with either too many regrets to resolve or not enough reasons to stay. But what happens to those we leave behind? How can people like Kurt Cobain bail on his numerous fans? Didn't he grasp how beloved his songs had become? Was his exit a cop-out on his wife, his daughter, his family and friends? What did his conversations with God sound like? Would God be peeved that such a passionate musician shortchanged his existence?

Suicide is the ultimate rejection of the gift of life. Yet I cannot understand why some people believe that necessarily consigns a person to hell. When I recall my two or three most haunted friends, I have to conclude that they'd already paid a great price prior to their suicides. They suffered through almost every day of high school. Their parents' divorces may have left them shuttered between two non-homes. They dove into drug use as a way to ease the pain, but that only made matters worse. Their suicides happened amid such isolation. They may not have been discovered for days (proof that their lives had gone almost unnoticed). Would God complete the cycle of rejection they experienced? Or would he extend the warm, open arms that they desperately needed (and could not find)?

Perhaps the most radical notion regarding suicide involves Judas Iscariot. In *The Gospel According to Judas,* theologian Ray Anderson considers the last hours of Judas' tragic life.[5] It is easy for us to assume that Judas died condemned. Is there a possibility that Judas could have repented? Did he get a hearing in heaven? The book is written as a conversation between Judas and Jesus. It deals with the sense of shame that drove Judas to commit suicide. Ray Anderson suggests that we may still see Judas in paradise. His case tests the limits of grace. Is Judas beyond forgiveness? What if his suicide represented the ultimate act of contrition? How else could he communicate the regret he felt for betraying his friend Jesus? As the full ramifications of his cooperation with the authorities sunk in, Judas revealed the depth of his sorrow.

This-World Christianity

Craig: So what do you believe?

John: For me, I can't pass the wall of experience. I'm one of those people who feel that he belongs here.

Craig: Guess what—so do I. I'm a this-world Christian.

If hell has lost its fury, heaven has also misplaced its bliss. Why have eternal resting places lost their appeal? Baby boomers seem to think they'll live forever. Whenever possible, they still dress like teenagers. Southern California surf and skate wear is (unfortunately) an all-ages affair. Has American affluence undermined the appeal of heaven? Many of us have such large, comfortable houses that a heavenly mansion in the sky lost its luster. Why do I need a room in the clouds if I already own a condo at a ski resort? Extreme sports could be the culprit. Perhaps we have experienced so many moments of exhilaration that heaven looks like a letdown. Who wants to lounge on a perpetual puffy couch when we still have powder to shred below?

Some of us have caught sneak previews of eternal bliss. U2 concerts approximate a heavenly choir. We gather as one, singing songs about liberty and justice for all. We take pride "In the Name of Love." We anticipate a place "Where the Streets Have No Name." As we "Walk On," we sing "Hallelujahs!" above guitars turned up to eleven. We've swayed our arms and followed the leader, St. Bono. But will we be allowed to bring our iPhones to light up the celestial stadium? Such an absurd question may seem disrespectful, but we spend so little time contemplating heaven. No one will accuse us of being too heavenly minded. The jury is out on whether we prove any earthly good.

Cemeteries remain rare strongholds of heaven. For centuries, graveyards were placed in proximity to churches. A weekly trip to church was a regular opportunity to remember the departed, the saints who'd already gone marching in. The rise in the urban population made burial plots a scarce commodity. Paris embarked upon a massive relocation project, burying their dead in the catacombs below the city.

Cremation becomes an attractive option where undeveloped land is in short supply.

My sister was buried in a new cemetery on the outskirts of Charlotte. With most of the plots in town already sold or occupied, my parents turned to the only available land in their time of crisis. The headstones of a disproportionate number of young people surround my sister. Unexpected deaths led many to this resting place. A stroll through the cemetery tells many sad tales. Too many teenagers perished too early. One was knocked off his bike, killed by a car. Another died of a weak heart. Their epitaphs talk of angels and a life beyond. We long to know our loved ones have crossed over to a better place. Didn't they exchange a world of pain for a place close to Jesus' side? My mother brought wind chimes to Dixie's grave. They hang from a tree, ringing out a tune of hope and comfort.

Cemeteries remain among the most placid and peaceful places on earth. Consider their soothing names: Forest Lawn, Grand View, Rose Hills. As a child, my grandparents used to take me and my siblings to play in cemeteries. We never considered it morbid. They were some of the greenest, grandest, open spaces around. Gravestones made convenient spaces for hide and seek. Frisbee throwing? Not so much. We danced on people's graves, not as mockery, but as a way to celebrate life. We pay tribute to the departed by living with more vigor and purpose. We prepare for the inevitable by playing hard, taking chances, doing more.

Our vision of heaven as a collection of clouds may need to be retired. It is too ethereal, too disembodied. I am intrigued by a phrase that repeatedly pops in our church liturgy: "that heavenly country." It is uttered within a Eucharistic prayer, connected to Jesus' triumph on the cross. We ask God, "In the fullness of time, put all things in subjection under your Christ, and bring us to that heavenly country where with all your saints, we may enter into the everlasting heritage of your sons and daughters; through Jesus Christ our Lord, the firstborn of all creation, the head of the Church, and the author of our salvation." What a massive statement! So much perspective packed into such a compact space. The prayer looks forward and back at the same time. This broad vision telescopes history, placing us within a long procession of saints. For rootless people, it provides a position of honor and renown, a heritage. It places us in proper relation to Christ. And Jesus' place rises above the incarnation. He was present at creation, he was at the foundation of the church, and he will be at the consummation of the age. We serve a living Lord. Yet the phrase that still pops out most Sundays is "that heavenly country." What does it look like? Will we recognize it?

Instead of a mansion, "that heavenly country" conjures up images of a park, a green space. A heavenly country contains echoes of the garden of Eden we left behind. But it looks forward to a destination we all know, "*that* heavenly country." Surely it is a verdant, well-watered place. It may include a pond, a fishing hole, and a place to cool off. It doesn't have any constraints or limitations. It provides room to wander, to get lost, to lounge in a hammock, to swing from a tree. Does it include a vineyard? Maybe an orchard or two? It must produce plenty of food because we've all got plenty of mouths to feed. Are the crops rotated? If so, what is in season now? Fresh strawberries? Tomatoes? Turnip greens?

The phrase comes from Hebrews 11. That heavenly country is the destination of Abraham, Sarah, and their numerous descendents. They are described as strangers and exiles on earth. They never quite reached their destination, never felt fully at home. Some may call them resident aliens.[6] What encouraging news for immigrants, refugees, and the homeless! You're part of a long line of sojourners, people forced to pack lightly, to constantly pull up stakes.

Abraham and Sarah sought a homeland. They weren't reminiscing on their distant past. They didn't wallow in a nostalgic longing for an idyllic childhood home. We don't go back to "that heavenly country." Instead, Abraham and Sarah desired "a better country—a heavenly one." It is a place we're heading toward, a distant but attainable goal. Lest we think it includes wide-open spaces reserved strictly for our pleasure, Hebrews 11:16 contains a surprise announcement. "Therefore

God is not ashamed to be called their God, for he has prepared a city for them." When we get to that elusive heavenly country, what will we find? A city!

We associate cities with crime, crowds, and pollution. We read about murder statistics in Baltimore and Atlanta. We've seen pictures of commuters shoved onto the trains in Tokyo. Beijing's infamous smog threatened to choke Olympic athletes. I live in Los Angeles, home of traffic jams, road rage, and riots. We are an international example of how unchecked growth, shortsighted policies, and poor planning can compound problems. Cities are seen as places to escape rather than to seek. They are anything but heavenly. And yet, despite it all, God promises to provide his people with a heavenly city.

The biblical vision begins with a garden and concludes in a city with streets paved with gold. We live between the garden of Eden and the New Jerusalem to come. It is tough to picture a place that works for all people. Yet in God's city, everyone prospers, so crime is eradicated. Although undoubtedly crowded, the heavenly city has plenty of room for everyone. No one sleeps on the streets. Shelter is provided for all. Despite the crowds, pollution has been abated through a self-sustaining economy. There is no hunger. Recycling must be rampant. Nothing wasted, spoiled, or rotten. It has plenty of green space, well-stocked ponds, gardens that yield abundant fruit. It is heaven.

Jesus talks about preparing a place for us. We have images of mansions, of banquets, of celebrations to come. But what steps do we need to take to get there? How do we get our name on the guest list? By acknowledging his name, we confirm our receipt of his invitation. By joining with his people and prioritizing his kingdom, we demonstrate our interest in his banquet. An embrace of his atoning work on the cross reserves our room in the mansion. But what do we do while we wait for that house to be finished? We invite others to join us. We work out our faith with fear and trembling, serving the poor, loving our neighbors. In these tangible actions, we make way for the kingdom to come. What direction do we walk en route to that heavenly country that Abraham and Sarah sought? Are we even moving in the right direction? We may sometimes feel as if we're wandering in the desert for 40 years.

Perhaps our eschatology (waiting for a new earth) can begin to coincide with ecology (preserving the gift we've been given). Plenty of scientists are supporting each side of the global warming debate. Plenty of money is being made by both camps as they engage in ongoing research. The environmental divide also falls along theological lines. Both sides may stake their claims in the garden of Eden. Are we called to fill the earth and subdue it (Genesis 1:28) or to tend and preserve the garden (Genesis 2:15)? The first Genesis account encourages fruitfulness and multiplication. It suggests that overpopulation will never be a problem. The second Genesis account puts humanity in the role of steward. We are more like managers of precious resources. Much of the exploration and conquering connected to the Industrial Revolution stems from the dominion extended in Genesis 1. The earth is our playground. The plants are made for our consumption. We are the crown of creation, the top of the food chain. The conservation movement finds a mandate in Genesis 2. Taking care of creation involves sensitivity toward the environment. Business expansion must take a backseat to the preservation of endangered species.

Genesis 1 served as the philosophical basis for scientific research. Christianity allowed us to treat nature as an object, worthy of study rather than worship. Unfortunately, we incorrectly assumed that there was an endless supply of natural resources. Lynn White famously suggested that "Christianity bears a huge burden of guilt" for our ecological crisis.[7] Science has slowly come to inform us that we have endangered our environment. Dominion has its limits. The curatorial or custodial role of Genesis 2 has emerged as a pressing need. Theologian Sallie McFague suggests, "The postmodern picture sees us as part and parcel of the earth, not only dependent on it and its processes, but since we are high on the food chain, *radically* dependent."[8] We have shifted from the freedom granted in Genesis 1 to the responsibility extended in Genesis 2.

We are coming to realize that creation care is not a liberal or conservative issue, but a core part of Christian discipleship. We care for earth because that is our God-given role. Groups like the Evangelical Environmental Network have offered visionary leadership (see www. creationcare.org). The Au Sable Institute in Michigan has allowed Christian college students to put their faith into active concern for the environment (see www.ausable.org). Newspaper columnist Rod Dreher suggests conservatism and conservation fit together to form "Crunchy Cons."[9] Boise Vineyard pastor Tri Robinson has taken all kinds of heat for teaching his congregation how to care for our Father God's "Mother Earth."[10]

We may even forge some unexpected partnerships. Sowing our wild oats may mean joining left-leaning vegetarians in buying organic foods. Harvard's famed entomologist Edward O. Wilson appeals to the Christian community to save life on earth.[11] Wilson draws from religious roots he abandoned long ago to compose a series of letters addressed to a Southern Baptist pastor. Whether we're environmentalists who fight for the biosphere or Christians caring for creation, we desperately need each other to solve pressing ecological problems.

I am the least likely environmentalist. I was born in South Florida, grew up in a Carolina boomtown, taught English in Tokyo, and now raise my family in L.A. I am a city slicker, accustomed to jostling for space at a rigorous pace. But one trip to the Galápagos Islands ruined a lifetime of rat racing. Swimming with penguins slowed me down. The birth of a baby seal stopped my progress. The stares of red- and blue-footed boobies got to me. They viewed me with such limited guile that I didn't know what to do. Why aren't the birds on the Galápagos Islands afraid of people? Shouldn't the massive albatross flee from my presence? Why do the frigate birds not shudder at the sight of humanity? How did Darwin fail to report this phenomenon?

My wife and I arrived at the Galápagos Islands during El Niño conditions. The islands were brittle and dry. Dead bird carcasses abounded. With their food supply diminished, the penguins, seals, and sharks struggled to survive in the unnaturally hot water. Was this local warming connected to global warming? We may never find a conclusive answer. In the meantime, how can I make a positive difference in the Galápagos? How do I ensure that tomorrow's children will commune with the red- and blue-footed boobies of the future?

I am an unlikely vegetarian. Raised on pulled pork Southern barbeque, I am shocked to admit I've given up the pig. No more chicken teriyaki either. I stopped grilling steaks and burgers too. Scientists warn us about livestock's greenhouse gas emissions.[12] Anyone who has driven between Los Angeles and San Francisco on Interstate 5 knows the noxious effects of cattle farms. You can smell their emissions for a solid ten miles. Fish are still on the platter for now. My mercury levels may end up rivaling a thermometer. I don't know if I'm getting back to the garden, to life before the fall, or trying to usher in the New Jerusalem. In the meantime, pass the lentils.

Good News

I meet plenty of people familiar with the biblical lake of fire. They've heard the bad news. They know they're in danger of being left behind. Yet almost no one realizes we're getting a new heaven and a new earth (Revelation 21:1). Imagine a place where there is no crying, no death, no sorrow (Revelation 21:4). Very few people realize that our greatest art, music, and film will have a place in the New Jerusalem (Revelation 21:26). Each culture's most enduring masterpieces will be preserved. All those discussions about the all-time greatest movies will finally be resolved. People may want to drink from a crystal fountain, flowing with the water of life (Revelation 22:1). For those fond of nature will come an opportunity to climb a tree whose leaves contain healing for the nations (Revelation 22:2). Imagine a city that requires no electricity (Revelation 22:5). God's presence lights it up instead. And who doesn't love a wedding? It is an honor to be invited. To all who are thirsty, the Spirit and the bride say, "Come." Who wouldn't be interested in that kind of gathering?

It is time to tell the other side of God's story. Not just the judgment to come, but the joy that awaits us. Can we begin to paint a picture of God's coming kingdom that resembles the finest fantasy films? Even better, can we start practicing our faith in ways that are beautiful, colorful, and compelling? We have been so busy deciding who isn't included that we neglected to extend an invitation. Jesus warns us that we may miss the party altogether. He had a firm sense of who's in and who's out, yet his guest list changed constantly (Luke 14:7-24). Those who are wrapped up in their busyness will likely forfeit their invitation. But the poor, the crippled, the lame, and the blind will take their place. They don't need to worry about clothes. He'll provide the party frocks.

We may want to start walking. Abraham and Sarah took a while to reach that heavenly country. If we're expecting a pastoral setting, we may be surprised. God's party is distinctly urban. It takes place in the most compassionate, functional, and cultured place possible: the city of God. Security may be tight at the door, but inside, the wedding party goes on and on and on…

New York

As college freshmen, John Marks and I bonded in New York City. In the Big Apple, we became friends for life. A spring break road trip introduced us to skyscrapers, art, and theater. We cruised down Fifth Avenue with our mouths agape. We were drawn to the museums, to the trove of artistic treasures gathered in such a compact space. We stood in awe atop the World Trade Center. So much life teeming beneath us! We were in the cultural capital of America and maybe even the world. John and I loved the pace. We were both intoxicated by the city, energized by its possibilities. What others decried, we considered fertile soil. We returned from the trip eager to room together as sophomores in college.

A decade later, John moved to New York City as a journalist. He covered arts and entertainment for *U.S. News & World Report.* His office was crammed with cultural artifacts, including the latest CDs and Criterion Collection DVDs. When he wasn't reporting on *Buffy the Vampire Slayer,* he was working on his first novel. John and his wife, Debra, bought a brownstone in Brooklyn. Park Slope is home to more writers than any neighborhood in America. It is celebrated in Paul Auster's short stories and the subsequent film *Smoke* (1995). It is also home to a vocal gay and lesbian community, raising their kids blocks from Prospect Park and the Brooklyn Museum. Park Slope is where the intelligentsia gathers over coffee and croissants.

Brooklyn also serves as a port of entry for recent immigrants.

Beckoned by the Statue of Liberty, these arrivals from Jamaica, Azer-baijan, Guatemala, Liberia, and China test the American experiment. They replicate their home cultures in storefronts and diners. Temples, synagogues, and mosques allow them to connect with their heritage. Can the multitude of voices be harmonized? Or should the variety of beliefs and practices be appreciated for their invigorating distinctives? Brooklyn's clash of cultures will tell us whether a new pluralism can make room for everyone.

Twenty-five years after my first visit, I was invited to New York City to give a lecture at the Damah Film Festival. Damah screens shorts that offer "Spiritual Experiences in Film" (www.damah.com). The 411, a new church planted within Times Square, hosted the fest. The church hoped to attract creative types from throughout the city. The Damah Film Fest coincided with a slightly charged weekend. Sunday marked the anniversary of 9/11.

John and I met for breakfast in Brooklyn on September 10. John was leaving New York, moving to Massachusetts. The pace of the city had exhausted his family. Simply getting to work and school every day took its toll. His wife and son had gone ahead, eager to get acclimated to a more relaxed environment. John tied up loose ends in Brooklyn, pausing to take a long brunch with me (and a film crew!). A local *trattoria* was kind enough to accommodate us.

Would we be able to cover our unfinished business? John arrived with a head full of questions. While I dug into my polenta, John pressed into the religious and political turmoil prompted by conser-vative Christians. It was an opportunity to explain the motivations behind the religious right. I tried to offer creative empathy for a move-ment that mostly created antipathy. If John could come to understand why Christians feel embattled, maybe we could find common ground with our perceived enemies. Our conversation might become emblem-atic of a purple state of mind across America.

Youth and Wisdom

9

My wife has a dream. Caroline wants to direct a daycare center for children and a senior center for adults housed in the same building. She wants to see the two groups often ignored by the world at work gathered in the same space. The energy of youth combined with the wisdom of age. Wouldn't that be a fine sight? Imagine the mutual benefits—the fresh perspective provided by little children married with the patience of elders. While the rest of us rushed past, they could get on with the creative business of play. Far too often we view children and grandparents as problems to solve. We outsource their care to professionals. Yet issues involving kids and the elderly continue to rise in importance.

From stem cell research and abortion to assisted suicide, the wedge issues that divide us are rooted in the humanity that unites us. The ethics of life and death swirling around our scientific era are complex, messy, and multifaceted. Just when we seem to have a firm handle on our position, another innovation alters the debate. How do we affirm God's gift of life in a contentious, scientific era? We may not all be pro-life, but surely we are all pro-children. A purple state of mind loves children, all children, and works to ensure they have the healthiest, heartiest life possible. It cannot separate abortion from health care, economics from education. A purple state of mind adopts a holistic approach to ministry. It nurtures people at all ages and stages, young and old, from birth through death. A purple state of mind brings the collective wisdom of the community together, across generations, for the benefit of all. The depth of our convictions can be measured by our attention to orphans and widows. A purple state of mind recognizes that abundant living must extend to the whole community; it must include justice for the orphaned and the oppressed.

> **John:** To me, the helium in my life often enough is my son. The birth of my child—that day reversed every dark engine in this life. It just did. I was there. I saw it. I've got a miracle that I can take with me to the grave. And if I don't see another one, that's okay.

You don't have to believe in God to consider children a miracle. The baby that emerges from the womb is so captivating. The skin is so soft. The tiny fingers so finely made. (In the 2007 film *Juno,* the mere idea of fingernails on a fetus drives Juno MacGuff out of an abortion clinic.) As babies wake up to sights and sounds, we are reminded of the beauty and splendor that surround us. Their focused stare reminds us of the gift of sight. Through their ears we're reacquainted with the wild world of sound. In their iron grip, we recall the comforting touch of others. Through our babies, we slow down long enough to hear the first word. Through our children, we celebrate each tentative step. We are born anew with every tiny accomplishment.

Unfortunately, my first experience with childbirth was decidedly less rosy than John's rapturous miracle. I nearly missed my daughter's arrival. I was too busy throwing up. I made the mistake of donating blood the day before. Already wound up by the baby's impending arrival, I weakened my defenses through bloodletting. On the morning of my wife's scheduled C-section, I woke up woozy. After ushering my very pregnant wife into the car, I lost my breakfast in the bushes. This was a late-breaking morning sickness. Was it solidarity with her anxiety? Caroline seemed fine—ready to deliver. As we waited for the delivery room, I had another attack. I contaminated the sterile hospital environment with my upset stomach. It was not a pretty sight. Just when the focus should have fallen on my wife and baby, I hogged the sick spotlight for myself.

Perhaps I was wound up by the full implications of it all. Parenting is a rather irreversible, long-term commitment. It is lifetime membership in a costly club. One must surrender certain freedoms. Goodbye to movies in the theater. Farewell to fall afternoons watching college football games. Bye-bye rounds of golf. A baby brings instant adulthood in a way that even marriage doesn't.

The wave of vomit-inducing anxiety that preceded my daughter's birth vanished upon first sight. All the clichés suddenly seemed true. It was an instant bond, a spontaneous love affair. Not just because she resembled my beautiful, bountiful wife. Zoë desperately needed a defender. She needed a champion, someone to make sure she was fed. She needed a father to go to work, to pay her bills, to keep her sheltered and clothed. By the time my son, Theo, arrived three years later, I had overcome my initial nausea. I greeted Theo's birth without even a headache.

Babies are living reminders of the elemental aspects of life. Children are utterly dependent upon the kindness of others. Their piercing cry is a demand for attention, from a change of temperature to a fresh diaper. They cannot feed themselves. Left alone, they may roll over on the wrong side and never right themselves. Child rearing is a moment-by-moment process. Toddlers are always one step away from catastrophe. Falling down a step, crashing into furniture, petting the wrong end of an animal...to simply keep a child alive is a challenge. Consider all the airborne diseases and viruses that threaten children's existence. What a surprise that any of us make it from birth canal to graduation day. We need a series of safety nets to get from young to old, from birth to death. No wonder issues of abortion and euthanasia are so emotionally loaded.

The birth of a baby alters our focus. We are no longer fighting for our own survival. A job promotion may mean more than additional luxury goods. It can be the difference in a home, in health care, in education, in opportunity. A baby may change how we vote. We start to view the future in a different manner. It is no longer about what I want *now,* but what they'll need *then.* A baby brings a built-in legacy, an appeal to something larger than us. It forces us to take the long view, to think about the interconnectedness of the planet. Decisions I make today will affect my kids' welfare down the road. How much debt should I assume? How can I protect the environment? How do I improve the public schools? The future is forged by policy decisions today.

John Marks said the birth of his son "reversed every dark engine in this life." Bringing a child into this world is the ultimate act of faith. It is also a profound act of hope. Parenting is an act of defiance; despite the evidence, we choose to believe in tomorrow. It is an assumption of enormous risk. Despite the substantial cost, we are willing to invest. We will pay for food, shelter, and clothing. We will figure out some way to pay for college. We may not live to see the benefits, but we are willing to mortgage our comfort for another's prosperity. Babies seem like blank slates of possibilities. They could grow up to become a president or a rock star. Our legacy becomes wrapped in their prosperity. Raising children forces us to focus on the future. Despite the forces that threaten to undo us, we will usher new life into a dark world.

The challenge is to extend the defense of our kids to all children. As I advocate for my daughter's best interests, do I remember to fight for others? She wants pizza. A few million hungry children in Africa would like a pizza too. She wants her room painted pink. So does a homeless child who has been camping in a tent on skid row. Zoë deserves the best education possible. And so do countless kids around the planet who are ducking bombs, braving the elements, sharing the few books in their village. A purple state of mind cares about all kids.

It also values the elderly. Rather than consigning people to categories of usefulness, a purple state of mind cares for those in the later stages of life. It adopts a holistic approach to ministry. A purple state of mind pushes past preestablished categories of red and blue, liberal and conservative, to deliver the basic life necessities children need to thrive and the elderly need to survive. It strives to pass the Bible's test of true religion: the care of orphans and widows.

Pro-women and Pro-life

Craig: The question is, where do personal morality and public policy intersect? Do my personal beliefs have a right to decide other people's practices? I don't think that's the case. I think in America there is a sense of freedom of choice, and that's the public contract all of us signed.

What a contentious issue! The arguments have grown so heated; Christians have been willing to kill in defense of life. Murdering doctors like David Gunn and Bernard Slepian is no way to claim the moral high ground. I write this chapter with trepidation. Efforts at moderation regarding abortion issues seemingly make one a target. Three decades after *Roe v. Wade,* I fear we still haven't thought through the full implications of a pro-life position. It has been a convenient dividing line, raising money for both sides. If a more conservative Supreme Court outlaws abortion, will that decision alter our behavior? When we take away a pregnant woman's choice, what alternatives will we provide? Despite our best efforts to ensure that children enter a nurturing environment, women may still choose to terminate unwanted pregnancies.

How will we deal with women who continue to seek abortions? Will we start registering pregnancies in a national database? Given privacy laws, who will have the right to access such conception information? Are we willing to put women in jail for having an abortion? What would be an appropriate sentence? Does an abortion at five months merit a longer sentence than one in the first trimester? What about cases of maternal caution? They are rare, but still a reality. Prior to *Roe v. Wade,* Christians argued for abortion as a compassionate defense of women.[1] Will we prevent doctors from making a difficult choice? Will they be hailed for sacrificing an expectant mother to save a child?

Abortion has a short history as a hot-button issue. Historian Randall Balmer demonstrates how indifferent evangelicals were toward abortion even after *Roe v. Wade*. He documents how the religious right was galvanized by an IRS threat against segregated Christian schools. When the racist policies of Bob Jones University threatened its tax-exempt status, conservative Christian leaders rallied to offer support. Searching for a host of issues to undergird their primary concern, these leaders latched onto the recent *Roe v. Wade* decision as an emotionally charged complement to prayer in schools and the Equal Rights Amendment. Only later was abortion identified as *the* wedge issue of the twentieth century. How ironic that a movement organized to sustain racist policies would eventually call its adherents "modern abolitionists."

Garry Wills points out that Catholic opposition to abortion is also a recent development. As a faithful Catholic, Wills finds "abortion is not treated in the Ten Commandments—or anywhere in Jewish Scripture. It is not treated in the Sermon on the Mount—or anywhere in the New Testament. It is not treated in the early creeds. It is not treated in the early ecumenical councils."[2]

After searching the scriptures, St. Augustine came to no conclusions about the origin of the soul. Wills writes that St. Thomas Aquinas "denied that personhood arose at fertilization by the semen. God directly infuses the soul at the completion of human formation." Wills considers abortion an issue of natural law and reason rather than theology. Yet the Democratic Party's support of exclusively pro-choice candidates has cost them the votes of countless Catholics.

The initial round of Christian protestors declared abortion is murder. They appealed to the biblical commandment "Thou shall not kill." As the rhetoric heated up on both sides, abortion became a surrogate for much more. By 1997, William Kristol suggested, "Conservatism's more fundamental mandate is to take on the sacred cow of liberalism—choice."[3] The lives of unborn babies were subsumed to arguments about women's self-determination. Kristol concluded, "The truth is that abortion is today the bloody crossroads of American politics. It is where judicial liberation (from the Constitution), sexual liberation (from traditional mores), and women's liberation (from natural distinctions) come together. It is the focal point for liberalism's simultaneous assault on self-government, morals and nature." So much weight thrust upon a fetus's still-forming shoulders.

Perhaps our frustration arises from tying the future of Western civilization to an issue with only a 30-year history. It is an unwieldy fulcrum in the culture wars. Libertarian Virginia Postrel makes this note:

> You cannot invoke dead babies to stop gay couples from living together, record companies from selling songs you don't like, women from pursuing careers, Wal-Mart from building new stores, developers from putting up condos, biotech companies from selling life-extending drugs, black men from marrying white women, farmers from leaving the land, companies from moving plants overseas, or any of the myriad choices one or another stasis-craving conservative has condemned as untraditional, unnatural, and immoral. To attack markets, to preserve central authority, you must attack choice.[4]

Taking choice away from women is a tough sell in a culture rooted in abundance. A trip down any supermarket aisle illustrates how sacred choice remains in a market economy.

Swarthmore College psychologist Barry Schwartz has suggested that our abundance of choices may be crippling us. Writing about shopping (not abortion), Schwartz notes, "As the number of choices keeps growing, negative aspects of having a multitude of options begin to appear...As the number of choices grows further, the negatives escalate until we become overloaded. At this point, choice no longer liberates, but debilitates. It might even be said to tyrannize."[5] Would women gladly be relieved of the burden of choice? Not likely. Virginia Postrel refuses to lay the blame upon choice itself. "Ultimately, the debate about choice is not about markets but about character. Liberty and responsibility really do go together; it's not just a platitude. The more freedom we have to control our lives, the more responsibility we have for how they turn out. In a world of constraints, learning to be happy with what you're given is a virtue. In a world of choices, virtue comes from learning to make commitments without regrets."[6] Abortion may never be removed as a choice. Can we change how people make such significant decisions?

The *Roe v. Wade* decision arose alongside a tumultuous debate about women's rights. Significant expansions of civil rights for black, Latino, and Asian Americans were followed by marches attacking gender bias. Caucasian Christians who had joined the marches for civil rights were poised to lobby for women's rights. The Women's Christian Temperance Union had been at the forefront of the women's suffrage movement earlier in the twentieth century. People of faith understood that equality for woman animated the life and ministry of Jesus. Unfortunately, *Roe v. Wade* become aligned with the Equal Rights Amendment. Christians who might have supported women's rights opposed women's rights to choose. Christian opposition to the Equal Rights Amendment turned women against themselves and their babies. They were forced into a Solomonic choice, dividing into either pro-women or pro-baby. Why not both? Arguments about rights grew so politicized that they were stripped from their source—the Bible. Abortion was turned into a matter for the state to decide. It proved disastrous for both the women's movement and the pro-life movement.

After three decades of heated divisions, we're finally seeing a slight thaw. It is no longer an oxymoron to say, "Pro-life democrat."[7] Will we see an accompanying rise in conservative feminists? Actress Patricia Heaton identifies herself as a "feminist for life." The organization (www.feministsforlife.org) seeks to tie the history of women's rights to its pro-life roots. It draws upon disparate pro-life feminists like Jane Addams, Mary Wollstonecraft, Dorothy Day, and Emma Goldman to suggest, "Women deserve better than an abortion." They "refuse to choose" between the limited options women have been presented: their rights or their unborn child.

Artists and filmmakers may provide the creative leadership that politicians have lacked. An unexpected trend of life-affirming films has emerged. I remember my surprise and delight at discovering the Polish film *Ono* (*The Stranger*) at the 2005 Sundance Film Festival. A young woman with limited job prospects and an unreliable boyfriend is surprised by an unplanned pregnancy. Eva heads to the doctor's office expecting to abort her child. The money for the abortion is stolen. She is inconsolable—until she finds out that the fetus can hear her voice. She decides to introduce her baby to as many sounds and experiences as possible. The second half of the film becomes a vibrant travelogue. *Ono* turns from a downbeat drama into a radical celebration of life's beauty. Unfortunately, director Malgorzata Szumowska's brilliant affirmation of women and children never was granted a commercial release in the United States.

The independent film *Bella* snuck into the 2006 Toronto Film Festival with limited acclaim. It takes viewers inside a Mexican restaurant in New York City. As a waitress, Nina struggles to pay her bills even before she finds out she's pregnant. Her boss offers no sympathy toward her plight. Only a thoughtful chef, Jose, rallies to her side. They skip work together, surprising his family for dinner. First-time director Alejandro Monteverde parcels out the chef's painful backstory to emotional effect. Nina's unwanted child becomes a source of healing for Jose. The little girl, Bella, arrives as a beautiful gift to all. This inspiring story captured the Audience Award in Toronto and became a modest indie box-office hit.

Two broad, Hollywood comedies from 2007 featured women in unwanted pregnancies. One-night stands and unprotected sex leads to comedic complications in *Knocked Up* and *Juno*. In *Knocked Up*, Alison Scott, a woman with broadcasting ambitions, celebrates a promotion by falling into bed with a shiftless slacker. Ben Stone focuses on getting high more than getting a job. Neither one knows how to respond to the unexpected pregnancy. Ben talks to his father, who offers the surprising declaration, "You're the best thing that ever happened to me." Alison refuses to follow her mother's advice. She decides to keep the baby and give the slacker father, Ben, a chance as well. *Knocked Up* suggests that a baby can arrive as a blessing even amid less than ideal circumstances. Director Judd Apatow finishes the film with a loving montage of baby photos from the cast and crew.

In *Juno,* a determined young woman attempts to deal with her unplanned pregnancy alone. She calls to "procure a hasty abortion." Outside the clinic, she encounters a high school classmate shouting, "All babies want to get borned." Su-Chin blurts out to Juno, "Your baby has fingernails." Juno rethinks her decision. She offers up the baby for adoption. First-time screenwriter Diablo Cody's clever script toys with classic adoption stories. Meeting the potential adoptive parents and their lawyer, Juno asks, "Can't we just, like, kick this old school? You know, like, I stick the baby in a basket, send it your way, like Moses and the reeds?" At her first ultrasound, she tells her best friend, Leah, "I am a sacred vessel; all you got in your stomach is Taco Bell." Some critics carped that Juno seemed too knowing and clever about her condition. After acting far too nonchalant, Juno starts to feel the weight of the moment. She recognizes her status, "They call me the cautionary whale." Juno has the baby and gives it away on her terms. She too becomes a feminist for life.

Do these films represent a shift in popular perceptions of abortion? They may only illustrate that having a child makes for more dramatic (and comedic) complications. Yet Hollywood has also provided strange cases of real teen parenthood. Sixteen-year-old actress Keisha Castle-Hughes took her role as Mary, mother of Jesus, quite seriously in *The Nativity Story.* Keisha missed all the prerelease publicity tours when it was discovered that she was pregnant. The pregnancy of Britney Spears' little sister, Jamie, surprised fans of her Disney Channel show, *Zoe 101.* Raised in a Southern Baptist family, Jamie never considered an abortion.

These young actresses placed Christians in an awkward situation. Pro-life activists were left with three conflicting messages, "Don't have sex." "Don't get pregnant." "Glad you're keeping the kid." These real-life scenarios demonstrate how much more complicated these issues of childbirth can become. Getting pregnant is easy. Having a baby is complicated. Raising a child is life-changing. In affirming the rights of women and their babies, we acknowledge how much support everyone needs to navigate the gauntlet called life.

Science: Partner in Life and Death

Scientific breakthroughs are also altering issues of life and death in surprising ways. Thanks to technology, we see early pictures of the fetus in the womb. Today's teenagers have grown up surrounded by ultrasound images. They are far more pro-life than generations before them.[8] Premature babies also have greater chances of survival. Newborns we could not save in an earlier era now survive under intensive care. So what about babies that fail to thrive? Women are still wise not to announce their pregnancy until 12 or 13 weeks. Miscarriage remains a painful possibility. It is God's way of sorting things out. While doctors fight for the health of babies and their mothers, we ultimately do not play God.

Science also allows more people to have children. Some of those parents conform to traditional notions of Mom and Dad while others include more surprising combinations. Our friend donated an egg to her sister (making her a very involved aunt). Another friend chose her mother to be a surrogate (creating a truly grand mother). Lesbians commonly seek out sperm donors. One of our gay friends sought out an egg from her sister. Increasingly, the person who bore the baby is not the person who is raising the child. We've come a long way from test-tube babies. The lines of family are blurring. Old fears that a proliferation of homosexuality threatens humanity's survival have been banished by science. Everybody can become a parent. How will churches that aspire to be pro-family respond?

We've only just begun to wrestle with issues of paternity, adoption, of being grafted into a family. As people marry and have children at later ages than in past generations, privacy related to childbearing affects the aging family. Personal rights related to in vitro fertilization, egg and sperm donation, adoption, and surrogacy grow in relevance with our aging society. For example, the recent publicity surrounding a 60-year-old woman's birth of twins required the woman to defend her autonomous rights.[9] Will pro-life Christians support new parents regardless of the circumstances that brought their child into the world? Will we provide parenting classes, child care, and support for all struggling parents?

Our children go to school with kids who have two mommies. Our children go to church with kids who have two daddies. Most of us have never discussed it with our children. Just as with differences of race or culture, we've waited for them to notice and bring it up. One day, my son, Theo, asked my wife, "Can people have two daddies?" She took a slight gulp. The long-awaited moment had arrived. We weren't any closer to having a prepared answer. We had plenty of role models to cite, from Brandt's daddies to Kate's mommies. But how do you explain all that to a three-year-old who already knows where babies come from?

My wife said, "Yes, people can have two daddies."

Theo said, "Jesus had two daddies."

This was not part of our script. Perplexed, my wife asked, "What do you mean?"

Theo concluded, "Joseph and God." (Out of the mouths of babes…) He wasn't thrown by the idea of multiple daddies.

I'm more concerned about kids with single mommies or daddies. What a daunting challenge! Kudos to any parent who raises a child on his or her own. Responsibilities are also extending in the other direction. With more parents waiting longer to have children, the next generation may have to serve as caregivers for their parents at an earlier age. We may be raising kids and caring for our parents in the same stressful time. We all need multiple support systems to navigate our complex world.

Quality of Life

Scientific advances have extended life expectancy. Frail babies can be sustained in incubators. The infirmed can hang on for years. Jesus' statement that he came that we might have life, life to the full, presents an interesting dilemma. Does the abundant life include comas? Can we love God in a vegetative state? The tragic case of Terri Schiavo demonstrates how messy the right to life (and death) is becoming. With a wave of baby boomers just approaching retirement, issues of elder care are about to explode. People who have lived vigorously may not want to hang on just because science makes it possible. Many will choose quality of life over quantity of life. How should people of faith respond?

Clashes between individual autonomy and government demands have barely begun. Pertinent privacy issues related to the aging family include the right to die, euthanasia, and assisted suicide. Additional complications can arise for those caring for family members. Decisions about health care treatments, institutionalization, the use of stem cells for therapeutic purposes, and experimental pharmaceuticals force us to explore new ethical terrain.

Even the case of reproduction is a privacy issue related to the aging family. It touches on issues of autonomy versus paternalism. Who holds power to decide? When can the government impede on someone's personal life?[10] Aging family members desire to maintain their privacy in relation to outside institutions, and professionals who work within the system have special codes of conduct to protect clients' and patients' privacy.[11] My wife is a geriatric social worker. Health care providers and social workers are obligated to respect privacy and autonomy. They are trained to honor people's requests.

This question of who makes the decisions wades into the controversial legal issue of the establishment of personal rights. The case of Terri Schiavo provides a public example of the emerging need for research and data to inform real-world issues of life and death.[12] Schiavo's case dealt with personal rights. Who should be making decisions for someone needing care? The legal morass indicates how ill-equipped our laws and policies are to deal with the right to life and death. In the absence of an advance directive that would have provided a health care proxy, or durable power of attorney to determine Schiavo's health care, the question of *who* was her decision maker arose. The publicity surrounding the case emerged from the lengthy public battle that pitted Schiavo's husband against her parents. When Terri was a minor, her parents exercised their moral rights to seek out the best possibilities for their daughter. The legal prerogative was clear. However, as Terri aged into adulthood and entered into a legal commitment in marriage to her spouse, her parents' paternalistic authority over her was severed twice. Their authority had no legal standing. Their relationships to Schiavo reflect the tension between autonomy and paternalism.

There is no legal precedent concerning the intergenerational issue of parents' caregiving for adult children. There is also no legal precedent on caregiving for adult children who are bound legally to another person through marriage. Lawmakers must grasp the increasing importance of multigenerational bonds and the growing varieties of families. Counterintuitive caregiving issues will rise in coming decades, beyond the traditional mother-daughter filial bonds. Laws concerning caregiver rights, family leave, domestic partnerships, and privacy are still being written. As people of faith, shouldn't we encourage even the youngest adults to establish living wills, durable powers of attorney, and advance directives? With life expectancy increasing and with the baby boomers aging, we will see more and more instances of adult children needing care and facing legal issues at the end of life.

Young Lives

John: Do you believe that *Roe v. Wade* is an attack on the sacredness of life?

Craig: Yes, in the same way that I believe not providing good health care for that kid after it's born is an attack on the sacredness of life.

Our efforts to change legislation regarding the rights of the unborn have been ineffective because we have been pro-fetus rather than pro-children. We bring kids into the world, and then social Darwinism kicks in. "Sink or swim, kids. We got you here—now it is up to you." The reversal of *Roe v. Wade* falls lower on my to-do list because I've seen the struggles that follow life after birth. Are we willing to pay the price to raise children? Hillary Clinton said, "It takes a village." Mike Huckabee demonstrated courage as governor of Arkansas on issues of health care and education. How do we better support struggling parents? We must be willing to invest in schools if we insist on babies being born. We must have courage of our convictions at every age and stage.

Working with teenagers in Young Life, I learned to value every kid, regardless of his or her background or potential "social contribution." As a student at Davidson College, I directed a team of volunteer leaders for Young Life. We walked into North Mecklenburg High School football games, basketball games, and band concerts. Jocks and cheerleaders were readily identifiable from their uniforms. They had considerable cachet within the high school culture. The preppy students lived on the lake in large houses. They went waterskiing every weekend. These affluent, college-bound students made a great nucleus for a Young Life club. They were popular, sociable, and had plenty of discretionary income. When we planned a trip to a Young Life camp, they could all afford to go. When we discussed a relationship with Jesus, they all nodded politely. Christian faith was a convenient way to round out their résumés.

Over time, we met students from different backgrounds, beyond the popular pack. Through a combination of economics and education, they weren't on quite as fast a track. "The Creekers" were good ol' boys in flannel shirts and scruffy beards. They were committed to getting roaring drunk at every occasion possible. Young Life was the first time they'd been noticed, singled out as worthy of honor and attention. One by one, these roughnecks committed their lives to Jesus. The leader of the pack is now a financial advisor living in a custom log cabin in the North Carolina mountains.

We also got to know teenage mothers who lived at Girls' Haven. Their group home was just up the road from North Meck. School buses roared past their campus with no notice or recognition of the girls who resided there. We decided to explode the social stigmas attached to teen moms. Instead of meeting at the usual, palatial lake homes, we held our Young Life club on the girls' turf. If we really believed that Jesus cared about every kid, we needed to demonstrate it. We put the girls on every kid's map. We communicated that Christ does not judge teen moms but loves them and their children.

We also met a cross section of black students. We befriended a group of sisters. None of them had the same last name, but they all lived in the same home. They shared the same foster mother, a gracious woman who took in five or six girls at a time. Sabrina Houston was the most dynamic foster daughter. She was a tiny spitfire, full of life. Her Jheri-curl bounced with energy. Sabrina could bend your ear, singing songs, joining school cheers. Sabrina did not know her mother or father. She was hoping to be adopted. At age 17, she had never experienced a steady home life, shifting from one facility or foster home to another. Her vibrant personality belied her status as an orphan.

Until I met Sabrina, I never thought much about the biblical challenges to care for orphans. Yet Deuteronomy 14:29 instructs God's people to set aside special tithes so that "the aliens, the fatherless and the widows who live in your towns may come and eat and be satisfied." Psalm 82:3 (ESV) calls us to "give justice to the weak and the fatherless; maintain the right of the afflicted and the destitute." James's letter to the early church suggests, "Religion that God our Father accepts as pure and faultless is this: to look after orphans and widows in their distress" (1:27). Was I failing that test? Isaiah 1:17 (NASB) offers a tangible action plan: "Learn to do good; seek justice, reprove the ruthless, defend the orphan, plead for the widow." It can involve peacemaking, social advocacy, letters to the editor. How could I have viewed orphans as an ancient problem?

I had once skied down a slope called the Widowmaker. I survived. But Sabrina's effervescent spirit made me consider our widow-making machinery. Orphans may be created by accidents. We have a neighbor who lost both her parents in a plane wreck. Forty years later, the mere mention of the event will reduce her to instant tears. Orphans can be created by a prison sentence. Children may end up paying for parents' mistakes. Addictions can create orphans. The state may separate drug-addicted parents from their children. Social workers in departments of Children and Family Services have tough, often thankless jobs. They serve children who often have no advocates. Sabrina put a human face on the highly criticized and misunderstood social system that protects children from abuse and neglect. A large percentage of homeless teens are emancipated foster youth. When they turn 18, they are often left to fend for themselves. How would you fare in similar circumstances?

AIDS has orphaned the next generation in Africa. The downward spiral often begins because of limited economic opportunity. Young fathers head to the city to find work. Mothers may resort to prostitution to feed their children. They contract AIDS while fighting for their babies' survival. Eventually, their orphaned children are forced to fend for themselves while battling their own HIV. The generous efforts of the Bill and Melinda Gates Foundation have paid for costly AIDS medicine in the far corners of Africa. Vaccines against tuberculosis and malaria go a long way toward prolonging life. Unfortunately, the riches associated with working for the Gates Foundation have taken nurses out of their local communities. Money spent to combat AIDS has directed attention away from everyday health care.[13] It is easy to fall into despair. Should we give up on big-budget programs aimed at eradicating social ills? Absolutely not. We must fight for the lives of all children. We need more nurses to serve in such vexing settings.

Probably our most consistent widow maker is the military. Hardened Marines pine from the frontlines for their spouses and children. The uncertainty of their status also creates a constant state of dread on the home front. Unfortunately, in an effort to honor the widows and orphans of 9/11, we created an equal number of widows and orphans in our American military. Lord knows how many Iraqi orphans have been created by our efforts to bring democracy to their soil. Some reports place the numbers around 20,000 per month. I understand why we have a military. We are all indebted to the men, women, and children embroiled in our Department of Defense. I simply grieve for their widows and orphans we create. True religion requires us to care for them all, regardless of nationality or belief.

Sabrina put a particular face on the plight of orphans. We made sure that students like Sabrina could join us for Young Life camp. Through the generosity of donors, she experienced her first big trip. She had her bag packed days before we departed. She screamed with glee as we pulled into Windy Gap. She'd never experienced such a pastoral setting. The lake, the pool, the mountains all mesmerized Sabrina. She was growing in faith and in confidence. As she saw more of the world, she considered the places she could go. When she graduated from high school, Sabrina enrolled in the army. She wrote letters from basic training and always signed them, "Your daughter." Within two years, she was married and stationed in Germany.

I've lost touch with Sabrina, but I have never forgotten the gift of life "my daughter" brought to me. I hope and pray she has not been widowed during the war in Iraq. Having forged a family, I question whether she could survive another loss. And what if she had a child? Will her son or daughter become an orphan because of the war? Will another wave of orphans result? Sabrina's spirit was undaunted despite her circumstances. Her life was nearly tossed away, but she deserved every possible opportunity we could afford her. I am forever changed by the infectious joy that emanated from her every pore.

Do we see all children as equal? How do we offer them a tangible hope? This conviction requires much more than a message; we must follow up with actions. What kind of comprehensive social network can we construct? My wife and I have attempted to improve one life at a time. Through programs like Compassion International, we have provided the tuition for students throughout the world. As a newly married couple, we supported a Korean boy, Jae Hoon, until Compassion indicated his family could afford his clothing and education. We started supporting Ricardo from Peru at age ten. He turned eighteen, finishing high school with our help. Our resources continue to be directed toward Peru. Our new child is named Jorge. We decided to "adopt" one child in every continent. Our children's "pen pals" are Dinalyn from the Philippines and Ramadani from Tanzania. Compassion allows us to send them birthday and Christmas gifts along with our monthly tuition payments. How precious to see photos of Ramadani wearing his new jeans. He always greets us with an enthusiastic, "Shick-a-moo." Our son writes back with the same greeting. Yet the reports provided by Compassion indicate that Ramadani is a below-average student. As he struggles in school, I wonder what employment opportunities await him? Can we offer economic uplift?

My family also believes in capitalization. We love to set people up in business. Opportunity International offers microloans to villagers around the globe. The recipients have a 98 percent rate of repayment. What a stirring testimony to a business and ministry that works. Instead of a handout, Opportunity International offers a hand up.

I desperately need the perspective gained from the world's poorest people. They help me remember what matters. Whatever my daily struggles, they are small in comparison to survival. Jesus' solidarity with the least of these compels me. He said, "Let the children come to me, and do not hinder them" (Luke 18:16). The kingdom of God belongs to them. They are God's most precious sight. This can mean letting them come into the world, making room for the next generation. But it also means let them be nurtured, fed, clothed, and educated.

I am encouraged by grassroots efforts like the Advent Conspiracy. Started in Portland by a group of churches, the Advent Conspiracy presents an alternative to our commercialized Christmas. This group is seeking to reclaim solidarity with the baby Jesus. He was born homeless. He traveled with refugees, with those who had no place to stay. He identified with the immigrants, fleeing to Egypt for safety. Even as a child, Jesus represented a revolt against an empire that was overtaxing its people. The birth of a boy king revealed the bankrupt fealty demanded by Rome. Each year, we are expected to pour thousands of dollars into a year-end splurge. While the roots of Christmas are in honoring Jesus, in the Western world that means enriching ourselves. The Advent Conspiracy reclaims the forgotten roots of Christmas, and not merely by arguing for the place of Nativity scenes in public squares. To truly capture the spirit of Christmas, these Portland churches encourage their members to craft homemade gifts for friends and family and give the money they would have spent to charity. If our annual Christmas gift-buying binge were redirected toward the two-thirds world, we could build enough wells to provide clean water across the planet. That is a celebration I am eager to join.

What can we conclude? It is tough to be completely pro-life. Scientific breakthroughs present even more ethical conundrums. Who can be parents? When does life begin? When does a fetus become viable? How long should an elderly person linger? Do we have the right to play God? Should Christians ever pull the plug for a person in pain? What is justice? What is mercy? We must stop pitting women against their children. We must offer more viable alternatives. A purple state of mind connects the dots between economics and education. It understands that affordable health care is a moral issue. If we insist that we bring more children into the world, we must provide an environment that enables them to thrive. Perhaps our future resides among the widows and the orphans. Rather than separating people by age and interest, perhaps the church can serve as a bridge builder—connecting youth groups with the elderly. As we learn to care for the least of these, we will discover the face of God among us. Only when youth and wisdom are both valued, both protected, and both secure will we have practiced true religion.

Suffering and Silence

10

For years, my evangelistic efforts focused on getting my friends to church. If only they entered God's house, perhaps they would meet the Almighty. A song may pierce their soul. The sermon may prick their conscience. God might speak to them from inside his sanctuary. I also invited friends to evangelistic events. I remember the look on a friend's face during the altar call at a Billy Graham crusade. I hoped to see tears of repentance. Instead, he appeared ready to vomit. Had the words of life made him sick? Was it too much truth that he couldn't handle? He looked like death warmed over. Maybe that is the face of defiance, a willful resistance to God. Or maybe he had so many things churning within him that he didn't dare open his mouth (or take a step forward). How much anger, doubt, fear, and resentment resides within us? We hold on to it until we explode with ulcers, psychoses, and regret.

Evangelism may be an event, but conversion is a process. It is about far more than information. It involves the depths of our being. It involves dredging up buried secrets, hidden pains, and the worst aspects of our life experience. No wonder that most religious conversions occur before the onset of adulthood. Who would dare to cough up a lifetime of tattered recollections and disappointments? Yet if we honestly consider ourselves ministers of the gospel, committed to wholeness and healing, we must enter into the anger, rage, and contempt that separates us from our community, our Creator, and ourselves.

This chapter is about getting to the root of things, drilling down to core questions. Beneath our many reasons for resisting God's ovations reside our deepest fears, our most galvanizing experiences. Did we utter a desperate prayer that wasn't answered? Have we seen too much pain and suffering? Maybe we're simply too scared to trust God with our lives. How do we respond to our friends' deepest objections to faith? A purple state of mind listens—really listens. It takes the suffering of others seriously. It doesn't minimize people's pain but rather attends to it through patient listening, pastoral caring, and long-term relationships. A purple state of mind practices compassion through suffering with others, affirming their anger, and upholding the unexplainable mysteries of life. It is comfortable with silence.

John: I can tell you that for many years, even after college, and after those letters and after you and I knew each other, I continued to believe in God. But I also know the exact moment when it became impossible for me for one more day to believe in God...It comes at the end of a long period in which I tried to continue to believe that there was this reality that connected me to the heart of things—as opposed to a Jesus that increasingly stood between me and the heart of things in this life.

As John Marks recounted the story, I just listened. His face flushed. A combination of rage and regret surfaced. His tears confirmed the gravity of his experience. We both got lost in his palpable recollection. John's breaking point came overseas, as a reporter in a time of war. As a journalist covering genocide in the Balkans, John saw unspeakable atrocities. Muslims and Christians practiced killing in the name of God. Yet John's crisis of faith did not come from such perversions of religion. He understood how ethnicity and faith had been intertwined in ancient struggles. No, the moment that crushed his belief came from playing God.

John was already struggling with his privileged position as an American abroad. His passport brought him protection, the ability to remain above the fray. So while Bosnia and Serbia imploded, John was able to move about with comparative immunity. As a reporter for *U.S. News & World Report,* John was interviewing a Muslim father whose only hope resided in his sons. The man had lost his homeland, but he pressed on with the knowledge that his name and his people would live on through his offspring. John happened to know that this man's sons were already dead, his only hopes dashed by another crossfire. To see such pain and yet feel helpless to change it was devastating. In this rare case of godlike foreknowledge, John questioned, "How can God preside over such a twisted scenario?" The silence was deafening.

The perversity of that moment severed John's last strains of faith. He couldn't cling to his own comfort in the face of such suffering. The injustice of it all weighed too heavily upon John's shoulders. He boiled with righteous anger. Some people might have prayed for an answer, but John lost hope for redemption. He couldn't picture God's heart breaking alongside the Muslim father. For John, nothing good could possibly come from such a tragic scenario in the Balkans. He adopted an attitude of defiance. Whoever presides over such a twisted reality does not deserve fealty. Such travesties require angry, active rebellion. He concluded, "If you could ever tell me that in this life, there is a God that presides over some meaning there, I would have to say, 'I don't give a crap.' Because if that God exists, I am in permanent contention with him."

It took four conversations, spread out over a year, to get this most painful and personal story out of John. How many previous reasons had he proffered for his loss of faith? Over the course of shooting our documentary, John's objections to Christianity shifted from art and theater to women and sex. Given a false choice between faith and art, John chose to pursue the writer's life. He worked out his faith through his art, putting faith in his ability to interpret events as he saw them unfold. Sheltered by his upbringing in Texas, John decided to cover the world as a reporter. The more colorful and painful moments would serve as fuel for his fiction. After refraining from sexual intercourse in high school, John dove into romantic entanglements with relish. He went on an idyll in India. He lived out the bohemian ideal in Germany. He fell in lust. He saw the fall of the Berlin Wall and the collapse of Communism. He witnessed the chaos that came with the breakup of Yugoslavia. He fell in love. At the end of his adventures, John was a published novelist with a strong commitment to marriage and monogamy.

His objections to Christian faith changed. John wanted to know if his Jewish bride was going to hell. Whatever lip service the Christian community may pay toward "chosen people," John pushed me toward core issues of salvation. "If my wife is going to hell, then what about me?" Why would he want to reside in a different place? Why choose eternal separation from the one you love? Moreover, how could he put asunder what God had joined together? The problem of hell is a significant stumbling block. It is tough to gloss over questions of eternal damnation when they involve our dearly beloved.

But finally I got the core objection. Beyond art, sexuality, and the question of hell was the haunting war in Bosnia. John couldn't stomach the religious conflict in Bosnia, at least not the level of perversion that resulted in senseless deaths. How could John support any killing in the name of God? How could anyone? As a reporter, John stood above the fray and saw the twisted mess below. And as his heart broke, he felt complicit in the atrocities. If John couldn't contain his disgust for humanity and himself, then surely God shared such contempt. And yet God's seeming indifference or his guilt by association in this repellent religious war broke John's faith (and heart).

How long did it take to get this story out of John, to get to the core of his objections? We must make room for people to share their stories. That takes time, patience, and silence. How many times could I have cut him off short? Corrected his thinking? I could have responded to his false objections while his root issues resided elsewhere. How often am I quick to speak but slow to listen? I could have called him a self-indulgent artist (except that I had the same pretensions). I could have derided him as a libertine (but I had indulged in a similar degree of sexual experimentation with my Christian girlfriends). I could have simply condemned him to hell and been done with the discussion. He and I would have both been satisfied that we had a closed case. And yet we soldiered on into the messy discussion of religious wars. And as John recounted a long rambling tale of Muslims and Christians and Bosnia, I simply listened.

A Response

How would you respond? I wish that I had been there, beside him, in Bosnia. I have no delusions that a hug would have sufficed. A shoulder to cry on is hardly a salve. And yet to have to walk through it alone seems so cruel. That was the fate of the father who lost his sons. That was John's assignment as a reporter, the Jews' situation in the Shoah, the Tutsis' predicament in Rwanda, the refugees' crisis from Darfur. That was Jesus' plight in the garden of Gethsemane. We must reassure people that God enters into their suffering. Christ experienced abject rejection on the cross. God the Father knows what it is like to lose a son. Yet all too often, that suffering feels more like silence.

I gave John a response, captured on tape but not in the movie. In the face of atrocities committed in the name of God, I cited the tangible models of relief and comfort offered by Christians in Jesus' name. The only acceptable response to such abject suffering is compassion. We suffer with, we minister alongside, we offer a cup of cold water and hands to help rebuild.

John's tale of atrocities in Bosnia came on the heels of my trip to Sri Lanka. I had just returned from a region hit hard by the tsunami of December 26, 2004. I went as a documentarian, covering the work of an organization called Asian Access. Even two years after the devastation, the tsunami's wake was still strong. Entire villages were still in ruins. I stood on the slabs of decimated homes where families and businesses once prospered. I talked to survivors who climbed up trees to avoid the waves. I saw the painful memories of the tsunami turned into artwork by children who lost their parents. I shared John's questions of how God could have created a world of such devastating possibilities. To lose mothers, brothers, daughters, and uncles all in a single event seemed too cruel. I sensed how the survivors struggled to move on. Their lives were hollowed out along with their homes. My faith was challenged by grim realities.

Yet I was also stunned by the practical ways people were helping the Sri Lankans rebuild. Acts of kindness surrounded me. I met Sinhalese still waiting for the Sri Lankan government to provide the loans they promised. I talked to Tamils energized in their ongoing rebel war by politicians' apparent indifference. I met Muslims who wondered why their local mosque refused to help them rebuild. And I followed Christians from Kithu Sevana Church who walked among the survivors, distributing microloans to rebuild homes, businesses, and lives. They offered help to people regardless of the survivors' beliefs. This local Christian community embraced Muslim families snubbed by their mosque.

I sat down for the famed Ceylonese tea with these survivors. Through translators, I heard the horrible, haunting details. Their combination of rage, confusion, and despair came through in their body language. And yet their appreciation was also equally palpable. They praised their Christian neighbors who entered into their suffering, who picked up hammers, who brought relief. Sinhalese and Tamils who had fought for centuries were united within Kithu Sevana Church. The indigenous pastoral leadership of Adrian DeVisser cut through old assumptions about Christianity as a colonial religion. I heard firsthand how Sri Lankan followers of Jesus were healing a fractured land.

The potency of my examples provided no comfort to John. Gracious rebuilding on one corner of the planet could not counterbalance the atrocities enduring elsewhere. When someone pours his heart out, that is no time to provide answers. Questions of theodicy have dogged people of faith throughout the centuries. How can a good God preside over such a fallen and demented world? Why do bad things happen to good people? Why is a fervent faith sometimes rewarded with unrelenting pain?

The biblical book of Job demonstrates how not to respond to a person in pain. Job's "friends" poured judgment on him, asking him to find the personal sin that prompted calamity. They urged him to renounce his faith, to curse God, to abandon hope. They poured salt in his wounds with ill-timed words. A purple state of mind listens carefully, taking the painful experiences of others seriously. It sits with those who are suffering, engaging in solidarity. It disdains easy answers, dignifying valid questions of theodicy. We must truly hear others' cry before we can even begin to respond. A purple-minded ministry repairs broken-down walls, restores the temple of God in our community, and mends our tattered hearts. It answers haunting questions with tangible actions.

Hearing and Doing

Prove yourselves doers of the word,
and not merely hearers who delude themselves.

JAMES 1:22 NASB

I appreciate the gracious ministry of pastors. They serve their flocks faithfully, dispensing wisdom, distributing communion. They are genuine heroes. New Testament scholar Scot McKnight notes that "rarely has so much been expected of so few. Those in ministry are expected to be competent in church history, systematic theology, ethics, apologetics, contemporary social analysis, Christian education, missions, evangelism, homiletics, and psychology."[1] Some are leaders who inspire by word and example. Others are teachers who clearly explicate the word of God. Others are more pastoral, better with one-on-one counseling. In times of crisis, we simply need a pastor with open ears and a patient heart.

When I graduated from college, I went to Japan to serve as a missionary. I had big dreams of mass conversions and a national revival. Teaching English in Japan was initially exhilarating. The colorful environs of Tokyo energized me. The many new foods and friends expanded my horizons. I was also inspired when several of my students decided to follow Christ. Our nascent church began. But after a year in Japan, the newness wore off. Ramen failed to satisfy. The *tatami* mats in my apartment felt sterile and cold. I grew tired of being a minority. I longed to see friends and family, who sent me signs of life from back home. I watched a videotape of the Super Bowl. I listened to cassettes of Sunday sermons from America. But halfway into my missionary endeavor, I began to burn out. Teaching felt tedious. My students' interest in Jesus waned. My missionary intentions seemed ill conceived. Had God tricked me? Was I the recipient of a cruel joke? What was I doing on the wrong side of the planet? My malaise grew into anger. Frustration eventually devolved into depression. Who could lift me out of it? I prayed vigorously, but that failed to alter my outlook or my surroundings.

My supervisors noticed my mood change. They assured me such letdowns were normal: "Don't worry about it, things will even out. Give it time." But nothing blew my blues away until one quiet missionary got involved. Kurt was one of the more taciturn teachers in Japan. Nothing about him was flashy. He had three very active, very young kids. Perhaps they kept Kurt on a rather slow burn. He spoke slowly, in a low voice. Kurt and I had little in common besides our setting and our calling. Yet he resolved to nurse me back to mental health. We met weekly for Bible study, prayer, and a little conversation.

Our first meeting was a little awkward. I didn't have much to say. The Bible seemed silent to my suffering. I had almost nothing to pray. Kurt listened carefully. He offered little advice. He mostly stared at me, ready to hear whatever aches and pains I brought with me. The silence was awkward. Slowly, I opened up. My frustration spilled out. He didn't correct my perceptions; he simply allowed me to vent. Afterward, I felt released to teach, at least for one more day. The next week was equally bland. Kurt didn't carry a plan or an agenda into our meeting. He sat still. My mind raced with questions. Why wasn't God showing up? When would he hear my prayers? How could I escape such spiritual torment? Kurt offered a short passage of scripture. He didn't elaborate. He closed the gathering by praying for me, bringing my frustration before God.

The meetings continued. I had never experienced such a steadying presence in my life. Kurt really listened. I realized that almost nothing I could say would shock, threaten, or arouse him. He seemed to have heard it all before. Similar struggles, recurring complaints. He never tried to tell me how he handled such situations in the past. Our regular meetings told me I mattered. They made me feel like the most important person in his week. His unflappable response assured me that I had nothing to worry about. This too shall pass. He spoke so rarely that I listened carefully. His measured tones made me pay attention to scripture, to prayer, to my own heartbeat.

Slowly life moved from feeling like a joke to becoming bearable. I had a marker to measure things by. I had a meeting that required me to pay attention throughout the week. Rather than blurring together, each day in Japan started to matter. It included moments I needed to pay attention to. Maybe God didn't bring me to Japan to trick me after all. Kurt Thompson discipled me. He never called it that, and I probably wouldn't have agreed to that. But his quiet, steady attention changed my posture. He showed me how to walk with a sense of the sacred. Kurt modeled the necessity of *listening to* God rather than *talking at* God. He nursed me back to life. Kurt heard my angry cry, but he didn't offer easy answers. He came alongside me, over the long haul, demonstrating his faith through conscientious commitment. His still, almost silent witness spoke volumes about the patience of God.

The Community in Action

> The secret things belong to the Lord our God,
> but the things revealed belong to us.
>
> Deuteronomy 29:29

My time in Japan spawned a psychic crisis. But what about physical calamities: fires, floods, and sudden deaths? Everyone experiences crisis moments. Unexpected calamities derail our best-laid plans. Our sureties are undermined by surprising tragedies. We end up so disarmed that we cannot plan our response. We are simply in the current, swept up in grief much larger than ourselves, beyond our ability to handle. The tsunami in the Indian Ocean was followed by the ravages of Hurricane Katrina. How do we even begin to process such devastation? My sister's death arrived in the wake of Hurricane Hugo. It devastated the Southeast. Hurricane Hugo hit land off Charleston, South Carolina, roared through Charlotte, North Carolina, and did damage all the way up to Charleston, West Virginia. As a city lined with trees, Charlotte was brought to a halt. Power lines went down. Streets were blocked. People were forced to cut and carve their way to grocery stores for supplies. The more heavily wooded an area, the more extensive the damage.

My sister died early on a Sunday morning. She was en route to a hospital to work a weekend shift. The news arrived before church. So at St. Stephen's United Methodist Church, where my parents had attended, the pastor shared the shocking news with the congregation. Everyone knew Dixie; they had watched her grow up. They shared our pain and sprang into action. As soon as the Sunday service ended, the women of St. Stephen arrived with buckets and brushes. They were determined to clean our house, upstairs and downstairs, in preparation for the wake. The ladies organized my mother's kitchen, making room for countless complimentary meals that followed. Our grieving relatives would arrive to a spotless house stocked with home-cooked food.

The men of St. Stephen descended on our yard. Like theirs, it was littered with fallen trees, covered with branches broken by Hurricane Hugo. The men poured out their grief with chain saws and axes. They stacked up massive piles of logs. They hacked through pine trees to find the grass growing underneath. They pushed mowers across our lawn. They bagged fallen leaves. They hauled all the debris away, making way for the wake to follow. They arrived unannounced. They departed without a thank-you. They did all this despite the fact that my father hadn't even entered the church in two or three years. These men had called, inviting and cajoling him to come to countless gatherings. My father turned his back on their pancake breakfasts, their men's retreats, and their morning Bible studies. And yet they still came, still cut, still served. I have never seen my father so humbled. The men of St. Stephen displayed such tangible love in a time of crisis.

These tangible acts of service were the first wave of an onslaught of kindness. Distant relatives drove in for the funeral. Friends called from all across the country. My sister's classmates from high school and college filed into the funeral home to pause before Dixie's casket. My mother seemed most moved by the appearance of Dixie's oldest friends. She wept at the sight of girls who played with Dixie's dolls. Memories of tea parties and pigtails hurt. Such innocence lost forever. The wake took two evenings. The lines of mourners stretched across four or five hours. How beautiful (and challenging) to receive so many condolences. We heard "I'm sorry for your loss" over and over. We were told "We're praying for you." We were convinced that "Dixie was loved," "She was special," and "We won't forget her."

Yet after so long on my feet, seeing so many people and memories pass by, I was overwhelmed. I was ready to collapse. Grief and fatigue collided at the three-hour mark. I felt ready to fall over. I could no longer be gracious. I didn't want another hug. I couldn't shake another hand. I was inconsolable.

Kimsey Koster was next in line. We had played football together in high school. He was a running back; I was one of his blockers. Kimsey hardly knew Dixie. She served as an equipment manager for the baseball team when he was starring in the outfield. She cheered for him from the dugout. He was always a handsome guy with a bevy of admirers. We weren't especially close friends. We hadn't talked too much about faith. I knew he was a committed Christian who tried to maintain a different standard of behavior. At the moment when I was about to fall, Kimsey propped me up. He leaned in close. He didn't offer any condolences. I couldn't accept another solemn sorry. Instead, Kimsey whispered in my ear. He was praying for me: *Strengthen Craig,*

*Father. Hold him up. Give him the grace to get through this. Come, Holy
Spirit, come. Send your comforting presence to Craig and his family, even
now.*

Kimsey wasn't just praying for me. He was praying *into* me. Kimsey
offered no speech. No wisdom. Just a direct invocation, "Come, Holy
Spirit, come." His prayers weren't rooted in the past. They weren't
predicated on a painful future. Kimsey invited God to break through
the present, to meet me in my moment of greatest need.

It worked. The Spirit swooped in. I felt strangely comforted, oddly
renewed. God didn't take away my pain or resurrect my sister. But the
Spirit showed up when I needed something, anything, to continue.
Kimsey moved on. A long line of mourners followed. I received a
thousand words of comfort and kindness. But one person stands out
from that blessed procession. While many told me they'd been praying
and many promised to be praying, only Kimsey *was* praying with his
hands on my head and his voice in my ear. I heard and experienced
what God was doing through Kimsey.

The galvanizing encounter with tragedy equipped me to enter into
others' suffering. I say very little at funerals. I stand beside those who
are suffering. I sit on their couch. I am simply there. The hard work
of grieving doesn't start until after the funeral. Once the relatives have
gone, after the gracious meals have been eaten, a house becomes eerily
quiet. In those long seasons, a mourner needs an encouraging word,
a shoulder to cry on. After the darkness has settled in, we desperately
need a glimpse of light. I try to remember death dates, to make a call
or send a note a year after significant loss. Those left behind remember
where they were, what they were doing a year before. They recollect
the sights, sounds, and smells of hospitals, funeral homes, and cemeteries.

Jesus implored us to remember his death. At the Last Supper, he
handed out bread and wine, the most elemental parts of any good
meal. He gave us tangible ways to commemorate his crucifixion every
time we eat, every time we drink. Our friends and loved ones deserve
similar treatment. Each life matters. When we visit a grave, we bring

a bouquet of flowers. We offer small signs that we remember. Ministry occurs amid such emotional minefields. Our absence when people desperately need a friend can undermine relationships. Our presence in times of crisis will often bind us to others for life.

I've been there for a friend who lost his father in a rafting accident. The family had no preparation time for such tragedy. Losing their dad amid an otherwise happy family vacation left a deep sense of shock. My friend simply wanted others around throughout the funeral process. I basically moved into his home, staying in the basement, sitting with him late into the dark nights. We rarely talk about what happened that week, but it cemented our friendship. Grief bonded us like brothers. I remember the triumphant song "How Great Thou Art" from the funeral. It seemed odd to me at the time. How can we call God great amid such pain? Yet the chorus became a desperate cry. Job had dared to proclaim, "Though he slay me, yet will I hope in him" (Job 13:15), and so we sang a song of affirmation at a moment of despair. Peter had asked Jesus, "To whom shall we go? You have the words of life" (John 6:68). So either as a statement of faith or simply as our only good option, we celebrated God's greatness.

My wife and I rallied around two people whose spouses left them. The jilted man and woman turned to each other for consolation. They ended up pregnant during the dual divorce proceedings. Not a good situation, and not many places they could turn. As Christians, they were determined to have the child. But they hardly felt like rushing into marriage to legitimize their baby. To even explain their story took so much work. What church setting could deal with the layers of mess residing behind their pregnancy? Yet the baby shouldn't be penalized for a series of the adults' mistakes. Caroline and I hosted a small baby shower. Life must be celebrated and embraced regardless of circumstances.

As a professor at a Christian college, I dealt with students still in transition toward adulthood. The faculty was striving to present them with an integrated Christian education, but we also wrestled with the hormones that raged within their dormitories. Many dealt with their libidos by getting married right out of college. They couldn't imagine postponing their sexual drive for another season. One of our more talented students evidently financed a fair amount of his education as a drug dealer. By his senior year, his off-campus apartment was the locus of all kinds of activities forbidden by the college code of conduct. None of this surfaced until his girlfriend got pregnant. Both students were outspoken pro-life advocates. They just never planned to put their convictions into such premature practice. For the sake of their unborn child, they ceased their drug use. They initially planned to get married. But as their parents got involved and fingers started pointing, the expectant parents were separated. Charges of sexual harassment and restraining orders followed. Passion turned to rage. The female student dropped out of school. The university could not allow our outstanding senior to graduate.

What would Jesus do? He would somehow manage to stand in solidarity with all sides. He certainly wouldn't bail on these confused kids in their hour of need. I offered myself as a sounding board. As the father went to court, he needed emotional support. He lost all his appeals. The baby would be born without him. The father has seen his child only once. Yet he remains quite proud of his daughter, showing off her photo. His talents have secured him a prime job. The couple could have married and raised their daughter together. It is hard to know where God was amid such a confusing process. But Jesus undoubtedly walked with them every painful, awkward step of the way.

I don't seek out such challenging situations. Ministers do not look forward to helping us process death, divorce, or disease. Yet that is our calling, to walk through the mud, the mire, and the messiest seasons of life. I admire the police, firefighters, and emergency medical technicians who offer a first response to crisis. I appreciate the doctors and nurses who serve on cancer wards. Unfortunately, we need judges and lawyers and mediators to settle our disputes. Social workers intervene for those who have no advocates. The vast majority of civil servants carry out their callings with dignity and respect.

I often wonder how they carry on amid overwhelming odds. Where do people find strength to share, to care, to give?

Silence

Silence of our eyes.
Silence of our ears.
Silence of our mouths.
Silence of our minds.
…in the silence of the heart,
God will speak.

MOTHER TERESA[2]

John Marks dared to go to church with me. On his last day living in New York City, John agreed to attend a house of worship. It was his first trip inside a Protestant church since he moved to the Big Apple. It was also the anniversary of September 11. Even Billy Graham would probably come up short in a sermon on that terrible topic. I had no illusions that John Marks would hear the word that would heal his rift with God. The praise songs struck him as silly. He didn't go with the flow as we raised our arms in worship. We cannot expect nonbelievers to make sense of a Sunday service. (We hardly know where our own traditions have come from.) Yet God showed up for me that Sunday morning. As we sang "How Great Thou Art," I burst into tears. It was the same chorus we'd sung at my sister's funeral. To the cynic, such praise to God may sound like folly. In the face of September 11, how can we shout, "My God, how great thou art"? It is an odd answer to a legitimate question. Such affirmations can only emerge from silent contemplation.

After the service, we headed toward Ground Zero. As we approached the site, we heard two disparate sounds. Police sirens wailed in the background. Were they a tribute to fallen firefighters and policemen? Or were they an eerie reminder that the work is never done? Not even on a memorial day do battles cease—in our homes, in our market-places, in our souls. The contrasting sound at Ground Zero was a bell, clanging at regular intervals. It shook the office buildings, bounding off the square. Firemen struck the bell. Perhaps one ring for every life lost. The call to action had been replaced by a call to remember. John and I stood quietly, taking it all in.

The sheer size of the hole left in the absence of the World Trade Center is staggering. To see so much unfilled space in New York City is disconcerting. The support beam that emerged from the wreckage formed a haunting echo of the cross. Was God within that fiery inferno on September 11? Surely everyone staring at the site still wanted to know. John and I engaged a few people in conversation. A group of Christian firefighters had set up a tent to honor the deceased. Most people stared at the fence in solemn silence. We studied the photos, flowers, and mementos attached to the chain links. Words are so utterly insufficient to summarize the experience. The combination of grief, disbelief, and horror belies simple interpretations. As we contemplate our conflicted thoughts about the tragedy, it is easy to overlook the victims' feelings.

Architects wrestled with a way to honor the dead. The debates over a design were fierce. Architects Michael Arad and Peter Walker created a design that was selected out of more than 5200 entries from 63 nations. Families of the victims protested the plan to list the names of the victims randomly across the site. The deceased will now be grouped according to their companies and colleagues.[3] Pastors will continue to struggle with September 11 sermons. It is tough to turn tragedy into inspiration.[4]

A few filmmakers have dared to posit some artistic statements. M. Night Shyamalan commenced the shooting of *Signs* (2002) as United flight 93 went down in a Pennsylvania field. The questions of theodicy emanating from his alien invasion story proved eerily prescient. Spike Lee slipped the sorting through the wreckage into the background of *The 25th Hour* (2002). *World Trade Center* (2006) reduced the troubling events to the fight for survival of two brave public servants. It puts the audience under the rubble, into the hearts and minds of the victims. Oliver Stone was a surprising choice as director, especially since the film concludes with a stirring affirmation of faith. God can speak through anyone at any time. Perhaps the most haunting film about 9/11 was the riveting recreation *United 93* (2006). Director Paul Greengrass adopts a documentary-style approach to the day's traumatic sequence. Both terrorists and terrorized are shown praying. The passengers rally to undercut the hijacking, but nobody wins the fight. *United 93* is a harrowing tribute to courage under fire.

The most humbling response to September 11 arrived in one of the smallest movies, *Land of Plenty* (2004). German filmmaker Wim Wenders juxtaposes a paranoid Vietnam veteran named Paul with an idealistic young missionary named Lana. They are separated by politics but bound together as family. The movie focuses on skid row in Los Angeles. It deals with ongoing issues of homelessness, of conflict in the Middle East, of war veterans we've ignored. The death of a Pakistani man draws Lana and Paul together. *Land of Plenty* becomes a road movie, concluding at Ground Zero. The characters stand on that fence in silence. They listen for the voices of the departed. *Land of Plenty* urges us to pause, reflect, and pray. It is a slow, contemplative film—on purpose. As Leonard Cohen sings of the promise of America, Lana closes her eyes. "Let's just be quiet and try to listen."

Art is an essential way to process overwhelming grief. The biblical book of Lamentations arose from the void left by the fall of Jerusalem. With their beloved city in ruins, the Israeli exiles poured their grief into poetry. Lamentations begins with the haunting question, how? "How deserted lies the city once so full of people. How like a widow is she who once was great among the nations!" (Lamentations 1:1-2). Visions of the hollowed-out World Trade Center expand to include Baghdad left in ruins. The ninth ward in post-Katrina New Orleans sits in disrepair. Coastlines in Sri Lanka, Thailand, and Indonesia still reel from the 2004 tsunami. The ancient Hebrew poet searches for words to describe the devastation, "Your wound is as deep as the sea. Who can heal you?" (Lamentations 2:13). It is hard to recognize through the ruins: "Is this the city that was called the perfection of beauty, the joy of the whole earth?" (Lamentations 2:15). Words cannot capture the magnitude of the loss. Yet the poet presses on, forging a fragile hope. Lamentations is rarely preached or read, but one passage stands out: "Because of the LORD's great love we are not consumed, for his compassion never fail. They are new every morning; great is your faithfulness" (Lamentations 3:22-23). We may not be able to make such an assertion. Not yet.

It takes time to process our grief. In the meantime, Lamentations 3:26 reminds us that "it is good to wait quietly for the salvation of the LORD." It is so easy to rush to judgment, to point fingers, to assign blame. Lamentations dares us to sit with our grief. Mourners are instructed, "Let him sit alone in silence, for the LORD has laid it on him. Let him bury his face in the dust—there may yet be hope" (Lamentations 3:28-29). Old Testament scholar Kathleen O'Connor turned to Lamentations as a highly appropriate post-9/11 meditation. She appreciates the holy silence emanating from the poetry. O'Connor writes, "Any words from God would endanger human voices. They would undercut anger and despair, foreshorten protest, and give the audience only a passing glimpse of the real terror of their condition. Divine speaking would trump all speech...The missing voice of God leaves suffering exposed."[5] It is out of respect and concern that God remains silent. O'Connor suggests, "God's silence in Lamentations leaves wounds festering, open to the air and possibly to healing. The benefit of exposed wounds is that they become visible and unavoidable. Left exposed, they require us to see, acknowledge, and attend to them, and then perhaps there can be energy to attend to the wounds of the world."[6] We have a rare opportunity to stand in solidarity with the least of these. Sheltered and comforted Americans have a chance to understand what it feels like to wait and wonder. We can develop ears full of compassion, eyes willing to witness suffering. As we address our own wounds, we can become wounded healers, empathetic to others' plight. When will we learn to sit with the silence of God?

Purple Reign

Conclusion

Christians in America have been engaged in a largely blood-less culture war. The victims are not cited in crime statistics, but the wounds become visible when we engage in conversation. Old grudges surface. People vent about a parochial school, a crazy aunt, the faith they left behind. I've listened to hours of invective about televangelists, pedophile priests, and the religious right. I have been tempted to abandon faith, to consign Christianity to an ash heap of its own making. Yet as these pages have testified, I've held on to an elusive hope. Jesus may have been dragged through all manner of mud, but his boundless love and compassion endures.

We're living in a dangerous time, laden with possibilities. Canadian singer and activist Bruce Cockburn suggests, "We kick out the darkness until it bleeds daylight." I am regularly grieved by the wars that continue to dominate our headlines. Yet I am also energized by the faith I see in the next generation of students. Despite the ugliness they've witnessed, they press on, determined to make a difference. The dismal tide may be rising, but they resist it with an abundance of grace and mercy. A purple state of mind abandons the politics of division for the crying need for justice. It longs to replace rancor with healing. This book is an effort to spur us on to love and good deeds (Hebrews 10:24).

> **John:** Let me ask you, what does the future hold for a Christian like you in a time like this? It does not seem to me like your version of Christianity is becoming this country's most widely accepted version of Christianity. Sometimes I look at you and I hear an endangered species. At other times I sort of hope, maybe you are the future. But my gut is, if you are the future, it is after quite a struggle. Because the forces of opposition toward the kind of Christianity you espouse are legion.
>
> **Craig:** We embarked upon this conversation because I've got a little shred of hope that things can change. If other people are digging a hole, then I guess I've got to do my part to help us dig out of that.
>
> **John:** Does it make you angry?
>
> **Craig:** It can't be about arguing. Even if you win the argument, you lose. Arguing about God, I don't see it helping anybody. I don't see it ever helping anybody.

Are you tired of fighting? Always having to explain, to defend, and to articulate what and why you believe can be exhausting. I see signs of fatigue on Facebook. Asked to define their political views, the next generation often checks "Other." The even more disengaged check "Apathetic." Invited to name their religious convictions, people will leave it at "Yes." They don't want to start an argument or to identify with that confusing word *Christian.* We may call ourselves Jesus followers, disciples of Christ, or even *Christianish.* I've seen religious views identified as "Love God," "Relationship, not religion," and "Difficult to see with all that glory around." We are clearly searching for new words, new images, and new metaphors to describe our deepest convictions.

The word *Christian* began as an epithet. We were identified as "little Christs." The name stuck. But after two centuries, the word has become tattered and frayed. It has come to be associated with judgment, hypocrisy, and intolerance. Brian McLaren fueled our current redefinition by talking about *A New Kind of Christian*.[1] The emergent movement has struggled to define a new Christian, mostly starting with "not that." The subtitle of Brian McLaren's *A Generous Orthodoxy* includes 22 qualities of the word *Christian*.[2] Clearly, *Christian* no longer serves as an effective identifier. Those who hoped to distance themselves from the religious right adopted the moniker *red-letter Christian*.[3] But it took too much effort to explain that Jesus' words were often highlighted in red-letter editions of the Bible. How sad that we have felt the need to suggest that a red-letter Christian does what Jesus said.

I have no delusions that we will soon be calling ourselves purple Christians, but the polarizing labels of red state and blue state are nearly exhausted. I am suggesting we build on the things we agree about rather than the differences that divide us. The missional church starts with conversation rather than conclusions.[4] It starts by putting faith into practice on a local level. While I appreciate the incarnational theology behind the movement, I cannot foresee a new word like *missional* passing into common parlance. We are searching for a language to describe the sea change occurring in faith and culture.

Perhaps our problem is that we have focused too much upon labeling ourselves. Instead of practicing our faith, we've been struggling to redefine it. Branding faith is a tricky business.[5] Perhaps we should leave it to our detractors to decide. They did a great job of naming us in the New Testament. So far, we've been identified as "unChristian."[6] How do we change that valid, earned perception? How do we move forward in our Christian faith? We must slow down long enough to relish God's beauty, to appreciate the wonders of the world, to come alongside those pondering the mysteries of life. A purple state of mind takes the long view. It adopts a sacramental approach to life in community. It is not enamored by political positions, by Hollywood takeovers, by any traditional power moves. It follows Jesus to the humbling and even humiliating cross. It is hopeful that despite the recent ugliness, God's beauty, Christ's grace, and the Spirit's power will prevail. A purple state of mind pledges allegiance first and foremost to Jesus, the reigning king, robed in purple majesty.

This book has been an effort to explain what we're for rather than against. After decades of either/or division, we have adopted a both/and approach to life. The breadth of sources and stories in these pages may have been daunting at times. To clarify, I offer this tidy summation. A purple state of mind...

1. exercises freedom responsibly

2. lives in the grace of God (while still pursuing goodness)

3. connects ancient creeds to tangible deeds

4. practices a visual faith rooted in the word of God

5. acknowledges depression and doubt but also embraces laughter

6. pours out love even when it disappoints us

7. seeks God's revelation in scripture and in everyday life

8. cultivates the garden (and leaves judgment to God)

9. defends orphans and widows

10. suffers with others

To these ten points, this conclusion will add two more. A purple state of mind...

11. celebrates beauty and wonder

12. follows and worships Jesus

We depend on the Spirit to accomplish these goals. We need wisdom, discernment, patience, courage, and energy to go the distance. Thankfully, the fruit of the Spirit is always in season.

Craig: Once a year. One night. And we're here tonight, in this moment. This is magic. This is miraculous. John, are you feeling it?

John: After all the arguments you have made to me, none of which are convincing in the least, that flower right there is the closest thing to an argument that there is for your view of the world. Right there.

My tearful testimonies didn't do it. My apologies never sufficed. No amount of patient bridge-building proved convincing. Even my Ph.D. in theology and culture fell short. After all the arguing, all the fussing, all the feuding, all the fuming, it came down to a flower. John Marks was silenced by an extraordinary houseplant.

On our final night in New York City, John and I had just finished a celebratory meal. With the shooting wrapped up, we felt free to unwind. Even the camera crew unplugged. On the walk back toward John's brownstone in Brooklyn, he offered one final reflection. He was explaining why he was leaving the city. It exhausted him. Just getting his son to school took so much work. The commuting into the city was wearing on his marriage. He longed for a simpler life in the country. As we walked down the block, a voice rang out, "You've got to see this!" Two women beckoned us from their basement apartment. They had something so profound that they longed to share it. We stopped, intrigued. They wondered if we had a camera. I had a compact digital camera in my bag. What did they want to take a picture of? They urged us to take a look.

The night-blooming cereus is classified as a desert plant. The technical name is *epiphyllum oxypetalum,* which might as well mean "playing possum." Most of the year, it is rather unexceptional and unnoticed. On only one midsummer night, it offers a fragrance and splendor that is staggering. This queen of the night is elusive. It sneaks up on its unsuspecting owners. One can easily miss it altogether. It requires patient observation. But what an extravagant reward it offers to those with eyes to see (and a nose to smell!). The flower's Brooklyn owners associated it with Sirius, the star. It served as quite a beacon to us. Whatever the derivation, the night-blooming cereus speaks volumes about the wonder of God, the splendor of creation.

John took the first whiff. He bent over, breathed in deeply, and emerged awed and refreshed. As I zeroed in on the flower, I noticed the petals' luminescence. The pistil and stamen were iridescent, a sparkly gold. What a luscious vision. Most of all, I was struck by the timing of the moment. As a screenwriter, I know how to construct dramatic peaks. Everything builds to a turning point, an axis upon which all the characters pivot. Here, in a completely unscripted, yearlong documentary, was the ultimate climax. Who else could coordinate such a perfect ending but the Original Screenwriter, the Author of our Faith, the Mighty and Mysterious One? I turned to John, glowing and gloating. John was brave enough, honest enough, man enough to admit what I was thinking: "If anyone wanted proof for the existence of God, we just stumbled across it in Brooklyn." John once told me he worshipped the earth. He honored everything that provided him with existence. This evening, he received a message from the earth. But it had nothing to do with survival. It was the most extravagant, disposable display of beauty imaginable. The night-blooming cereus is a useless beauty, a pure gift.

During the Enlightenment, we dissected plants, animals, and the natural world. We broke things down to an elemental, even subatomic level. We cracked the code for DNA. We tackled the human genome. We cloned sheep. In our efforts to categorize and label the natural world, we also drained it of much of its mystery. In an either/or universe, science and religion were placed in separate spheres. Everything was subjected to the burden of proof. Now our arguments for and against God have reached a dead end. Having desacralized the pagan world, we now need to resacralize God's creation. We must recover beauty, mystery, and wonder.

Thankfully, others have gone before us. Mother Teresa understood the relationship between beauty and wonder, nature and God. She wrote, "We need to find God, and he cannot be found in noise and restlessness. God is the friend of silence. See how nature—trees, flowers, grass—grows in silence; see the stars, the moon and the sun, how they move in silence…We need silence to be able to touch souls."

Hans Urs von Balthasar risked the rejection of his church and his peers to forge a new theological method. In his magisterial work *The Glory of the Lord,* Balthasar suggests that our theology should begin where God begins, with creation. Life starts with beauty. God's beautiful actions lead to beautiful ethics, to right and wrong. Beautiful doctrine flows out of creation rather than sprouting *ex nihilo.* Balthasar considers the incarnation to be the most beautiful sight in history. He is obsessed with the mystery of Christ. The cross transformed the most horrific sight into the most redemptive moment. It became our beautiful symbol of salvation. Christ provided us with the Eucharist, the most beautiful ceremony.

Balthasar understood the theatrical and dramatic actions of Jesus. He thought of the gospel as "Theo-drama."[7] God breaks into history, pulling back the curtain to reveal Jesus. God not only writes the play but also casts himself in the lead role—an epic tragedy that ends in a comedic surprise. The fallen hero rises! Kevin Vanhoozer extends the implications of Balthasar's theology.[8] God calls us to act, to play the part. As the director, he invites us to rehearse. After memorizing and internalizing our lines, we are ready to perform. The drama of doctrine provides a script. We are called to make our lives beautiful, to make our liturgy poetic.

Whom do we worship? The Most Beautiful One, garbed in splendor. We don't worship power. We don't worship culture. We don't worship results. We don't worship approval. We don't worship political expediency. A purple state of mind bows before a king robed in purple. We have our hearts set on a true purple reign. A purple state of mind offers allegiance to our one and only king and his kingdom. But our allegiance must be displayed with Christlike compassion and tolerance toward those beyond the gates. Let every heart prepare him room (while heaven and nature sing a glorious prelude).

From ancient Roman times to medieval Europe, purple was the color of kings, reserved for regal apparel. Violet or purple was a cherished and expensive color in the ancient world. During Jesus' time, the dye used to make the color was painstakingly acquired by massaging the neck of a Mediterranean shellfish that secreted a special fluid. It was therefore afforded only by the rich and worn most exclusively by the royalty.

Jesus, the king of the Jews, wore a purple robe only once. As soldiers mocked and tormented him, they placed on him a purple garment in order to ridicule him and belittle the claim that he was a monarch. How ironic that the most legitimate king was mocked as a pretender. Our holiest season in the church calendar, Easter, is robed in purple. During the penitential season of Lent, purple colors remind us of the contempt and scorn Jesus endured and the subsequent sacrifice he made for our salvation. Purple in a worship context reminds us to lead a life of humble repentance. Jesus may have been born under blue (the season of advent), but his death unfolded in a sea of red. A purple reign resulted from the mixing of red and blue, Jesus' life, death, and resurrection.

What colors should we be flying? Where does our loyalty reside? I love my country. I am grateful for the freedom it offers. We have such a wealth of educational opportunities. We have so many possibilities for jobs and careers. The opportunity for riches is unparalleled in human history. Are resources distributed equally? Absolutely not! Do we still have improvements to make in education, health care, and employment? Definitely. But I am proud to be an American.

I also love other countries. I am fascinated by the heritage of Europe. I am impressed by Japanese design. I am humbled by the hospitality of Thailand, Sri Lanka, and Ecuador. I am intrigued by the artistry in Barcelona. Chile's rugged peaks in Torres del Paine National Park awe me. I still need to see Africa and the Middle East. My heart breaks for people besieged by poverty, famine, and war. I am a global citizen. We all are, whether we realize it or not.[9] What kind of citizenship does Jesus ask for and deserve? We're called to a purple state of mind, an allegiance to our one and only king and his kingdom.

Unfortunately, his flag has been dragged through the mud. It has been yoked to some unholy alliances. We have claimed to serve King Jesus, yet we have betrayed him by our actions. It is time to restore the beauty to his kingdom. It will not arrive with more bluster. To clean up the mess will take a while. We must fill plenty of holes and patch up all manner of structural damage. We must scrub vigorously, submitting ourselves for close inspection. We must attend to the garden. We will never accomplish the task alone. Some will toil in silence. Others will be tapped for high-profile service. We must take on the restoration as a long-term project. We may never reap the benefits personally. But for our children, we start painting now. Guess what color we use?

Notes

Introduction—Beyond Red and Blue

1. For a more complete take on post-9/11 faith, see Scott Bader-Saye, *Following Jesus in a Culture of Fear* (Grand Rapids, MI: Baker Books, 2006).

2. Garry Wills, *Head and Heart: American Christianities* (New York: Penguin Press, 2007).

3. "Rep. Tom DeLay Delivers His Farewell Address," Congressional Quarterly, June 8, 2006. Available online at www.washingtonpost.com/wp-dyn/content/article/2006/06/08/AR2006060801376.html.

4. Cal Thomas and Bob Beckel, *Common Ground: How to Stop the Partisan War That Is Destroying America* (New York: William Morrow, 2007).

5. John W. Whitehead, "Crazy for God: An Interview with Frank Schaeffer." Available online at www.rutherford.org/Oldspeak/Articles/Interviews/oldspeak-frankschaeffer.html.

6. Charles Taylor, *A Secular Age* (Cambridge, MA: Harvard University Press, 2007).

7. Dan Kimball, *They Like Jesus but Not the Church* (Grand Rapids, MI: Zondervan, 2007), 236.

8. Gregory A. Boyd, *The Myth of a Christian America* (Grand Rapids, MI: Zondervan, 2006).

9. David Kinnaman and Gabe Lyons, *unChristian* (Grand Rapids, MI: Baker Books, 2007), 26.

10. For a complete account of John's experience at *60 Minutes* and his book-length answer to the question, see John Marks, *Reasons to Believe: One Man's Journey Among the Evangelicals and the Faith He Left Behind* (New York: Ecco Press, 2008).

11. Ray Anderson, *The Soul of Ministry: Forming Leaders for God's People* (Louisville, KY: Westminster John Knox Press, 1997), 179.

12. I am indebted to the insights of Fr. Richard Rohr. A good starting place for his profound thoughts is *Radical Grace: Daily Meditations by Richard Rohr* (Cincinnati: St. Anthony Messenger Press, 1995).

Chapter 1—Freedom and Responsibility

1. The most comprehensive introduction is James Davison Hunter's *Culture Wars: The Struggle to Define America* (New York: Basic Books, 1991).

2. Check out the insights of Morris P. Fiorina with Samuel J. Abrams and Jeremy C. Pope, *Culture War? The Myth of a Polarized America* (New York: Longman, 2005).

3. Ronald Brownstein, *The Second Civil War: How Extreme Partisanship Has Paralyzed Washington and Polarized America* (New York: The Penguin Press, 2007).

4. Probably the most oft-cited study is Robert Putnam, *Bowling Alone: The Collapse and Revival of American Community* (New York: Simon & Schuster, 1995).

5. See Tom Sine, *Cease Fire: Searching for Sanity in America's Culture Wars* (Grand Rapids, MI: Eerdmans, 1996). The next generation has extended the call, especially in Eric Bumpus and Tim Moranville, *Cease Fire, the War Is Over!* (Fairfax, VA: Xulon Press, 2005).

6. Neil Howe and William Strauss, *Millennials Rising: the Next Great Generation* (New York: Vintage Books, 2000), 46.

Chapter 2—Grace and Goodness

1. Neil Howe and William Strauss, *Millennials Rising: The Next Great Generation* (New York: Vintage Books, 2000), 214.

2. For a sample of new organizations and projects started by young activist filmmakers, visit www.invisiblechildren.com, www.thesoldproject.org, and www.burningheartproductions.com/thefairtrade/.

3. To understand why adults consistently prefer to use alarmist language about teen behavior, see Mike A. Males, *Framing Youth: Ten Myths About the Next Generation* (Monroe, ME: Common Courage Press, 1998).

4. For a thorough report on the layers within which adolescent culture operates, check out Chap Clark, *Hurt: Inside the World of Today's Teenagers* (Grand Rapids, MI: Baker Books, 2004).

5. See J. Keith Miller, *Sin: Overcoming the Ultimate Deadly Addiction* (New York: Harper Collins, 1987).

6. See Cornelius Plantinga, *Not the Way It's Supposed to Be: A Breviary of Sin* (Grand Rapids, MI: Eerdmans, 1995).

7. Lorraine Ali and Julie Scelfo, "Choosing Virginity," *Newsweek,* December 9, 2002, 61-66.

8. Walter Kirn, "Saving It for Jesus," *Gentleman's Quarterly,* April 2006.

9. Jake Tapper, *Nightline,* New York: ABC News, May 26, 2006.

10. Samantha Shapiro, "All God's Children," *The New York Times Magazine,* September 5, 2004.

11. Philip Yancey, *What's So Amazing About Grace* (Grand Rapids, MI: Zondervan, 1997), 14.

12. Cited in Yancey, *What's So Amazing About Grace,* 15.

Chapter 3—Creeds and Deeds

1. Josh McDowell, *Evidence that Demands a Verdict* (Nashville: Thomas Nelson, 1992).

2. Lee Strobel's popular *The Case for Christ* (1998) and *The Case for a Creator* (2005) represented the apogee of the modern apologetics movement. It will be interesting to see what forms postmodern apologetics takes.

3. See Crystal Downing, *How Postmodernism Serves My Faith* (Downers Grove, IL: InterVarsity Press, 2006).

4. Nancey Murphy, *Bodies and Souls, or Spirited Bodies?* (Cambridge: Cambridge University Press, 2006).

5. Gerardus van der Leeuw, et al., *Sacred and Profane Beauty* (New York: Holt, Rinehart, and Winston, 1963), 55.

6. Van der Leeuw, *Sacred and Profane Beauty,* 54.

7. Van der Leeuw, *Sacred and Profane Beauty,* 55.

8. Jim Forest, *Praying with Icons* (Maryknoll, NY: Orbis Books, 2006), 40.

9. Forest, *Praying with Icons,* 40.

10. See Marvin R. Wilson, *Our Father Abraham: Jewish Roots of the Christian Faith* (Grand Rapids, MI: Eerdmans, 1989).

11. See Hans Urs von Balthasar, *Theo-Drama: Theological Dramatic Theory,* vol. 1, *Prolegomena,* (San Francisco: Ignatius Press, 1988).

12. Kevin J. Vanhoozer, *The Drama of Doctrine* (Louisville, KY: Westminster John Knox Press, 2005), 6-7.

13. Ramsey MacMullen, *Christianizing the Roman Empire* (New Haven, CT: Yale University Press, 1984), 28.

14. Cited in MacMullen, *Christianizing the Roman Empire,* 29.

15. Cited in MacMullen, *Christianizing the Roman Empire,* 54.

16. Vanhoozer, *The Drama of Doctrine,* 13.

17. Vanhoozer, *The Drama of Doctrine,* 21.

18. David Kinnaman and Gabe Lyons, *unChristian* (Grand Rapids, MI: Baker Books, 2007).

19. Brian McLaren, *Everything Must Change* (Nashville: Thomas Nelson, 2007).

20. Mother Teresa, *In My Own Words,* ed. Jose Luis Gonzalez-Balado (New York: Random House, 1997), 21.

Chapter 4—Word and Image

1. Mitchell Stevens, *The Rise of the Image, the Fall of the Word* (New York: Oxford University Press, 1998).

2. See Frederick Hartt, *Art: A History of Painting, Sculpture, Architecture,* vol. 1 (New York: Harry N. Abrams, 1976), 54-56.

3. Gerardus van der Leeuw, *Sacred and Profane Beauty* (New York: Holt, Rinehart, and Winston, 1963), 11.

4. Van der Leeuw, *Sacred and Profane Beauty,* 77.

5. Van der Leeuw, *Sacred and Profane Beauty,* 90.

6. Robert Hughes, *The Shock of the New* (New York: Alfred A. Knopf, 1991).

7. Eusebius, *The History of the Church,* chapter 7, section 18.

8. See Jim Forest, *Praying with Icons* (Maryknoll, NY: Orbis Books, 2006), 5.

9. St. John of Damascus, *Three Treatises on the Divine Images,* tr. David Anderson (Crestwood, NY: St. Vladimir's Seminary Press, 1980).

10. Van der Leeuw, *Sacred and Profane Beauty,* 185.

11. Leonid Ouspensky, "The Meaning and Language of Icons," in Leonid Ouspensky and Vladimir Lossky, *The Meaning of Icons* (Crestwood, NY: St. Vladimir's Seminary Press, 1982), 48-49.

12. Shane Claiborne, *The Irresistible Revolution: Living as an Ordinary Radical* (Grand Rapids, MI: Zondervan, 2006).

13. See William Dyrness, *Visual Faith: Art, Theology and Worship in Dialogue* (Grand Rapids, MI: Baker Academic, 2001).

14. Jane Daggett Dillenberger, *The Religious Art of Andy Warhol* (New York: Continuum, 1998).

15. Richard Blake, *Afterimage: The Indelible Catholic Imagination of Six American Filmmakers* (Chicago: Loyola University Press, 2000).

16. Andrew Greeley, *The Catholic Imagination* (Berkeley, CA: University of California Press, 2000).

17. Van der Leeuw, *Sacred and Profane Beauty,* 180.

18. I am indebted to my friend Eric Kuiper for his insightful contributions to this discussion.

19. Jürgen Moltmann discusses such protest theology in *Experiences in Theology,* tr. Margaret Kohl (Minneapolis, MN: Fortress Press, 2000).

20. Walter Brueggemann, *The Prophetic Imagination* (Minneapolis, MN: Fortress, 2001).

21. Examples of Lunn Aldrich's smart and provacative work can be found at www.geocities .com/a4theroad/blog/la-art.html.

Chapter 5—Doubt and Laughter

1. Jennifer Michael Hecht, *Doubt, a History* (San Francisco: HarperOne, 2003).

2. Jürgen Moltmann, *Experiences in Theology,* tr. Margaret Kohl (Minneapolis, MN: Fortress Press, 2000), 17.

3. Moltmann, *Experiences in Theology,* 17.

4. The best-selling atheists include Sam Harris, *The End of Faith,* Richard Dawkins, *The God Delusion,* and Christopher Hitchens, *God Is Not Great,* 2007.

5. David van Biema, "Mother Teresa's Crisis of Faith," *Time,* August 23, 2007.

6. Don S. Browning, *A Fundamental Practical Theology* (Minneapolis, MN: Fortress Press, 1996), 6.

7. C.S. Lewis, *A Grief Observed* (San Francisco: HarperOne, 2001), 78.

8. Frederick Buechner, *Wishful Thinking: A Theological ABC* (San Francisco: Harper & Row, 1973), 25.

Chapter 6—Love and Disappointment

1. David Kinnaman and Gabe Lyons, *unChristian* (Grand Rapids, MI: Baker Books, 2007), 92.

2. C.S. Lewis, *The Four Loves* (Fort Washington, PA: Harvest Books, 1971).

3. Elizabeth Huwiler and Roland Murphy, *Proverbs, Ecclesiastes, Song of Songs* in *New International Biblical Commentary* (Peabody, MA: Hendrickson Publishing, 1999).

4. Cal Thomas and Ed Dobson, *Blinded by Might: Why the Religious Right Can't Save America* (Grand Rapids, MI: Zondervan, 1999), 193.

5. "Is the Religious Right Finished?" *Christianity Today,* September 6, 1999.

Chapter 7—Revealed and Revealing

1. Gerhard Maier, *Biblical Hermeneutics,* tr. by Robert Yarbrough (Wheaton, IL: Crossway, 1994), 57.

2. Two brilliant books that place God as the center of the dramatic Christian story are Jack Miles, *God: A Biography* (New York: Vintage, 1996) and Kevin J. Vanhoozer, *The Drama of Doctrine* (Louisville, KY: Westminster John Knox Press, 2006).

3. Mark Twain, *Letters from the Earth,* Letter X. Available online at www.sacred-texts.com/aor/ twain/letearth.htm.

4. Thomas Jefferson, *The Jefferson Bible: The Life and Morals of Jesus of Nazareth* (Boston: Beacon Press, 2001).

5. Maier, *Biblical Hermeneutics,* 193.

6. Gordon D. Fee, *New Testament Exegesis* (Philadelphia: Westminster Press, 1983), 25.

7. See Philip Jenkins, *The New Faces of Christianity: Believing the Bible in the Global South* (New York: Oxford University Press, 2006) and Philip Jenkins, *The Next Christendom: The Coming of Global Christianity* (New York: Oxford University Press, 2002).

8. See Peter C. Phan, *Christianity with an Asian Face* (Maryknoll, NY: Orbis Books, 2003) and Tokunboh Adeyemo, ed., *Africa Bible Commentary* (Grand Rapids, MI: Zondervan, 2006).

9. Gordon D. Fee and Douglas Stuart, *How to Read the Bible for All Its Worth* (Grand Rapids, MI: Zondervan, 1982), 15-16.

10. Carol Adeney, ed., *This Morning with God* (Downer's Grove, IL: InterVarsity Press, 1978).

11. Annie Dillard, *Teaching a Stone to Talk* (San Francisco: Harper Perennial, 1988), 40.

12. John Goldingay, *Models for Scripture* (Toronto: Clements, 2004), 342.

13. See Eugene H. Peterson, *Eat This Book: A Conversation in the Art of Spiritual Reading* (Grand Rapids, MI: Eerdmans, 2006).

14. James D.G. Dunn, "The Challenge of New Testament Study for Evangelicals Today," in *Introducing New Testament Interpretation,* ed. Scot McKnight (Grand Rapids, MI: Baker Book House, 1989), 15-16.

15. Quoted by William Lee Miller in *Arguing About Slavery: The Great Battle in the United States Congress* (New York: Alfred A. Knopf, 1996), 139.

16. For some practical ways to push past our differences, see Michael O. Emerson and Christian Smith, *Divided by Faith: Evangelical Religion and the Problem of Race in America* (New York: Oxford University Press, 2001).

17. Ben Witherington III, *The Living Word of God: Rethinking the Theology of the Bible* (Waco, TX: Baylor University Press, 2008), 12.

18. Walter A. Henrichsen, *A Laymen's Guide to Interpreting the Bible* (Colorado Springs: NavPress, 1978), 77.

19. I appreciate the thorough historical background and exegesis offered by Jack Rogers in *Jesus, The Bible and Homosexuality: Explode the Myths, Heal the Church* (Louisville, KY: Westminster John Knox Press, 2006).

20. F.F. Bruce, *The Hard Sayings of Jesus* (Downer's Grove, IL: InterVarsity Press, 1983), 56-62.

21. Garry Wills quotes the full letter in *What Jesus Meant* (New York: Penguin Books, 2006).

Chapter 8—In and Out

1. Eric Lax, *The Mold in Dr. Florey's Coat: The Story of the Penicillin Miracle* (New York: Henry Holt, 2004).

2. See Thomas Molnar, *The Pagan Temptation* (Grand Rapids, MI: Eerdmans, 1987).

3. See Gregory A. Boyd, *Letters from a Skeptic: A Son Wrestles with His Father's Questions* (Colorado Springs: Cook Communications, 1994).

4. Harold S. Kushner, *When Bad Things Happen to Good People* (New York: Anchor Books, 2004).

5. Ray S. Anderson, *The Gospel According to Judas: Is There a Limit to God's Forgiveness?* (Colorado Springs: NavPress, 1994).

6. Stanley Hauerwas and William H. Willimon, *Resident Aliens: Life in the Christian Colony* (Nashville: Abingdon Press, 1989).

7. Lynn White Jr., "The Historical Roots of Our Ecological Crisis," *Science*, vol. 1, no. 55, 1967, 1203-7.

8. Sallie McFague, *Life Abundant: Rethinking Theology and Economy for a Planet in Peril* (Minneapolis: Fortress Press, 2001), 102.

9. Rod Dreher, *Crunchy Cons* (New York: Three Rivers Press, 2006).

10. Tri Robinson and Jason Chatraw, *Saving God's Green Earth: Rediscovering the Church's Responsibility to the Environment* (Bloomington, MN: Ampelon, 2006).

11. E.O. Wilson, *The Creation: An Appeal to Save Life on Earth* (New York: Norton, 2006).

12. Brad Knickerbocker, "Humans' Beef with Livestock: A Warmer Planet," *Christian Science Monitor*, February 20, 2007.

Chapter 9—Youth and Wisdom

1. Randall Balmer, *Thy Kingdom Come: An Evangelical's Lament* (New York: Basic Books, 2006).

2. Garry Wills, *Head and Heart: American Christianties* (New York: Penguin Press, 2007).

3. William Kristol, "On the Future of Conservatism," *Commentary*, February 1997.

4. Virginia Postrel, "Laissez Fear: Left and right agree the market is their enemy," *Reason*, April 1997. Available online at www.reason.com/news/show/30224.html.

5. Barry Schwartz, *The Paradox of Choice: Why More Is Less* (New York: Ecco Press, 2003).

6. Virginia Postrel, "Consumer Vertigo," *Reason*, June 2005. Available online at www.reason .com/news/show/36172.html.

7. Kristen Day, *Democrats for Life: Pro-Life Politics and the Silenced Majority* (Green Forest, AR: New Leaf Press, 2006) and David R. Carlin, *Can a Catholic Be a Democrat?* (Manchester, NH: Sophia Institute Press, 2005).

8. Stephanie Simon, "The new abortion warriors," *The Los Angeles Times*, January 22, 2008, A1.

9. J. Springer, "Woman defends decision to give birth at 60," www.msnbc.com, May 24, 2007.

10. Kenneth R. Wing, "Government Power and the Right to Privacy," *The Law and the Public's Health*, 6th ed. (Chicago: Health Administration Press, 2003).

11. Marshall B. Kapp, "Aging and the Law," *Handbook of Aging and the Social Sciences*, 6th ed. (Boston: Elsevier, 2006).

12. George J. Annas, " 'Culture of Life' Politics at the Bedside—The Case of Terri Schiavo," *The New England Journal of Medicine*, April 21, 2005.

13. Charles Pillar and Doug Smith, "Unintended Victims of Gates Foundation Generosity," *The Los Angeles Times*, December 16, 2007.

Chapter 10—Suffering and Silence

1. Scot McKnight, *Introducing New Testament Interpretation* (Grand Rapids, MI: Baker Books, 1989), 76.

2. Mother Teresa, *No Greater Love* (New York: MJF Books, 2000).

3. Phil Hirschkorn, "Names Will Be Grouped at WTC Memorial," CBS News, December 13, 2006.

Notes

4. Sermons delivered following the tragic events are collected in Forrest Church, ed., *Restoring Faith: America's Religious Leaders Answer Terror with Hope* (New York: Walker & Company, 2001).

5. Kathleen M. O'Connor, *Lamentation and the Tears of the World* (Maryknoll, NY: Orbis Books, 2002), 85-86.

6. O'Connor, *Tears of the World,* 86.

Conclusion—Purple Reign

1. Brian D. McLaren, *A New Kind of Christian* (San Francisco: Jossey-Bass, 2001).

2. Brian D. McLaren, *A Generous Orthodoxy* (Grand Rapids, MI: Zondervan, 2004).

3. Tony Campolo, "What Is a Red-Letter Christian?" http://www.beliefnet.com/story/185/story_18562_1.html.

4. Darrell L. Guder and Lois Barrett, eds, *Missional Church* (Grand Rapids, MI: Eerdmans, 1998) and Alan Roxburgh and Fred Romanuk, *The Missional Leader* (San Francisco: Jossey-Bass, 2006).

5. Phil Cooke, *Branding Faith: Why Some Churches and Nonprofits Impact Culture and Others Don't* (Ventura, CA: Regal Books, 2008).

6. David Kinnaman and Gabe Lyons, *unChristian* (Grand Rapids, MI: Baker Books, 2007).

7. Hans Urs von Balthasar, *Theo-Drama: Theological Dramatic Theory,* vol. 1, *Prolegomena* (San Francisco: Ignatius Press, 1988).

8. Kevin J. Vanhoozer, *The Drama of Doctrine: A Canonical Linguistic Approach to Christian Theology* (Louisville, KY: Westminster John Knox Press, 2005).

9. Tony Campolo and Gordon Aeschliman, *Everybody Wants to Change the World* (Ventura, CA: Regal Books, 2006).

Crazy,

Beautiful,

Messed Up,

Breathtaking

World...

And People Are Talking About It...

conversant life .com

engage your faith